Highlights of Jewish History

VOLUME THREE

DANIEL TO THE RAMBAM

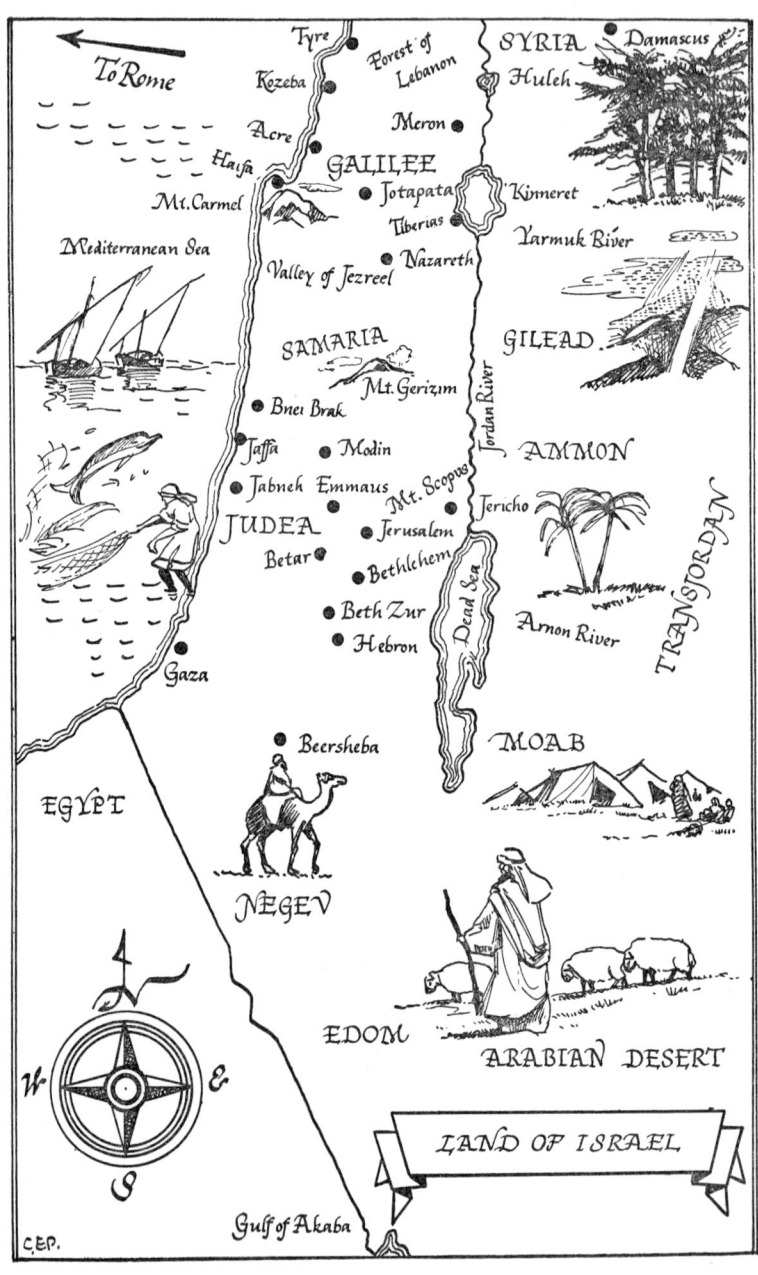

HIGHLIGHTS OF JEWISH HISTORY

VOLUME THREE

From Daniel to the Rambam

WITH EXERCISES,
PROJECTS AND GAMES

By
MORDECAI H. LEWITTES

Illustrations by
CHARLES E. PONT

HEBREW PUBLISHING COMPANY
NEW YORK

Copyright 1955
by Hebrew Publishing Company, New York
Printed in the United States of America

PRINTED AND BOUND IN U.S.A. BY
MONTAUK BOOK MANUFACTURING CO., INC., NEW YORK

Dedicated in loving memory to Benjamin Cohen, grandfather of Hedva and Don.

Preface

Highlights of Jewish History is a sequel to *Heroes of Jewish History: Abraham to Moses* and *Heroes of Jewish History: Joshua to Jeremiah*.

The change of title reflects a slight change in point of view. The student in the intermediate grades, for whom this book is intended, is maturer than the one who studied the earlier books. He is interested not only in heroes but in other aspects of Jewish history as well. The return to Zion, the rebuilding of the Temple and of the Land of Israel, the struggle for religious and political freedom, the development of the oral law, the spread of Judaism, the emergence of new centers in East and West—these themes are basic.

The heroes of Jewish history, however, still play an important part in this narrative. Instead of devoting but a few lines to each of the many, many leaders who have glorified Jewish history, the author has carefully selected representative figures for each period. Thus it has been possible to devote entire chapters to men such as Ezra and Nehemiah, Judah the Maccabee, Hillel, Johanan ben Zakkai, Akiva and Bar Kochba, Judah the Prince, Saadia, Rashi, Judah Halevi and the Rambam. Each one emerges as a vivid, colorful personality who has made a unique contribution to Jewish history.

It is difficult to make ancient history come alive for a young person. The author has tried to write in a simple and dramatic style that will prove a source of enjoyment to the reader. He has also sought to establish a point of contact with the modern child through those Jewish experiences that are real to him such as Purim and Chanukah, synagogue and Sabbath. In describing Mishnah, Talmud and the writings of the great Rabbis he has chosen excerpts dealing with charity, the golden rule, Passover, pupils and teachers, justice, the yearning for Zion and the striving for a better world. It is hoped that these concepts will prove significant to the pupil.

Maps, illustrations, exercises, review tests, topics for discussion, games, suggestions for projects and many other pedagogic aids have been added.

The teacher must seek to appeal to both mind and heart. Jewish history is more—much more than a mere list of battles and persecutions. In the Book of Maccabees we read how Nehemiah found the sacred fire which had been hidden at the time of the fall of the Temple. But the fire had become frozen, hardened, congealed. At that moment the sun shone forth and the frozen fire burst into flame. Many of our pupils seem indifferent and apathetic—yet the sacred flame is there. The teacher of Jewish history must seek, above all, to ignite the inner spark.

Contents

PAGE

UNIT ONE
The Return to Zion

1.	Daniel	19
2.	From Babylon to Jerusalem	31
3.	Strengthening Jerusalem	43
4.	The Reforms of Ezra and Nehemiah	51
5.	The Story of Purim	58

UNIT TWO
The Glorious Maccabees

6.	The Coming of the Greeks	71
7.	Chanukah—the Festival of Lights	81
8.	The Maccabean Struggle for Independence	95

UNIT THREE
Rome and Jerusalem

9.	Under Roman Rule	111
10.	In the Days of King Herod	119
11.	Hillel—Teacher of the Golden Rule	128
12.	The Gathering Storm	139
13.	War Against Rome	146

UNIT FOUR
The Struggle for Survival

14.	Johanan Ben Zakkai—the Man Who Saved Judaism	161

15.	Akiva—Master of the Oral Law	172
16.	The Bar Kochba Rebellion	183
17.	Judah the Prince—Editor of the Mishnah	195

UNIT FIVE
Jews in Babylon

18.	A New Center of Learning	209
19.	The Talmud	217
20.	Under Arab Rule	227
21.	Saadia Gaon—Babylon's Greatest Scholar	234

UNIT SIX
New Centers of Jewish Life

22.	The Kingdom of the Khazars	247
23.	The Golden Age in Spain	255
24.	Rashi—Prince of Commentators	264
25.	Judah Halevi—Sweet Singer of Zion	276
26.	Rabbi Moses Ben Maimon (Rambam)	284
	Index	300

Illustrations

	PAGE
Land of Israel (*Map*)	*Frontispiece*
The Handwriting on the Wall	25
Queen Esther before the King	64
Rededicating the Temple	91
The Wailing Wall	154
Israel and Her Neighbors (*Map*)	168
Akiva and Rabbis at the Seder Table	179
Studying the Talmud	221
In the Middle Ages (*Map*)	249
Rashi's Synagogue	266
The Rambam	285

TO THE STUDENT

We have already met many of the greatest heroes of Jewish history.

It might be fun for your class to produce a dramatic pageant telling about these heroes. You might call it, "The Story of Our People," or "Meet Our Heroes," or "The Pageant of Jewish History."

You would have to write a script, make costumes and plan the staging of the pageant.

Of course, you couldn't include everything. But the narrator could briefly mention those heroes whom you didn't present on stage.

Abraham, Isaac and Jacob, the fathers of the Hebrew people, would be the first ones to cross the stage in flowing shepherd robes. The narrator might tell about Abraham as a boy in Ur breaking the idols, about his search for the promised land, about his heroism in battle, about his hospitality and kindness.

The pageant might portray Rebecca and Isaac and their two sons, Jacob and Esau. It would describe Jacob's wonderful dream when he saw angels climbing up and down the ladder that reached from earth to heaven. It would tell about God's promise to Jacob to give Canaan unto his children if only they obeyed God's law of truth and justice. The final scene in Part I would describe Joseph as prime minister of Egypt.

Part II would tell about the slaves in Egypt. It would show how Moses and Aaron pleaded with Pharaoh, "Let My people go," and how they freed the slaves from bondage. Some Passover songs might be sung at this point.

The pageant might then describe the granting of the 10 commandments, while some Shavuot music was played in the background. The next scene would show how the Israelites wandered in the desert for 40 years, and would tell about the *sukkot* or booths in which they lived.

Part III might be devoted to Joshua and the Judges. It would present, through narration and song, the battle of Jericho, the division of the land, the heroism of Deborah, the loyalty of Ruth and the power of Samson.

Part IV might be called "The United Kingdom." This act would probably be the most dramatic and colorful of all. Who does not thrill to hear the exciting tales of Saul's being anointed first king of Israel by Samuel, of David and Goliath, of Jonathan's friendship for David, of David's exploits as warrior and as king? The visit of the Queen of Sheba to Solomon would make a colorful scene. We would also hear about the building of the Temple, about Solomon's wisdom and about his great ships that sailed to Spain and to India.

The final part would have some sad moments. It would show how a rebellion brought about a division into two kingdoms, Israel in the north and Judah in the south. It would tell how the ten tribes of Israel fell before Assyria and how the Temple in Jerusalem was destroyed by Babylon.

The script would portray the prophets as the real heroes of the Hebrew people. Elijah, Isaiah and Jeremiah taught the people not to worship idols but to believe in one God, to pursue peace, to love justice and to treat all men as brothers.

The pageant would end on a note of hope as Jeremiah's voice was heard proclaiming, "There is hope for thy future. Thy children shall return to their own border."

At this point the curtain might fall.

In reality, however, the pageant of Jewish history never ends. What happened after the destruction of the Temple? How did the Jewish people in Babylon live? When did Jeremiah's prophecy of a return to Zion come true? How did the Jewish people fight for their freedom? What great ideas and ideals did they teach the entire world?

This book is a continuation of the pageant of Jewish history.

It will help you find the answers to these questions. You will hear about Babylon, Persia, Greece, Rome, Arabia, France, Spain.

Some of these nations were friendly, others unfriendly. But always the Jewish people fought bravely to preserve their freedom, and to maintain their right to worship one God and to obey the laws of the Torah.

The curtain never falls on Jewish history.

UNIT ONE

The Return to Zion

CHAPTER I

DANIEL

1. IN THE LAND OF BABYLON

THE JEWS who had been exiled from Jerusalem swore:

"If I forget thee, O Jerusalem,
 Let my right hand forget her skill."

Daniel was one Jew who did not forget Jerusalem even though he was only a young boy when he was carried into exile.

Daniel, like Moses, grew up in the king's palace. He and several other Hebrew lads were chosen because of their beauty and wisdom to serve the king.

Like Moses, the young Daniel never forgot his people. He would gather with other Hebrews to pray to God. Three times a day, at the times when sacrifices were offered in the Temple, Daniel and his friends sang the songs of David. They turned to Jerusalem as they prayed.

Sometimes the people would grow discouraged.

"All hope is lost! We will never return to Zion!"

Daniel and the other leaders would comfort them.

"Did not Jeremiah warn us not to lose hope?"

In the group was Baruch the scribe, the man who had been Jeremiah's companion for so many years.

"What were Jeremiah's exact words?" they would ask.

Again and again, Baruch would describe the prophet's vision about Rachel who pleaded before God to have pity on the exiles. He would relate how God comforted Rachel, telling her to wipe the tears from her eyes.

"Refrain thy voice from weeping,
And thine eyes from tears;
For thy work shall be rewarded, saith the Lord;
And they shall come back from the land of the enemy.
And there is hope for thy future, saith the Lord;
And thy children shall return to their own border."

"What must we do in the meanwhile?" asked the people.

"Do as Jeremiah asked you to do. Build houses, plant vineyards and work for the welfare of the cities in which you dwell."

Daniel rejoiced that the people followed the advice of Jeremiah. They planted gardens, built houses and worked hard.

The exiles began to prosper.

From day to day Daniel grew in wisdom. The king of Babylon, Nebuchadnezzar, often called on Daniel to interpret his dreams.

Daniel warned the king that God would punish Babylon because of its sins.

2. OUR HOPE IS NOT YET LOST

Once the prophet Ezekiel came to visit the Jews in the city of Babylon. Ezekiel lived in a city, not far from Babylon, called Tel-Aviv. Here he had preached to the Jews ever since the beginning of the exile, eleven years before the destruction of the Temple.

Daniel and the Jews of Babylon gathered eagerly to hear the words of Ezekiel.

"Why did God allow Jerusalem to be destroyed?" asked one person.

"Because our nation had sinned," replied Ezekiel.

"Then all hope is lost. We can never hope to return," said one of the Jews of Babylon.

"God will not punish us for the sins of our fathers," replied Ezekiel. "If we worship Him in truth and do justice, then our captives will be brought back to Jerusalem."

Raising his voice so that all could hear, Ezekiel continued.

"Hear my vision, O children of Israel. I dreamed that a wind came from God and carried me into a valley. And the valley was full of dried-up bones. They were the bones of those who had died and whose flesh had withered away."

Those in the crowd pressed closer to the prophet so that they would not miss a single word.

"And God said to me, 'O son of man, can these bones live?'

"And I answered, 'O Lord, you know best.'

"And God said, 'Prophesy over these bones and cause breath to enter these bones, and cause sinew and flesh and skin to cover these bones. They will live again!'

"So I prophesied as I was commanded. And as I prophesied there was a great noise, and the bones came together, bone to its bone. Sinews were upon the bones, and flesh came up, and skin covered the bones. But as yet there was no breath of life.

"Then said God unto me: 'Prophesy unto the breath to come from the four winds, and to breathe upon these slain that they may live.'

"So I did as I was commanded and prophesied, 'Come from the four winds, O breath, and breathe upon these slain that they may live.'

"And the breath of life entered these bones, and they lived, and stood up on their feet.

"And I asked, 'What is the meaning of this vision?'

"And God replied, 'The dead bones represent the house of Israel. They think that the nation is dead. They cry that all hope is lost and that the Hebrew nation can never be restored to life. But the dead nation will be revived like the dry bones of the valley. I shall bring back the people of Israel and of Judah to their own land. There they will enjoy a new life as a nation reborn.'"

"Indeed," added the prophet, "our hope is not yet lost! That is my message to you. Israel will be restored!"

Daniel looked around as Ezekiel concluded his words. He

seemed to have cast a spell over the people. Daniel knew that Israel would never forget the message of Ezekiel.

We have remembered Ezekiel's words for over 2500 years. When, in our own day, Hebrew pioneers dreamed of returning to Zion they began to sing the words of Ezekiel, "Our hope is not yet lost." These words became the new national anthem, the Hatikvah, or song of hope.

When a new garden city was built on the shores of the Mediterranean, the colonists said, "Let us call this city Tel-Aviv, which means Hill of Spring."

This was the name of the city in which Ezekiel had lived in far-off Babylon. It was a fitting reminder of the great prophet who taught the people never to lose hope.

3. THE HANDWRITING ON THE WALL

After the death of King Nebuchadnezzar, the Hebrew captives were treated more kindly. The members of the Hebrew royal family were released from prison and were given many honors.

Daniel remained an adviser in the king's palace.

Once Belshazzar, a prince of Babylon, made a great feast to a thousand of his lords.

"Bring the golden vessels of the Temple in Jerusalem," ordered Belshazzar.

The golden vessels which once were used as part of the Temple service were quickly brought.

The vessels were filled with wine and Belshazzar and his lords drank merrily from the Temple vessels. As they drank they sang songs of praise to their idols of wood and of stone.

"Look!" suddenly cried one of the nobles in horror.

Belshazzar and his guests quickly turned to look. Clearly visible was a giant hand. Horrified, Belshazzar watched as the moving fingers wrote on the wall.

For a moment the hand stopped writing. The palm of the

hand was now turned away from the wall toward Belshazzar.

Then, as suddenly as it had appeared, the hand disappeared.

The nobles and lords examined the words written by the giant hand. Alas, the words were in a strange language and none could read the handwriting on the wall.

"Bring me my wise men," shouted Belshazzar. "I shall not rest until I learn the meaning of these words."

In great fear the prince anxiously waited for the wise men to explain the strange words. None could understand what the hand had written.

"Is there nobody who can help me?" cried Belshazzar. His face had turned an ashen white, and his body shook.

"Peace, O Belshazzar, live forever!" said his wife. "Call for Daniel. He will surely know what this strange writing means."

When Daniel appeared before the prince, Belshazzar said, "If you can read the handwriting on the wall, and explain its meaning you will be richly rewarded. You will wear purple and a chain of gold around your neck like one of the royal family. You will rule with me and my prime minister as one of the first three in the kingdom."

"I shall gladly read the words and explain their meaning," replied Daniel, "but I do not wish to receive any gifts or any reward."

"Hide nothing from me! I must know all, no matter what it may lead to!" urged Belshazzar.

"God has warned you of punishment for your wickedness," said Daniel. "The words written by the hand are MENE MENE TEKEL UPHARSIN. This is their meaning:

"MENE MENE—these words mean 'numbered.' God has numbered the days of your kingdom and has brought them to an end.

"TEKEL means 'weighed.' You have been weighed on the scales of justice, and have been found guilty because of your wicked deeds.

"UPHARSIN means 'broken.' Your kingdom will be broken up and given to your enemies, the Medes and the Persians."

That night the Persians and Medes under King Cyrus swept into Babylon. Belshazzar was slain and mighty Babylon fell.

4. DANIEL AND THE IDOL BEL

Daniel, the man of wisdom and of faith, became the hero of many legends. One of these legends is found among the later writings not included in the Bible.

According to this legend, Daniel was a trusted adviser of King Cyrus, the Persian who had conquered Babylon.

In the city of Babylon was a giant idol called Bel.

"Why do you not worship Bel?" King Cyrus asked Daniel.

"I do not worship idols," replied Daniel. "I worship the living God."

"But Bel is a living god," argued Cyrus. "Each day he devours the huge sacrifices brought before him."

Daniel laughed. "Bel is an idol of brass and clay. He cannot eat or drink. His priests have deceived you. The food is eaten by human beings."

When Cyrus called the 70 priests of Bel before him, they said, "To prove that we speak the truth why do you not seal the temple with your own lock and seal? If the food disappears even though nobody enters the temple, then you will know that Bel devours the food."

The king thought this a good plan. He brought large baskets of food before Bel, and ordered that the temple be emptied of all people except for him and Daniel.

Just before the temple was locked Daniel requested permission to spread a fine powder on the floor. The king granted permission.

The temple was then locked and sealed with the king's seal.

The next morning Cyrus and Daniel returned to the temple of Bel. The seal was unbroken.

THE HANDWRITING ON THE WALL

"You see," said the king. "Nobody could have entered the building."

They broke the seal and entered the temple. The food had disappeared.

"Bel is god," exclaimed Cyrus. "He has devoured the food."

"I do not think so," replied Daniel with a smile. "Glance at the footsteps shown by the powder."

The king glanced down at the floor of the temple. There was the clear imprint of human footsteps. The marks led to a secret trap-door behind the idol.

When the trap-door was opened the king found a large tunnel in which many of the priests of Bel slept. Each night they would open the trap-door and take the food placed before the idol.

The king punished those who had tried to deceive him, and showered rich rewards on the wise Daniel. The king then ordered that the idol be destroyed.

This story is only a legend. Yet it teaches us a great deal about Jewish history, for it is true that in Babylon the Jews learned at last not to worship idols.

For hundreds of years the prophets had pleaded in vain with the Hebrew nation not to worship idols. At last in Babylon the people learned this great lesson.

5. IN THE LIONS' DEN

The last king whom Daniel served was Darius the Mede.

When the king's officers saw how Daniel was honored, they were very jealous.

"Let us disgrace him in the eyes of King Darius," they said to each other.

But Daniel's actions were so fair and just that the officers could find no cause for complaint.

"Only in one way can we make trouble for Daniel," said one officer. "Daniel worships God. Let us ask the king to sign a decree allowing his subjects to worship only the king for the next 30 days. Daniel will never obey such a law."

The officers came before Darius and said, "O, King Darius, live forever! We wish to propose a new law."

"What is your proposal?" asked the king.

"O King Darius," they replied, "let us see whether all of your subjects are loyal to you. For the next 30 days let nobody worship any god but you."

"Let it be as you say," replied the king, pleased that his subjects worshiped him as a god.

"Let anybody who disobeys your word be thrown into a den of lions."

"So shall it be."

The law was sealed with the king's seal and proclaimed in the lands over which Darius ruled.

Daniel was not frightened by the new law. Three times a day he turned toward Jerusalem and prayed unto God.

Daniel's enemies spied on him and soon found him praying to God. Daniel was quickly brought before the king.

"Have you not ordered that anybody who disobeys your law is to be thrown into a den of lions?" demanded Daniel's enemies. "We have found him praying to God."

"Surely you do not expect me to harm my trusted adviser, Daniel?" said Darius.

"You have signed a law with your seal. No law passed by the Medes and Persians can ever be changed."

Darius knew that this was the rule of the Medes and Persians. No law could ever be changed. There was nothing he could do now to save Daniel.

Sadly he called Daniel before him.

"I shall pray for you," said Darius, "and I shall refrain from food and drink. Maybe God will hear my prayer and save you."

Daniel was then cast into the den of lions. A stone was

rolled to the mouth of the cave so that Daniel could not escape.

The king fasted that day and night, and prayed unto God to deliver Daniel from the mouth of the lions.

As soon as dawn came the king hurried to the den of lions.

"Daniel! Daniel!" called the king anxiously.

"Here am I," replied Daniel. "I am unharmed."

To the king's delight and joy Daniel had not been touched by the lions.

"God has answered my prayer," said Darius. "Praised be the God of Daniel and of the Hebrews."

Daniel lived to a ripe old age, honored and respected by all as a man of wisdom, of faith and of courage.

EXERCISES

I. Select the correct name or phrase. (Review the section called "To the Student," pages 13 to 15.)

1. Abraham is considered the father of the Hebrew people because _____. (he was a hero in battle, he was the first to believe in one God)
2. God promised Canaan to the descendants of _____. (Jacob, Esau)
3. _____ commemorates the freeing of the slaves. (Passover, Shavuot)
4. Moses _____. (received the 10 commandments, conquered Canaan)
5. _____ led the people into Canaan. (Joshua, Samson)
6. _____ was a heroine in battle. (Ruth, Deborah)
7. _____ was the first king of Israel. (Samuel, Saul)
8. The Temple in Jerusalem was built by _____. (David, Solomon)
9. The Temple was destroyed by _____. (Assyria, Babylon)
10. Jeremiah told the people that _____. (they must not lose hope, Jerusalem would never be rebuilt)

THE RETURN TO ZION

II. Eliminate the name or phrase that does *not* belong. (Review sections 1 and 2, pages 19 to 22.)
   1. (Daniel, Elijah, Moses) grew up in a palace.
   2. The Jews swore never to forget (Egypt, Jerusalem, Zion).
   3. (Baruch, Jeremiah, Zedekiah) urged the Jews of Babylon to work for the welfare of the cities in which they lived.
   4. The bones that came to life represented (Babylon, Israel, the Jewish people).
   5. We are reminded of Ezekiel by (Haifa, Hatikvah, Tel-Aviv).

III. Select the correct word or name to complete each sentence. (Review section 3, pages 22 to 24.)
   Belshazzar, Daniel, Persians, Tekel, Upharsin
   1. _____ was frightened by the handwriting on the wall.
   2. The words on the wall were Mene Mene Tekel _____.
   3. _____ means "weighed."
   4. _____ warned that Babylon would be destroyed.
   5. The _____ conquered Babylon.

IV. Who said to whom? (Review sections 4 and 5, pages 24 to 26.)
   1. "If the food disappears even though nobody enters the temple, then you will know that Bel devours the food."
   2. "Bel is god. He has devoured the food."
   3. "For the next 30 days let nobody worship any god but you."
   4. "I shall pray for you. Maybe God will hear my prayer and save you."
   5. "Here am I. I am unharmed."

V. Questions for discussion:
   1. "The curtain never falls on Jewish history." Explain.
   2. How did Jeremiah and Ezekiel help to keep the Jewish people alive?
   3. Daniel is a greater hero than Samson. Why?
   4. The story of the idol Bel is a legend. What can we learn from legends?

THINGS TO DO

1. *Research*—Babylon was one of the great powers of ancient times. What are some of the things for which Babylon is famous?

2. *Dramatization*—The story of Daniel and Bel is one of the first detective stories in world literature. Dramatize the story.

3. *Picture Collection*—There have been many pictures drawn of Daniel. Bring to class a picture of Daniel in an illustrated Bible or in a magazine or pamphlet.

PUZZLE

Answer these questions. The initial letters of the answers should spell out the name of a person mentioned in this chapter.

1. In what country was Moses born?
2. What is another name for Jerusalem?
3. Which prophet, according to the legend, visits every Jewish home on Passover?
4. Who was Nebuchadnezzar?
5. What is the name of the new Jewish state?
6. Who was Jacob's brother?
7. Who was Rachel's sister?

CHAPTER II

FROM BABYLON TO JERUSALEM

1. THE PROCLAMATION OF KING CYRUS

CYRUS THE GREAT, the king of Persia, was one of the best friends the Hebrew nation ever had.

After Cyrus had captured many of the cities of Greece and most of Asia he said to his captains, "Let us conquer Babylon and we will be masters of Asia."

Cyrus attacked Babylon with a large army. There was a pitched battle outside of the walls of Babylon. Cyrus was the victor, but the Babylonian army quickly withdrew behind the walls of the city.

The Babylonians were prepared for a long siege. It had once taken their army 13 years to lay siege to the city of Tyre. They were sure they could resist for an even longer period of time since they had stored vast supplies in their city.

Cyrus saw that it was almost impossible to storm the walls of Babylon. He decided to use a stratagem.

Cyrus ordered his soldiers to dig a canal just where the Euphrates enters the city of Babylon. The waters of the Euphrates River were turned aside, and the river bed became almost shallow.

The Persian soldiers waded in the shallow waters along the river-bed and entered the city. There was nobody to resist them.

They found the Babylonian nobles and lords drinking and feasting and making merry. The Persians were soon masters of the city.

The handwriting on the wall had come true.

The many people who had been exiled from their lands by the Babylonians rejoiced.

King Cyrus was soon told, "The Hebrew prophets warned the Babylonians that you would overthrow their city because of their sins. God has given you this great victory."

"If it is true that the Hebrews prophesied my victory they shall be greatly rewarded," said Cyrus.

The leaders of the Hebrew people were called before Cyrus.

"Tell me your history," ordered the king.

"We are Hebrews who worship one God," was the reply. "But Babylon destroyed our Temple in Jerusalem. Our prophets told us never to lose hope. God would punish Babylon, they said, and would give you victory over the sinful city. This is the day for which we prayed so that we could return to build our city and our Temple."

"So shall it be," answered the generous king. "You may rebuild your Temple and Jerusalem. I shall issue a proclamation ordering all my subjects to help you. Also, the holy vessels of your Temple you may take back with you."

Cyrus appointed many of the wise men among the Hebrews, like Daniel, to be his advisers. He treated all of his Hebrew subjects very kindly.

King Cyrus soon issued his proclamation. This is what the proclamation said:

"Thus saith Cyrus, king of Persia. All the kingdoms of the earth has the Lord, the God of heaven, given me. And He has charged me to build Him a house in Jerusalem, which is in Judah. Whoever there is among you of all His people—let him go up to Jerusalem to build the house of the Lord, the God of Israel!"

King Cyrus also urged his subjects everywhere to help the Jews return to their land by giving them generous gifts. The cost of the Temple was to be paid by the king.

There was great rejoicing among the Jews when they heard that they could return to the Land of Israel. At last the words of Jeremiah, Ezekiel and Daniel had come true!

2. BACK TO JERUSALEM

The exiles who decided to return to Jerusalem soon picked Zerubbabel, grandson of a former king of Judah, as their leader.

Over 50,000 Jews set out on the road back. A long line of camels, horses, mules and donkeys extended for several miles.

Many of the older men and women were among those who had been exiled 50 years before.

Once they had sworn:

> "If I forget thee, O Jerusalem,
> Let my right hand forget her skill."

But now they sang a song of joy:

> "When the Lord brought back those that returned to Zion,
> We were like dreamers.
> Then was our mouth filled with laughter,
> And our tongue with singing.
> They that sow in tears
> Shall reap in joy."

Led by Zerubbabel the exiles arrived safely in Jerusalem and in the surrounding villages after several months of travel.

Shortly after their arrival they celebrated the holidays of Rosh Ha-Shanah, Yom Kippur and Sukkot. A small altar was set up on the spot where once the Temple stood.

Jeshua, grandson of the last *Kohen Gadol*, was appointed High Priest.

Zerubbabel then sent messengers to the city of Tyre saying, "King Cyrus has given us permission to rebuild our Temple. He has also granted us a large sum of money for the purchase of wood. Send us, therefore, cedars from the forest of Lebanon with which we shall rebuild God's house."

Zerubbabel and Jeshua soon laid the foundations of the Temple. The people gathered to celebrate when the foundations had been completed.

The *Kohanim*, or priests, blew on the trumpets and the Levites played with the cymbals. As they played they sang:

"Praise the Lord, for He is good,
 For His mercy endures forever."

The people shouted with great joy and sang praises unto God. The old men, however, who remembered the Temple of Solomon wept, for they knew that the new Temple could never equal the old in splendor.

But soon they too gave thanks that their exile had ended. They too joined in the singing:

"Praise the Lord, for He is good,
 For His mercy endures forever."

3. THE SAMARITANS

Zerubbabel and Jeshua soon learned that the neighboring tribes were very hostile.

To the south of Jerusalem lay the land of Edom whose people claimed descent from Esau. They sought in every way to prevent the growth of the villages in the south.

Most dangerous of all were the Samaritans in the north. The Samaritans lived near Samaria, the city which once had been the capital of the 10 tribes of Israel.

When the 10 tribes were exiled, Assyria brought in captives from all parts of Asia. These new settlers intermarried with the Israelites who had remained in the Land of Israel. From them they learned the belief in one God. They too studied the 5 Books of Moses and celebrated holidays such as Passover, Shavuot and Sukkot.

The Samaritans, however, were very unfriendly to the

Hebrews who had returned from Babylon. They might not have allowed them to settle in Jerusalem at all were it not for the fact Cyrus had sent 1000 Persian soldiers with Zerubbabel to protect the pilgrims.

The Jews who settled in the villages north of Jerusalem were in great fear. Travel was dangerous. The Samaritans might attack at any moment and wipe out the new settlements.

When the Samaritans saw that the foundations of the Temple had been laid, they approached Zerubbabel and Jeshua with these words:

"Let us build with you. We too believe in God and have sacrificed unto Him ever since the Assyrians brought our fathers to this land."

Zerubbabel and Jeshua were greatly troubled. Hastily they called together the leaders of the people.

"Shall we allow the Samaritans to build the Temple with us?" they asked.

"We are in favor," replied some of the leaders. "They too believe in one God. If we allow them to build with us we shall be one strong nation. If we do not, they will be our enemies forever."

"We are not in favor of allowing the Samaritans to build the Temple with us," replied other leaders. "They are not really our friends. They are our enemies and are only looking for ways to prevent our growth. They will gain control of our nation and prevent us from worshiping God in truth. Although they study the 5 Books of Moses they know nothing about the words of our prophets. They will turn us astray into false ways."

Most of the leaders did not believe that the Samaritans really wanted to help. They were afraid too that the Samaritans would prevent the people from worshiping God with pure hearts as commanded by the prophets.

Zerubbabel and Jeshua agreed with those who opposed the

Samaritans. It was decided not to accept the Samaritan offer.

"We cannot build the Temple with you," they replied to the Samaritans, "for we are not one nation. King Cyrus of Persia has commanded us to build the Temple, and we will carry out his command by ourselves."

The Samaritans knew that King Cyrus was too busy waging war to protect the Jews. They attacked the caravans bringing wood and supplies to Jerusalem. They sent messengers to the Persian military commanders claiming that the Jews had no right to build the Temple.

Their attacks succeeded. Zerubbabel and Jeshua soon found that the people grew discouraged and that they refused to continue the building of the Temple.

Zerubbabel, however, pleaded with the settlers to hasten the building of the wall around Jerusalem.

"If we do not build this wall," he said, "the Samaritans and Edomites can attack and destroy us all."

Zerubbabel hoped that Cyrus would return from war and order the Samaritans to cease their attacks. Alas, King Cyrus was killed in battle. The Jews knew that they had lost one of their greatest friends.

The son of Cyrus reigned as king of the Persians.

The Samaritans lost no time in writing to the new king with the help of the Persian captain stationed in Samaria.

"Be it known unto the king," they wrote, "that the Jews are building a wall around Jerusalem without permission. Once the wall is completed the Jews will refuse to pay tribute to Persia. Let a search be made in the records and it will be found that Jerusalem has rebelled many times in its history against its rulers. Such a rebellion can spread to all of the countries west of the Euphrates River."

The new king replied to the Persian captain in Samaria:

"The letter which you sent was read to me. We have searched the records and have found your words to be true. Jerusalem rebelled many times and was laid waste for that reason by Babylon. Hasten and prevent any further building in Jerusalem. Why should we allow the seeds of rebellion to grow?"

Thus, all work on the wall of the city and on the Temple soon ceased.

4. THE MENORAH

Fifteen years had now passed since Zerubbabel had led the Jews back from exile. He had been a wise and righteous governor, but little progress had been made in building the Temple or the wall around Jerusalem.

The son of Cyrus died and Darius the Mede ascended the throne as king of the Medes and Persians.

A new prophet named Zechariah now arose to encourage the leaders to resume the building of the Temple.

"Let your hands be strong," said the prophet, "for God will help you."

The people would gather in the market-place to hear the words of the prophet as once they had listened to Isaiah, Jeremiah and Ezekiel.

"What will become of us?" asked the people, "Will we be able to rebuild Jerusalem?"

"In my mind's eye I see a picture of Jerusalem in the future," replied the prophet Zechariah. "The streets of the city are full of boys and girls playing, unafraid. Many men and women who have lived happily to a ripe old age walk through the city. They worship God with pure hearts, and show mercy to the stranger and to the poor. And the city is called by all, 'The city of truth.' "

"How can we worship God if His Temple is not restored?" asked the people.

"Soon, soon, you shall see the builder's tools in the hands of Zerubbabel," replied Zechariah. "His hands have laid the foundation and his hands will complete the Temple."

The prophet then continued, "Hear my vision, O men and women of Jerusalem.

"As I slept I dreamed that an angel of God awakened me. I followed him to the Temple site.

" 'What do you see?' asked the angel.

"I looked and saw a beautiful *menorah*. The candlestick was all of gold. And the candlestick had seven lamps. Each lamp was connected with a little pipe that drew oil from a central bowl. Near the bowl stood two olive trees, one on each side.

"A beautiful light shone from the *menorah*. The gold of the candlestick glittered. I turned to the angel and asked what these meant.

" 'The Temple will again spread light to all mankind,' replied the angel, 'just as this *menorah* spreads light.'

" 'But how can the Temple be restored?' I asked. 'We have no power to fight against our enemies.'

" 'Just as the *menorah* draws its light from an unseen source, so too the house of Israel will draw its strength from an unseen source—from God. Not by might, nor by power, but by My spirit, says the Lord of hosts.'

" 'And what is the meaning of the two olive trees?' I asked.

" 'These are the two leaders who will finish the work of God—Zerubbabel and Jeshua. Nothing shall stand in their way.'

"I awakened," said the prophet, "and knew that our strength must come from God. Do not worry about our enemies. The Temple will be rebuilt and will shine like the *menorah*, spreading truth and light unto the whole world."

The people heard the words of Zechariah and were comforted.

5. THE COMPLETION OF THE SECOND TEMPLE

Encouraged by Zechariah and by other leaders, Zerubbabel and Jeshua resumed their work on the Temple and on the city wall.

The Samaritans immediately turned to the Persian officers, and asked them to interfere.

"Who gave you permission to build this house?" demanded the Persian governor.

Zerubbabel and Jeshua replied:

"King Cyrus issued a proclamation saying that we could return from Babylon to Jerusalem to build a Temple to God. And the gold and silver vessels which were taken from Jerusalem by Nebuchadnezzar were restored to us by King Cyrus. Search in the records and you will find that our words are true."

The Persian officers wrote to Darius, but meanwhile allowed the work to continue.

The Jews sent a delegation to King Darius in Persia to plead for his help. It is possible that Zerubbabel himself headed the delegation. This is the same king about whom we read in the story of Daniel.

King Darius ordered that the records be searched. He found a scroll which recorded the proclamation of Cyrus.

He immediately wrote to his officers in the Land of Israel to permit the work to continue.

"Let the work of this house of God alone," he wrote. "Let the governor of the Jews and his helpers build this house of God. Let their expenses be paid from the king's treasury. If anybody disturbs them, let a beam be pulled out from his house, and let him be fastened to the beam. May God protect the builders from all their enemies. I, King Darius, have made a decree. Let it be carried out as soon as possible."

The Persian officers hastened to Jerusalem to carry out the decree of King Darius. The work now continued without interruption. Soon there was a wall around the entire city protecting Jerusalem from enemy attacks.

Zerubbabel finally finished the building of the Temple 20

years after he had led the exiles back from Babylon. 70 years had passed since the first Temple had been destroyed.

Again there was great rejoicing. And the people sang a song of thanksgiving:

> "Enter into His gates with thanksgiving,
> And into His courts with praise
> Give thanks unto Him, and bless His name,
> For the Lord is good,
> His mercy endures forever."

And the rejoicing continued for eight days just as in the time of King Solomon when the First Temple was dedicated.

EXERCISES

I. Answer each question in a complete sentence. (Review sections 1 and 2, pages 31 to 34.)

1. Why were the Babylonians sure that they could withstand a long siege?
2. How did Cyrus gain entrance to Babylon?
3. What did Cyrus state in his proclamation to the Jews?
4. Who led the Jews back to Jerusalem?
5. When did the people sing, "Praise the Lord"?

II. Choose the right word or phrase. (Review section 3, pages 34 to 37.)

1. The Samaritans lived (north, south) of Jerusalem.
2. The Samaritans worshiped (God, idols).
3. The Samaritans were (friendly, unfriendly) to the Jews in Jerusalem.
4. Zerubbabel decided (to permit, not to permit) the Samaritans to help rebuild the Temple.
5. The Samaritans wrote that the Jews (would not worship the king, would rebel against the king).

III. What did Zechariah say about each of the following? (Review section 4, pages 37 to 38.)
   1. Jerusalem
   2. boys and girls
   3. the Temple
   4. the enemies of the Jewish people
   5. Zerubbabel and Jeshua

IV. True or false? (Review section 5, pages 38 to 40.)
   1. Zerubbabel was encouraged by Zechariah to resume work on the Temple.
   2. The Egyptians interfered with the rebuilding of the Temple.
   3. The Jews sent a delegation to King Darius.
   4. Darius found the proclamation of King Cyrus.
   5. Darius ordered that the work be stopped.
   6. 70 years passed between the destruction of the First Temple and the building of the Second Temple.

V. Questions for discussion:
   1. Compare the proclamation of Cyrus and the Balfour Declaration of 1917. The Balfour Declaration states:

   "His Majesty's Government view with favor the establment in Palestine of a National Home for the Jewish people, and will use their best endeavors to facilitate the achievement of this object, it being clearly understood that nothing shall be done which may prejudice the civil and religious rights of existing non-Jewish communities of Palestine, or the rights and political status enjoyed by Jews in any other country."

   2. Zerubbabel has been called the greatest Jewish political leader since Solomon. Why?
   3. Compare the problems of those who returned to the Land of Israel with Zerubbabel and those in Israel today.
   4. What was meant by Zechariah when he said, "Not by

might, nor by power, but by My spirit, says the Lord of hosts."?

THINGS TO DO

1. *Posters*—Print posters containing the words of the proclamation by Cyrus; the Balfour Declaration; the Zechariah prophecy, "Not by might, nor by power, but by My spirit, says the Lord of hosts."

2. *Council of Leaders*—Pretend you have been selected as delegates to a council of leaders. Debate the question, "Should the Samaritans be permitted to help in the rebuilding of the Temple?" The person chosen as Zerubbabel can preside.

3. *Model of Temple*—Build a model of the Second Temple. Pictures of the Temple can be found in the Jewish Encyclopedia.

CALENDAR PROBLEMS

1. The First Temple was destroyed in 586 B.C.E. (Before the Common Era). 70 years passed before the Second Temple was completed. In what year was the Second Temple finished?

2. Cyrus gave the Jews permission to return to Jerusalem in 536 B.C.E. How many years ago did this event take place?

CHAPTER III

STRENGTHENING JERUSALEM

1. EZRA

JEWS throughout the world heard the good news about the rebuilding of Jerusalem, and they rejoiced. They repeated the words of the prophet, "Comfort ye, comfort ye My people."

From all parts of the world Jews streamed back to the Land of Israel. They came from Egypt, from Assyria, from Babylon. They came one by one, or by families, or in large groups.

About a generation after the death of Zerubbabel a group of 1600 Jews arrived from Babylon under the leadership of Ezra.

Ezra was a scribe; that is, a man who wrote copies of the holy books. Carefully, word for word, Ezra would copy the 5 Books of Moses and the teachings of the prophets.

When messengers arrived from Jerusalem, Ezra and the other Hebrew leaders in Babylon would eagerly inquire, "What news do you bring from the Land of Israel?"

But Ezra was disappointed by what he heard. Jeshua's son served as *Kohen Gadol*, but the governors who succeeded Zerubbabel were weak and selfish. The children of the settlers were growing up without knowledge of the teachings of Moses.

"I will go up to Jerusalem," said Ezra, "and settle there. I will do all that I can to teach the Torah to the Jews of Jerusalem."

The king of Persia, who admired Ezra's wisdom and learning, gave him a large sum of money as a present to the Temple.

The king also gave him a letter ordering all Persian officers to protect Ezra and his group of pilgrims. The *Kohanim* and Levites who served in the Temple were freed from all taxes.

Ezra was also given authority to appoint judges who would judge the people in keeping with the laws of the Torah.

Ezra and the 1600 pilgrims arrived peacefully in Jerusalem. The people of Jerusalem rejoiced to greet this large band of pilgrims.

Ezra soon discovered that things were even worse than he had been told. The people of Jerusalem had intermarried with the many surrounding tribes. The children spoke strange languages, and knew nothing about the teachings of the Torah.

Once more the fear of the Samaritans gripped Jerusalem. The wall had broken down in many places, and there was nobody to repair the wall. In case of an attack Jerusalem would be defenceless.

Ezra called the leaders to him and declared, "We cannot allow intermarriage. Even King Solomon was led astray by his foreign wives. If we permit such marriages, our children will forget the teachings of our Torah. They will worship false gods and bring disaster on the house of Israel."

Recognizing the truth of Ezra's words, the people agreed not to allow such marriages.

Ezra then appointed judges, and devoted his efforts to teaching the word of God.

2. NEHEMIAH

Ezra had no authority to repair the wall of Jerusalem. The city remained defenceless. There were several years of drought when the crops were ruined. The farmers were in great debt and complained bitterly.

In the city of Shushan, capital of Persia, lived a great Jewish leader named Nehemiah. He served as the king's cupbearer. The king relied on Nehemiah as one of his most trusted advisers

Nehemiah's brother, Hanani, lived in Jerusalem. When Hanani returned to Shushan for a brief visit Nehemiah asked, "How do the people fare in the Land of Israel?"

"They are in great trouble," replied Hanani. "Those outside of Jerusalem are in constant danger of attack by unfriendly tribes. The wall of Jerusalem is broken down, and the gates in the wall have been burnt by fire."

Nehemiah prayed to God for the strength to help his people.

When Nehemiah next appeared before King Artaxerxes, the king noticed how sad Nehemiah looked.

"Why are you so sad?" asked the king.

"Why should I not be sad?" replied Nehemiah. "Jerusalem, the city of my fathers, still lies in ruins."

"What is your request?" asked the king.

"If it please the king, send me to Jerusalem that I may rebuild it."

"Your request is granted," said the king, "provided you return to Persia after your work is done."

The king then gave Nehemiah a letter appointing him governor of Jerusalem, and ordering the Persian officers to provide him with all the materials that he needed.

Nehemiah arrived in Jerusalem accompanied by several Persian captains and horsemen. Secretly, Nehemiah made a tour that night around the wall of the city.

In most places the wall built by Zerubbabel was completely thrown down. The gates leading into the city were burnt by fire. In some places the road had so many obstructions that it was almost impossible for Nehemiah to pass by.

The next day Nehemiah showed the officers of the city his letters from the king appointing him governor. Ezra rejoiced to hear of the coming of Nehemiah.

"Jerusalem lies in ruins," said Nehemiah. "Come let us build its walls."

"Our enemies are strong," replied the officers. "The Samaritans, the Ammonites and the Arabs led by Sanballat will destroy us."

"God will protect us," answered Nehemiah. "We will fight back bravely to defend what we build."

Inspired by Nehemiah, the officers consented.

"Let us rise up and build," they said.

Sanballat, leader of the Samaritans and hostile tribes, soon heard what had happened.

"We laugh at your efforts," said Sanballat's messengers. "The foxes and beasts of the field will throw down whatever you build!"

"We are not afraid of your threats," replied Nehemiah. "We shall build without fear."

3. THE WALL IS BUILT

The people at first gave many excuses for not repairing the wall.

"We are not strong enough to bring the wood and stone here," they complained. "There is so much debris, it is impossible to clear it away."

Nehemiah knew that the real reason for their complaints was fear of the Samaritans. He calmed their fears, saying he would set up a guard to warn them of danger.

Now the work proceeded quickly. Each family or group was assigned a special task, and all worked hard to carry out their duties.

When Sanballat saw that the wall was being quickly repaired, he secretly planned an attack.

"We will take them by surprise, slay all who are building and destroy what they have built," boasted Sanballat.

Nehemiah, however, was well prepared. His spies soon informed him of Sanballat's plans.

Nehemiah armed half of his men with swords, shields, bows

and arrows and spears. The other half were engaged in building but they too carried swords at their sides.

Near Nehemiah stood a man with *shofar* or ram's horn. At the sounding of the horn the builders would leave their work and rush to assist those who were being attacked. There were trumpeters placed at every 500 feet.

Thus with tools in one hand and a sword in the other the Jews continued to build.

Sanballat now sought to destroy Nehemiah by strategy. He would invite Nehemiah to a peace conference, seize him and kill him.

"Why do we quarrel?" said Sanballat's messenger to Nehemiah. "Let us meet in the open valley and make peace."

Nehemiah understood that Sanballat planned to seize him and to kill him. Knowing that he could not bring an army with him to such a meeting to protect him, Nehemiah refused.

"I am engaged in a great task," replied Nehemiah, "and I cannot interrupt my work for even a day."

Sanballat sent several delegations but could not persuade Nehemiah to leave Jerusalem.

Sanballat now tried another scheme. He sent a spy to Nehemiah who pretended he was trying to save Nehemiah's life.

"Sanballat has hired men to murder you," said the spy. "There is only one way to save your life. Escape to the Temple and hide in the Holy of Holies. The murderers will not dare follow you into the Holy of Holies."

Sanballat knew that only the *Kohen Gadol* entered the Holy of Holies once a year, on Yom Kippur. If Nehemiah entered, the people would be outraged by such a sin. Nehemiah might then lose his influence with the people who would refuse to continue their work.

Nehemiah understood Sanballat's plan.

"I will not sin by entering the Holy of Holies," he told the spy. "I am not afraid. Men like me do not run away!"

Nehemiah knew that he really was in danger. Some of the families in Jerusalem that had intermarried were eager to destroy him. They wrote letters to Sanballat informing him of every move made by Nehemiah. But he was carefully guarded day and night.

As a last resort Sanballat wrote to Nehemiah accusing him of rebellion.

"It has been reported to me," wrote Sanballat, "that you are planning to rebel against the king of Persia. You are building this wall so that you can withstand a siege by the Persians. I have been told that you have hired men to proclaim you king of Jerusalem."

Sanballat hoped that Nehemiah, out of fear of the Persians, would discontinue the rebuilding of the wall.

Nehemiah replied, "God knows that I have no such plan. The king of Persia has given me permission to rebuild. This is only another of your schemes to delay our work."

At last, after two years of hard work the wall was finished. Sanballat knew that his plans were defeated.

Jerusalem was now too strong to be attacked. The Jews could live in their capital city unafraid. Peace had come to Jerusalem.

EXERCISES

I. Complete each sentence. (Review section 1, pages 43 to 44.)
  1. From all parts of the world Jews returned to the Land of _____.
  2. 1600 Jews came from Babylon under the leadership of _____.
  3. One who writes copies of the holy books is called a _____.
  4. Ezra went to Jerusalem to teach the _____.
  5. Ezra was angry because some of the Jews of Jerusalem had married _____.

THE RETURN TO ZION 49

II. Match. (Review section 2, pages 44 to 46.)

Column A   *Column B*
Ezra   1. leader of Samaritans
Shushan   2. king of Persia
Nehemiah   3. capital of Persia
Artaxerxes   4. scribe
Sanballat   5. cup-bearer

III. Why? (Review section 3, pages 46 to 48.)
  1. Why did the people complain about rebuilding the wall?
  2. Why did Nehemiah order the builders to carry tools in one hand and weapons in the other?
  3. Why did Nehemiah refuse to meet Sanballat at a conference in the valley?
  4. Why did Sanballat want Nehemiah to hide in the Holy of Holies?
  5. Why did the Jews now feel safe?

IV. Questions for discussion:
  1. Compare the problems that Zerubbabel had to solve and the problems that Ezra and Nehemiah had to solve.
  2. "Babylon was an enemy of the Jews, but Persia was a friend." Show how this is true.
  3. "Sanballat" now means a treacherous, scheming villain. Why?
  4. Zerubbabel and Nehemiah both refused to allow the Samaritans to join the Jews in building the Temple. Were they justified?

THINGS TO DO

1. *Meet the Press*—Pretend you are arranging a television broadcast similar to "Meet the Press." Let the reporters ask Nehemiah challenging questions. Here are some possible questions: a—Why weren't the Samaritans permitted to join in building the Temple? b—Is it true that Nehemiah was building the wall in order to rebel against Persia? c—Did Nehemiah have any ambitions of becoming king in Jerusalem? d—Could the Jews defend

themselves against their hostile neighbors? e—What was the attitude of the Jews who had intermarried to the rebuilding of the wall? f—Why didn't Nehemiah arrange a peace conference with Sanballat?

2. *Original Story*—Write a story about a Jew from Jerusalem who was captured by Sanballat's soldiers. Let the story end happily.

A GAME

Each student selects the name of a person important in Jewish history. When your name is called, respond by quickly mentioning one fact about the person selected. You then continue by calling another name. For example, if "Nehemiah" is called, the student might say, "Governor of Jerusalem." He in turn then calls out a name such as Abraham.

The same fact can be mentioned only once. A student who fails to answer within a few seconds is out of the game.

CHAPTER IV

THE REFORMS OF NEHEMIAH AND EZRA

1. PROTECTING JERUSALEM

INSIDE the wall Nehemiah built a strong fortress. The captain of the fortress, Hananiah, and Nehemiah's brother, Hanani, were given military control of Jerusalem. Both were reliable and faithful men.

"Let the gates of Jerusalem be shut and barred every night," ordered Nehemiah. "Appoint guards to watch the gates. Every man in Jerusalem must take his turn. Let not the gates be opened until morning when the sun is hot. On the Sabbath let no merchants enter to sell their wares, for the Sabbath is holy unto God."

Both men promised to guard Jerusalem against all danger.

Nehemiah, however, was worried because Jerusalem had so few inhabitants. The city was large, but the houses were few. In case of attack there would not be enough defenders.

Nehemiah called the Jews of the villages together and asked that one out of every ten reside in Jerusalem.

Lots were cast, and those chosen by lot built houses in Jerusalem.

Jerusalem was now strong and secure.

2. HELPING THE POOR

Then there arose a great outcry because of the lack of rain. Crops failed and many went hungry. Those who tried to borrow were forced to pay back two pieces of silver or two measures of grain for every piece of silver or measure of grain they borrowed.

"Give us food," the farmers demanded of Nehemiah. "We have no bread for our children. Give us food so that we may eat and live."

"The king demands heavy taxes," added other farmers. "When we cannot pay we must mortgage our fields, our vineyards and our houses. And when we cannot pay those from whom we have borrowed, we must sell our daughters as servants to pay our debts."

Nehemiah was very sad when he heard these complaints.

In great anger he called together the princes and the nobles.

"You have done an evil thing," said Nehemiah. "We are commanded to redeem our brothers. Instead you have bought their children as slaves."

The nobles, ashamed, asked, "What shall we do to help our brothers?"

"Return their fields, and their vineyards and their houses. Free those who have been sold as servants. Lend them food and money. They will repay when they can, but do not force them to pay interest. This is what our Torah commands us to do."

"We shall do as you say," replied the nobles. "We shall restore their property, and lend them money and food without charge. In this way they will live and not die."

The nobles carried out their promise and helped their neighbors in time of trouble.

"Now we see how wonderful the Torah is," said the people. "The Torah commands us to help our brothers in need and not to take advantage of their poverty."

And all praised Nehemiah, the great governor, who had saved the poor from hunger and from slavery by enforcing the laws of the Torah.

3. THE GREAT ASSEMBLY

When Rosh Ha-Shanah came the people gathered in the Temple to celebrate the New Year.

They then turned to Ezra the scribe saying, "Read to us from the law of Moses."

A special platform had been built in the largest open square of Jerusalem. Ezra the scribe mounted the platform. He took the scroll of the law and blessed the name of God. The people stood up and answered, "Amen! Amen!"

Ezra then read from the scroll. He read from early morning until midday. The people heard the wonderful laws of Moses, and resolved that they would carry out these laws.

At first many began to weep, for they knew that not always had they obeyed the laws of Moses.

When Ezra and Nehemiah saw the people weeping they comforted them saying, "Go your way; eat and drink, and send portions to the poor. Do not weep, but rejoice for this day is holy unto the Lord."

Ten days later the Jews observed Yom Kippur, and then, on the fifteenth of the month, they began the celebration of Sukkot.

Each person built a *sukkah*, or booth, of olive branches and wood. Processions were formed during which the people carried palm branches, citrons, myrtle and willow leaves. The booths reminded them of the wandering of the Israelites in the desert for 40 years. The palm branches and citrons were a sign of thanksgiving for the crops they had just harvested.

For eight days they celebrated the feast.

On the day after the feast, Ezra and Nehemiah called a great assembly. All the princes, nobles and *kohanim* were present at this assembly.

For many hours Ezra read from the scroll of the law. After this, the people confessed their sins. All present then stood while a prayer was recited thanking God who had guided the Hebrew nation since the days of Abraham.

The people concluded with the words, "For all this we make a sure covenant, and set our seal unto it."

85 leaders of the nation then approached to sign their names

to the covenant. This was a great day in Israel for it meant that the people had accepted the Torah as their constitution.

This was the beginning of the Great Assembly. In Hebrew this group was called the *Knesset Ha-g'dolah*. The Great Assembly continued to meet for many years under the leadership of Ezra, and made many wise and just laws for the people of Israel.

Nehemiah rejoiced that he had lived to see the day when the Torah was accepted as the constitution of the house of Israel.

He felt that his work was done, and that it was now time for him to return to Persia. He had been governor for 12 years.

"I shall come back to Jerusalem if I am needed," said Nehemiah at the time of his departure.

He did return several years later when a serious dispute arose in the Temple. Although the king allowed him to remain only a short time, he was successful in his new mission.

The people of Jerusalem thanked Nehemiah for all he had done. He had built the city wall, strengthened Jerusalem, helped the poor and defended the Jews against their enemies.

Nehemiah was one of the greatest leaders in Jewish history.

4. THE BIBLE

The Torah was the constitution of Israel. On Sabbaths and on market-days, the people gathered to pray and to study the Torah. This custom had also been followed in Babylon.

Ezra and the leaders of the Great Assembly drew up a schedule of Torah passages to be studied and of prayers to be recited.

Thus began the first Jewish synagogues.

Throughout the land Ezra sent *Kohanim* and teachers to teach the words of the Torah. Ezra carefully copied the writings of Moses and of the prophets, and arranged them in clear order.

Were it not for Ezra and the Great Assembly many of these

writings would have been lost. We might call Ezra the editor of the holy scriptures.

In Hebrew the writings of Moses and the prophets were called Torah. Later when these holy writings were translated into other languages they came to be known as the Bible.

Bible means "book." The Bible is really "the book of books"; it is the most important book ever written.

All nations later learned to read the Bible and to accept its teachings. They began to believe in one God. The ten commandments were accepted as the basis of civilization. "Love your neighbor as yourself" became the golden rule of society.

Men were inspired by the words of the prophets teaching peace, justice and brotherhood. In time of trouble people read the Bible for comfort and for hope.

2000 years after Ezra, when printing was invented, the Bible was the first book to be printed.

The Bible was translated into English many times. In Shakespeare's day, King James of England ordered the great scholars to prepare a new translation. This translation was so beautiful that the King James Bible became the glory of English literature.

When the Pilgrims came to America they prepared their own translations. The first book published in America was the Bay Psalm Book, which contained translations from the psalms of David.

The Pilgrims accepted the Bible as their constitution. They gave their children Biblical names and called their cities after the cities of ancient Israel. Their holidays, like Thanksgiving, were modeled after Biblical holidays.

The founders of the American republic often turned to the Bible for guidance. They were inspired by the words of Moses inscribed on the Liberty Bell, "Proclaim liberty throughout all the land unto all the inhabitants thereof." The struggle of the children of Israel against Pharaoh for liberty encouraged the American patriots to fight for independence.

Everywhere the Bible has helped people to lead a good life. It has been translated into every spoken language. Thus far it has been translated into more than 2000 languages.

The world owes a great debt to Ezra who helped preserve the Bible. That is why Ezra has often been called "The second Moses."

EXERCISES

I. Explain the reason for each of the following commands by Nehemiah. (Review sections 1 and 2, pages 51 to 52.)
   1. "Let the gates of Jerusalem be shut and barred at night."
   2. "On the Sabbath let no merchants enter."
   3. "One out of every ten Jews must move from the villages to Jerusalem."
   4. "Restore the fields, and vineyards and houses."
   5. "Lend the people food and money."

II. Choose the correct name or phrase. (Review section 3, pages 52 to 54.)
   1. The scroll of the law was read on Rosh Ha-Shanah by (Ezra, Nehemiah).
   2. Booths were built on (Sukkot, Yom Kippur).
   3. The covenant was signed by (12, 85) princes and leaders.
   4. *Knesset Ha-g'dolah* means (Great Assembly, Temple).
   5. Nehemiah returned after 12 years to (Babylon, Persia).

III. Complete, each sentence. (Review section 4, pages 54 to 56.)
   David, Ezra, Moses, Pharaoh, Torah
   1. _____ was the leader of the Great Assembly.
   2. The Jews gathered in synagogues to pray and to study _____.
   3. The first book published in America contained the psalms of _____.
   4. On the Liberty Bell are inscribed the words of _____, "Proclaim liberty throughout all the land unto all the inhabitants thereof."

5. American patriots were encouraged to fight for freedom by the struggle of the children of Israel against _____.

IV. Questions for discussion:
1. In your opinion which was Nehemiah's greatest achievement? Why?
2. Why is Ezra called "The second Moses"?
3. When the new state of Israel was formed in 1948, the founders chose the name *Knesset* for the law-making body. Do you think this was a good choice of name? Why?
4. What has been the influence of the Bible on America?

THINGS TO DO

1. *Model of Jerusalem Wall*—Build a model of the wall around Jerusalem. Consult the Jewish Encyclopedia for pictures of this wall.

2. *Scroll of Law*—Make a miniature scroll of the law by pasting sheets of paper together in horizontal order. Attach at each end to wooden spools or rollers. Copy some quotations from the Bible with a quill (feather used as a pen).

Examine a real scroll in the synagogue as a model.

3. *Research*—The Samaritans later built their own temple on Mt. Gerizim. Today, there are only a few hundred Samaritans left.

Find out more about the history of the Samaritans. In what way does their religion resemble Judaism? Tell about their Passover sacrifice which they still offer each year on Mt. Gerizim.

SCRAMBLED NAMES—A PUZZLE

Unscramble the following names. When properly arranged the letters will spell out the names of people who are well known in Jewish history.

1. ZERA
2. RYCUS
3. ANDELI
4. RADIUS
5. AEHJSU
6. EEEIKLZ
7. HAIMEREJ
8. HAIMEHEN
9. HAIRAHCEZ
10. ABBBEELRUZ

CHAPTER V

THE STORY OF PURIM

1. TWO QUEENS

PERSIA was friendly not only to the Jews of Jerusalem but to the Jews in all of Persia.

Once King Ahasuerus, who ruled over the 127 provinces of Persia, made a banquet for his nobles and servants. This was followed by a feast for all the people of Shushan, the capital city. Queen Vashti arranged a special feast for the women of Shushan.

The people swarmed through the royal gardens, and drank wine from vessels of gold. For seven days the Persians ate, and drank, and feasted.

On the seventh day, when the king was merry with wine, he ordered beautiful Queen Vashti to appear before the people.

"Let all Persia know how beautiful you are," said King Ahasuerus.

If Ahasuerus had not been drunk he would never have made such a request. In Persia a queen never appeared in public.

Queen Vashti refused to appear before the people of Shushan.

In great anger Ahasuerus called his wise men and asked, "What shall be done to a queen who refuses to obey the king's command?"

"This is a crime not only against the king but against all Persia," replied one of the chamberlains. "When the women of Persia hear of the queen's disobedience they too will disobey the commands of their husbands. Let the crown be taken from Queen Vashti! Let the women throughout Persia know they must give honor to their husbands!"

The king was pleased with this advice and removed Vashti from the throne.

The king's servants then said, "Let us search throughout Persia and find a beautiful maiden to take the place of Queen Vashti."

The most beautiful girls in Persia were brought before the king, but none found favor in his eyes.

In one of the provinces of Persia the servants found a beautiful Jewish girl named Esther (her Hebrew name was Hadassah). Esther was an orphan girl who had been adopted by her older cousin, Mordecai.

Before Esther was taken to the castle, Mordecai warned her not to reveal that she was a Jewess.

"Some day," said Mordecai, "you may be able to help your people in time of trouble."

Each day Mordecai walked before the court of the women's house to find out what had happened to Esther. At last, after 12 months of waiting, Esther was brought before the king.

Ahasuerus fell in love with the beautiful Esther at first sight.

"You shall be my queen," said the king joyfully.

Esther was crowned queen and a special feast was declared in her honor. And all Persia rejoiced that the king had found a new queen.

2. MORDECAI AND HAMAN

In those days, while Mordecai sat before the king's gate, he overheard two chamberlains plotting against the king. Mordecai reported the plot to Esther who informed the king.

The two chamberlains, Bigthan and Teresh, were immediately arrested. Upon investigation they were found to be guilty and were hanged. The scribes recorded the details of the plot in the king's chronicle and wrote that Mordecai had saved the life of Ahasuerus.

Several years later the king appointed Haman his prime minister.

"Let all my servants bow before Haman," commanded the king.

Mordecai, however, refused to bow, for he said, "I am a Jew and I bow only before God."

When Haman saw that Mordecai refused to bow he became very angry.

"It is beneath my dignity to take notice of this man alone," said Haman. "Instead I shall wipe out his whole nation."

Haman then commanded his servants to bring before him *purim* (lots), so that he could cast lots to find out on what day to destroy the Jews. The lot fell on the thirteenth day of the month *Adar*.

Appearing before the king, Haman said, "O your Majesty, there is a certain nation scattered throughout Persia whose laws are different from those of all other people. They deserve death since they do not obey the king's laws. If it please the king, let it be written that they be destroyed. In return for their destruction I will pay 10,000 pieces of silver."

"Here is the king's seal," replied Ahasuerus. "You may inscribe this law in my name, and stamp the decree with the king's seal. But no money is necessary. You may do with this nation as you please."

Letters were soon sent to the 127 provinces of Persia ordering the death of all Jews, young and old, on the thirteenth day of *Adar*.

Mordecai heard the sad news and mourned greatly. Weeping and wailing he clothed himself in sackcloth and ashes, and sat before the king's gate.

When Esther's servants told her that Mordecai was in mourning she sent her chamberlain to find out the reason for his grief.

Mordecai informed Esther, by means of her chamberlain, of Haman's wicked decree.

Then Mordecai added these words to the chamberlain, "The

queen must go before the king to plead that her people be saved."

"Tell Mordecai," said Esther to the chamberlain, "that I have not been called before the king for the past thirty days. He knows that anybody who dares to approach the throne uninvited is immediately put to death, unless the king holds out his golden sceptre."

Mordecai asked the chamberlain to bring back this message to Esther, "Do not think that you will escape if all other Jews are slain. If you fail to help at this time, then God will deliver the Jews in some other way, but you will perish. Who knows—perhaps you have come to royal estate to help in just such a time as this."

"I will do as you say," consented Esther. "Gather all the Jews of Shushan and ask them to fast and to pray for me. I will approach the king's throne, even though it is against the law. And if I perish, I perish!"

3. THE MAN WHOM THE KING DELIGHTS TO HONOR

The king smiled when Esther approached, and extended his golden sceptre. Ahasuerus loved his beautiful queen with all his heart.

Esther drew near and touched the top of the sceptre.

Then said the king, "What is your wish, Queen Esther? Even if you request half of my kingdom it shall be given to you."

And Esther replied, "If it seem good unto the king, let the king and Haman come this day unto the banquet that I have prepared for him."

At the banquet of wine the king again asked what Esther's request was.

"Let the king and Haman come again tomorrow to another banquet. Then I shall tell you what my wish is," said Esther.

Haman went forth that day joyful and glad of heart. But

when Haman saw Mordecai in the king's gate, he was filled with anger.

Haman turned to Zeresh, his wife, and to his friends for advice.

"I have been invited by the queen to a banquet that she has prepared for the king and for me. The king has placed me above all other officers. Yet these honors mean nothing to me as long as I see the impudent Mordecai at the king's gate."

"Let a gallows be made fifty cubits high," advised Zeresh and Haman's friends. "In the morning ask the king to allow you to hang Mordecai on the gallows. Then you can go merrily to the banquet."

The advice pleased Haman, and he ordered that the gallows be made.

On that night the king was restless and could not sleep.

"Bring the book of chronicles to me," commanded Ahasuerus.

All that night the king's servants read from the book of chronicles. When Ahasuerus heard how Mordecai had saved his life, he asked, "What reward has Mordecai received?"

"He has not received any award," replied the servants.

"He shall be honored without any further delay," said Ahasuerus. "See who is in the outer court."

Haman stood in the outer court waiting to speak to the king about hanging Mordecai.

When Haman was brought before the king, Ahasuerus asked, "What shall be done unto the man whom the king delights to honor?"

"Surely he means me," thought Haman.

Aloud he said, "Let the man be clothed in royal garments. Let him ride on the king's horse. Let one of the king's nobles lead this man through the streets of Shushan. And let the noble proclaim, 'Thus shall be done to the man whom the king delights to honor.'"

"That is an excellent suggestion," said the king. "Go find

Mordecai the Jew and do exactly as you suggested, for Mordecai is the man whom the king delights to honor."

In great anger Haman carried out the king's command. He clothed Mordecai in royal garments, and placed him on the king's horse.

Haman then led Mordecai through the streets of Shushan proclaiming as he went, "Thus shall be done to the man whom the king delights to honor! Thus shall be done to the man whom the king delights to honor!"

Head bowed, downcast and humiliated, Haman returned to his home.

"Perhaps you should never have entered into a dispute with Mordecai," said Zeresh sadly. "I am afraid that he will be the victor, and that you will suffer a terrible defeat."

4. ESTHER SAVES HER PEOPLE

The king's chamberlains soon came to Haman's house, and brought him to Esther's banquet.

When Ahasuerus was merry with wine he turned to Queen Esther and said, "Tell me what your wish is. Even if you request half of my kingdom it shall be granted to you."

Then Esther replied, "If I have found favor in your sight, O King, save my life and the lives of my people. We have been sold—I and my people to be destroyed, to be slain and to perish."

"Who is he?" demanded Ahasuerus. "Where is the man who dares to threaten you?"

Pointing to Haman, the queen replied, "There is our enemy —wicked Haman!"

The king was furious when Esther informed him of Haman's wicked plans. Haman fell on his knees and begged the king for mercy.

At that very moment Harbonah, one of the chamberlains, entered.

"Your Majesty," said Harbonah, "we have just heard that

QUEEN ESTHER BEFORE THE KING

Haman has prepared gallows 50 cubits high on which to hang Mordecai."

"The evil he planned for others will fall on his own head," said Ahasuerus. "Hang him on the gallows 50 cubits high!"

Since the laws of the Persians and Medes could never be changed, the king could not revoke Haman's decree to slay the Jews on the thirteenth day of *Adar*.

"I cannot change Haman's decree," said Ahasuerus. "I shall give the Jews the right, however, to defend themselves."

Messengers were quickly sent to the 127 provinces over which Ahasuerus ruled. The Persian officers were ordered to help the Jews defend themselves.

The Jews won a great victory over their enemies who sought to destroy them. On the next day, the fourteenth of *Adar*, there was a splendid victory celebration.

It was a day of gladness and joy for all Jews!

Mordecai then wrote to Jews throughout Persia, "Let us never forget this great day on which God gave us victory over wicked Haman! For on this day He turned sorrow into gladness and mourning into rejoicing. Let us make it a day of feasting, of exchanging presents, and of sending gifts to the poor."

Each year the Jews celebrate this joyous holiday. It is called Purim because of the *purim*, or lots, which Haman cast in choosing a day on which to slay Mordecai and his people.

What a joyous day Purim is!

There are masquerades, carnivals, operettas and parties. We bake delicious *hamantashen*, cakes baked in the shape of Haman's hat.

We read from the *megillah*, or scroll, which tells the wonderful story of Esther and Mordecai. And when Haman's name is mentioned we loudly turn our *groggers*, or noise-makers, to show that we disapprove of Haman and of all who spread hatred and prejudice.

And we all join in singing jolly songs about brave Mordecai and beautiful Esther who with the help of King Ahasuerus defeated the evil plans of wicked Haman:

> So we sing,
> So we sing,
> So we sing and raise a row,
> For Haman he was swinging
> While Mordecai was singing
> In Shu-shu-shushan long ago!

EXERCISES

I. Arrange these sentences in the order in which the events happened. (Review section 1, pages 58 to 59.)
  1. "You shall be my queen," said Ahasuerus to Esther.
  2. Vashti refused to appear before the people of Shushan.
  3. Ahasuerus made a feast for the people of Shushan.
  4. The servants found a beautiful girl named Esther in one of the provinces of Persia.
  5. The king removed Vashti from the throne.
  6. Ahasuerus ordered Vashti to appear at the feast before the people of Shushan.

II. Who? (Review section 2, pages 59 to 61.)
  1. Who conspired against the king?
  2. Who discovered the plot?
  3. Who became prime minister?
  4. Who refused to bow down?
  5. Who gave Haman permission to do as he pleased?
  6. Who consented to plead before the king to save the Jews from destruction?

III. What is my name? (Review sections 3 and 4, pages 61 to 66.)
  1. I prepared two banquets for the king and pleaded with him to save my people.
  2. I was the capital of Persia in ancient days.
  3. I advised my husband to build a gallows 50 cubits high.

4. I was honored by the king because I once saved his life.
5. I tried to destroy all Jews but was sentenced to hanging by the king.
6. I loved my queen and punished the man who tried to destroy her nation.
7. I am a joyous holiday. I come each year on the fourteenth day of the Hebrew month *Adar*.
8. I am a delicious cake. Some people think I look like Haman's hat.
9. I am a scroll in which you can read a wonderful story about a day of mourning that was turned into a day of joy.
10. I am a noisemaker. I make noise to show I don't like those who spread hatred and prejudice.

IV. Questions for discussion:
1. Mention some interesting Persian customs.
2. Do Mordecai and Esther deserve to be elected to a Jewish Hall of Fame? What arguments would you give to support their election?
3. Haman was guilty of prejudice against an entire people. Is prejudice still alive today? How can we eliminate such prejudice?
4. Purim is a holiday we all remember. Mention some memories of previous Purim holidays that you have celebrated.

THINGS TO DO

1. *Purim Arts and Crafts*—Most students like to make *groggers* and masks. The making of an illustrated *megillah* is an interesting project. And of course what's more fun than baking *hamantashen* for the class party!

2. *Purim Projects*—a) Arrange a masquerade. Present prizes for the most appropriate costumes and the most original costumes. b) Prepare a Purim play or operetta for the school assembly. c) Plan a Purim *Adloyada* (Carnival). Arrange booths and games. Proceeds can be sent to some worthy charity.

3. *Mishloach Manot*—Mordecai requested that Purim be celebrated through *mishloach manot* or exchange of gifts. a) A

Purim grab-bag may be arranged as *mishloach manot*. Agree in advance what the approximate value of each gift should be. b) Send a gift as *mishloach manot* to a charitable organization.

FINISH THE JINGLE

On Purim day we love to sing
Of Ahasuerus, the tipsy _____.

As soon as lovely Esther was seen
The king resolved to make her _____.

Praise Mordecai, so brave and true,
Because he was a noble _____.

Oh Haman was a wicked man
But Esther foiled his evil _____.

To turn the *grogger* in joyous noise
Is the custom of Jewish girls and _____.

UNIT TWO

The Glorious Maccabees

CHAPTER VI

THE COMING OF THE GREEKS

1. ALEXANDER THE GREAT

PERSIA continued to rule over the Land of Israel for more than a century after the death of Ezra and Nehemiah.

Persia treated the Jews very kindly. Of course, there was a tax to pay to the king, but there was little interference in the affairs of the Jewish people.

The High Priest and the Great Assembly ruled over Judea in peace. The Jews built houses, planted fields and prospered. They kept the laws of the Torah, worshiped God and helped each other in time of trouble.

The Jewish way of life was best described by the great High Priest, Simon the Just, who said, "The world depends on three things: on Torah, on worship and on kindness to one's fellow-man."

Suddenly a new world conqueror arose—Alexander the Great.

Alexander defeated Persia and Egypt and ruled over Europe, Asia and Africa.

Judea now had a new master!

How did Alexander conquer Judea? The account which has come down to us seems to be part legend and part fact.

When the city of Tyre refused to surrender, Alexander laid siege to the city. He sent a message to Simon the Just in Jerusalem saying, "Send me food for my army. Pay me the taxes that you have always paid to Persia, and I shall treat your nation kindly."

Simon the Just replied, "I have sworn loyalty to the king of Persia and cannot break my oath."

As soon as Alexander conquered Tyre and Gaza he began to march toward Jerusalem.

Knowing that it was impossible to resist, Simon the Just decided to open the gates of Jerusalem. He ordered the *Kohanim* to dress in their priestly garments of linen. He clothed himself in the purple and scarlet robes of the High Priest, and wore the full adornments used when he entered the Temple. The people who accompanied Simon the Just were dressed in white.

Led by Simon, the procession left the gate of Jerusalem and slowly marched toward Mount Scopus, above Jerusalem. Here they met Alexander and his army.

Alexander's soldiers were already prepared to snatch much booty and spoil. But then a strange thing happened.

Alexander dismounted from his horse, approached the High Priest and bowed down before him.

When Alexander had risen, his officers crowded around him in amazement.

"The whole world bows down to you," said one of the officers. "Why do you bow down before the High Priest?"

"I bow not to him but to the God whom he serves," replied Alexander. "When I was still in Macedonia I dreamed that a man dressed in purple and scarlet came to me. He urged me not to be afraid but to carry out my plans without delay. The man in my dream looked very much like the High Priest. Maybe God, in this way, has given me His blessings."

Alexander entered Jerusalem peacefully and offered sacrifices to God in the Temple.

There is a tradition that Alexander wanted a statue of himself placed in the Temple. Simon the Just told Alexander that this was not allowed by the Torah.

"Instead we shall call every child born this year by your name," said the High Priest.

Alexander was pleased and consented. Surely this was a more lasting memorial than any statue could be.

Of one thing we are certain. Alexander treated the Jews with great kindness. He did not demand any taxes during the seventh year when the Jews allowed the land to rest. Jews who joined his army as soldiers were permitted to rest on the Sabbath and on holy days. Jews were invited to settle in Alexandria, Egypt and in other Greek cities that had just been founded.

The Jews rejoiced that Alexander had proved to be such a good friend.

2. THE LEGEND OF ALEXANDER

Many legends about Alexander sprang up among the Jewish people. Most of these legends were later recorded by the Rabbis in the Talmud and have become part of Jewish folklore.

According to one legend Alexander once attacked a city whose inhabitants were all women.

"How foolish it would be for you to attack us," said the women. "If you conquer, people will say you are cruel because you slew women. If we conquer, people will mock you because you were defeated by women."

"Bring out bread for me and my soldiers," commanded Alexander.

The women brought out golden loaves and golden fruit on a golden table.

"Do you eat gold in your country?" asked Alexander in amazement.

"If it is bread that you seek why did you come here? Surely you have enough bread in your own country."

Alexander then wrote on the gate of the city:

"I, foolish Alexander of Macedonia, have been taught wisdom by the women of this city."

Alexander then marched to a city named Katzya where he

was received in friendly manner by the king. Two farmers appeared before the king.

"Your Majesty," said the first. "I bought a field from my neighbor and found a treasure in the field. I want to return the treasure to my friend since it really belongs to him, but he refuses to accept it."

"I sold you the field, and therefore all that is in it belongs to you," replied the second farmer.

"Do you have a son?" asked the king.

"Yes," said the first man.

"Do you have a daughter?"

"I do," answered the second farmer.

"Let the two marry and give them the treasure as a wedding present."

Alexander laughed when he heard the king's decision.

"In my country we would probably slay both men and take the treasure for ourselves," said Alexander.

"Do you have cattle in your country?" asked the king of Katzya.

"Of course," replied Alexander.

"And does it rain in your country?"

"Certainly," said Alexander.

"If it does, it's only by virtue of the cattle in your country that the sun shines or that the rain falls!"

Alexander praised the wise king and then departed.

Finally after much travel, the legend tells us, Alexander reached the walls of Paradise.

"Prove to me that this is the land of the dead," shouted Alexander to the keeper of the gate.

A skull was thrown to him. To Alexander's amazement the skull, when placed on the scale, outweighed all his silver and gold.

"What is the meaning of this?" Alexander asked his wise men.

"This skull contains the human eye," was the reply. "No

matter how much silver and gold is acquired, the eye is never satisfied but yearns for more and more."

The wise men then took a speck of dirt and covered the eye with it. The scale was immediately tipped as the gold and silver outweighed the skull.

"When man is covered by dust, as death comes, the eye loses all desire" explained the wise men.

The many legends about Alexander the Great are proof of the deep impression he made on the Jewish people.

His coming was a turning-point in Jewish history.

3. THE FIRST TRANSLATION OF THE BIBLE

Alexander died after reigning for 12 years. Through Alexander, the Jews made their first lasting contact with the West. Jews were encouraged to settle in great cities, such as Alexandria, and were treated as full citizens.

Alexander left no heir to the throne. After his death his generals began to quarrel about the division of his kingdom. The Greek general who ruled over Egypt gained control of Judea after much bloodshed.

There grew up a close contact between the Jews of Judea and the Jews of Egypt. The Jewish community of Alexandria began to prosper. It soon became next to the most important Jewish community in the world, second only to Jerusalem.

The Jews of Alexandria were very anxious to teach their children the laws of the Torah.

"Our children speak Greek," said the Jews of Alexandria. "How can we teach them the words of Moses which are written in Hebrew?"

The Jews of Alexandria taught their children the Hebrew language. They were overjoyed when the king of Egypt ordered the scholars to translate the 5 Books of Moses into Greek. Such a translation, they knew, would help to spread a knowledge of the Torah.

Why was the king interested in the Torah? This is the legend that has come down to us.

Philadelphus, the king of Egypt, decided to collect the greatest books that had ever been written. His librarian began to assemble all the great books that he could find.

After some time Philadelphus inquired of his librarian, "How many books have you collected?"

"I have collected 995 books," replied the librarian. "But the five greatest books of all are not yet to be found in our library. With these five added there will be 1000."

"And which are the five greatest?" asked Philadelphus.

"The 5 Books of Moses," replied the librarian. "These books are in Hebrew. If it please your Majesty, write to the High Priest of the Jews in Jerusalem. Let him send to us scholars of the Hebrew nation who will translate their laws into Greek."

Philadelphus sent beautiful gifts to the High Priest, Eleazar, the brother of Simon the Just. He requested 70 scholars who would be able to translate the Bible into Greek.

Eleazar was pleased with the king's request. He chose 70 scholars who were received with great honor by the king of Egypt.

Each scholar was given a separate room in a large house on an island. For seventy days, according to the legend, the scholars worked diligently without comparing notes. Each one translated the entire 5 Books of Moses.

At the end of the 70 days the work was finished. When the translations were compared they were all found to be identical in every respect.

When the king heard the words of the Torah he rejoiced because he found such great wisdom in the 5 Books of Moses. Each scholar was given a generous gift by the grateful king.

This translation came to be known as the "Translation of the 70." The anniversary of the day on which the translation was completed became an annual holiday in Alexandria. This holiday was celebrated by both Jews and non-Jews for many years.

Of course, some of the details that have come down to us are legendary. But the legend is a sign of the great importance of the Greek translation written at the request of King Philadelphus.

This was the first translation of the Bible into another language. Since then there have been translations into more than 2000 other languages, thus making the Bible the most widely read book in the history of mankind.

4. UNDER GRECIAN RULE

King Philadelphus was kind to the Jews in many ways. He freed the Jewish captives who had been made slaves in war. He encouraged Jews to settle in Alexandria, which was then the capital of Egypt.

Under the Greeks, the country of Judea began to grow. The farmers were able to export wine, olive oil and fruit. Products of many lands were brought to Judea and sold in the market-places.

Jews who had settled in large Greek cities in Asia, Africa or Europe sent gifts to the Temple so that Jerusalem prospered.

The Jews were unhappy, however, for many reasons.

1. Judea was not independent. The people yearned for the days of King David and Solomon when the Hebrews were completely free.

2. Judea suffered because of the wars between the Greek rulers of Egypt and the Greek rulers of Syria. Judea was caught between two fires. Sometimes Egypt would win and sometimes Syria would win. The wars continued for 150 years after the death of Alexander. The victor would often enter Jerusalem, take many of its inhabitants captive and kill all who tried to resist.

We are told that Judea was like a ship on the ocean tossed

from wave to wave in the storm. Judea was once given away as part of the wedding dowry to Egypt when the king of Egypt married the daughter of the king of Syria.

3. Taxes were very heavy. The king would appoint tax-collectors who were often very cruel. Tax-collectors would hang the leaders of a village if taxes were not paid.

Once at a banquet in the palace of the king of Egypt the guests placed all the bones on the plate of the tax-collector of Judea.

"Why have you done this?" asked the king.

"The tax-collector has stripped the land bare," replied the guests. "He has left nothing but the bones."

4. The Greeks built many new cities in the Land of Israel that were inhabited by non-Jews. These people were often unfriendly. In time of trouble they attacked their Hebrew neighbors.

5. Many Jews began to imitate the Greeks. They took Greek names, dressed like Greeks and spoke Greek. Like the Greeks they took part naked in Greek athletic games. They celebrated the holiday in honor of the Greek god of wine through drunken feasts.

They forgot the laws of the Torah. They no longer observed the Sabbath or Jewish holidays. Some even sacrificed to the Greek gods and tried to deny that they were Jews.

Those who were loyal to the Torah warned the Jews to repent before it was too late. They prayed and hoped for the day when Judea would be free.

EXERCISES

I. Answer each question in a complete sentence. (Review sections 1 and 2, pages 71 to 73.)

1. How did the Persians treat the Jews?
2. According to Simon the Just what are the three most important things in the world for Jews?

3. Why did Alexander bow down before the High Priest?
4. What did Alexander write on the gate of the city of women?
5. When did the silver and gold outweigh the eye?

II. Who? (Review section 3, pages 75 to 77.)

1. Who told the king that the five greatest books in the world were not found in the library?
2. Who invited the scholars to Alexandria?
3. Who selected the scholars to translate the Bible?
4. Who translated the Bible into Greek?
5. Who celebrated the anniversary of the translation of the Bible?

III. True or false? (Review section 4, pages 77 to 78.)

1. Philadelphus was kind to the Jews.
2. The Temple was not well supported while the Greeks ruled Judea.
3. Judea was torn between two fires—between Egypt and Syria.
4. Taxes were very heavy under Greek rule.
5. Jews were proud of the new cities built by the Greeks in the Land of Israel.
6. Some Jews imitated the Greeks.

IV. Questions for discussion:

1. Who did more for the Jewish people—Cyrus or Alexander?
2. Why was the story of the skull from Paradise especially appropriate for Alexander?
3. Why is the translation of the Bible into Greek so important?
4. Were the Jews satisfied with Greek rule?
5. In what ways do Jews today try to carry out the statement made by Simon the Just about Torah, worship and kindness?

THINGS TO DO

1. *Dramatization*—Act out the story of Alexander. Include the following scenes: Alexander and the High Priest; Alexander in the Temple; Alexander before the city of women; Alexander and the King of Katzya; Alexander and the skull from Paradise.

2. *Research*—a) Find out more about Alexander's life. b) Tell an interesting Greek legend such as the story of Pandora, or the story of Damon and Pythias, or the story of Hercules.

3. *Proverb*—Print a poster containing the words of Simon the Just. ("The world depends on three things: on Torah, on worship and on kindness to one's fellow-man.") If possible print this saying in Hebrew and in English. Your teacher will help you find the Hebrew in the *Ethics of the Fathers* (chapter 1, verse 2).

A GAME

Each student selects the name of some person connected with Jewish history. The group also picks a key name such as "Jerusalem," "Jews," "Persia." The teacher or narrator then relates some incidents from Jewish history. As a person's name is mentioned he must bow, stand up or make some amusing gesture. If he forgets to do so, he is out. When the key name, such as "Jerusalem," is mentioned, everybody stands up and twirls. Those who fail to do so are eliminated. The narrator, of course, may skip from one narrative to another. Those not eliminated within the time set in advance are the winners.

CHAPTER VII

CHANUKAH – THE FESTIVAL OF LIGHTS

1. WICKED ANTIOCHUS

THE JEWS were finally forced to rebel against the Greeks because of the cruelty of Antiochus IV of Syria.

Antiochus called himself "Epiphanes" (godly), but in jest his subjects would call him "Epimanes" (madman). Madman he was, for often he would wander, drunk, with horn and bagpipe through the streets of his city.

His first crime against Judea was to sell the position of High Priest to the highest bidder. The man who bought the office was an evil person named Menelaus.

Menelaus was one of the worst traitors in Jewish history. To raise the money he had pledged to the king he stole from the Temple treasury. When the Jews sent three of their leaders to Antiochus to protest, the king slew the three leaders.

Antiochus now made war against Egypt but was forced by Rome to withdraw his armies.

A false rumor spread through Jerusalem, "Antiochus has been killed! The king is dead!"

The people rejoiced. In fear the hated Menelaus took refuge in a fortress opposite the Temple.

When Antiochus heard what had happened he entered Jerusalem with his army. He cruelly put to death thousands of men and women.

Then, led by Menelaus, he ransacked the Temple stealing whatever silver and gold vessels he could find. Menelaus even showed him the Holy of Holies which only the High Priest was allowed to enter once a year, on Yom Kippur.

Antiochus waited until Rome was engaged in war.

"Now I can attack Egypt, and Rome will be unable to interfere," thought Antiochus.

He soon conquered most of Egypt and laid siege to Alexandria.

Rome's answer came quickly.

Three Roman messengers arrived at the camp of Antiochus in the sands outside of Alexandria.

"Rome orders you to leave Egypt immediately!" was the message they brought.

"Give me three days time to consider my reply," answered Antiochus.

One of the Romans took his staff and drew a circle in the sand around Antiochus.

"You must give us your answer before you leave this circle," warned the Roman.

Sadly, Antiochus withdrew a second time from Egypt. Rome had proved how weak his kingdom really was.

"Maybe my own subjects will rebel," thought Antiochus in fear.

He resolved to unite all the people over whom he ruled. The best way to do this, he believed, was through the Greek gods. All must worship as he did.

"Let there be but one law for all my subjects," declared Antiochus. "Let all worship before Jupiter. Worshipers of the God of Israel will be put to death!"

Antiochus must have been madman indeed for he thought he could destroy the Jewish religion.

Antiochus sent soldiers to Jerusalem to enforce the new law. The statue of Jupiter was set up in the Temple and pigs were sacrificed on the altar. This happened on the 25th day in the month of *Kislev*.

Aided by the traitor Menelaus, the Syrians seized all scrolls of the law and burned them. Parents were forbidden to bring their sons into the covenant of Abraham. Those who continued to observe the laws of the Torah or who refused to worship Jupiter were cruelly slain.

Sometimes entire families were wiped out. This was the sad fate that overtook Hannah and her seven brave sons who preferred death to idol worship.

Jerusalem and the Temple lay in ruins. Thousands had been killed, but the Jews fought bravely for their freedom and their religion.

2. MATTATHIAS

In the village of Modin, not far from Jerusalem, lived the aged Mattathias and his five sons. The sons were named John, Simon, Judah, Eleazar and Jonathan. The people admired Mattathias and his sons because of their wisdom, their courage and their loyalty to the Torah.

Mattathias was saddened by the destruction of so many innocent men and women.

"Alas, that I was ever born to see Jerusalem and the Temple in ruins," he mourned. "Strangers have invaded our land and have destroyed both young and old."

When the officers of Antiochus arrived in Modin they tried to bribe Mattathias.

"You are respected by all the inhabitants of this village," they said. "Carry out the command of the king by sacrificing to Jupiter. You will be richly rewarded with silver and gold. We know that the others will follow your example."

"All the silver and gold in the world cannot induce me to betray the Torah," replied Mattathias. "I will not obey the king's command."

The Syrian officers commanded all the inhabitants of the village to gather near the altar that had been set up to Jupiter.

"In the name of King Antiochus I command you to sacrifice to Jupiter," said the Syrian general.

Spurred on by hope of reward one Jew approached the altar and began to sacrifice to the idol.

Mattathias could no longer restrain his fury.

"Death to the traitor!" he shouted. Rushing forward he drew a concealed sword from beneath his cloak and slew the renegade.

The Syrian general and his soldiers tried to capture Mattathias. The five sons soon came to their father's assistance. In the struggle they slew the general and forced the soldiers to flee.

"Let those who are zealous for the Lord—follow me!" called out Mattathias.

Knowing that they had little time to lose the brave Mattathias and his followers fled to a cave in the wilderness. They left behind all that they owned, well aware that their houses would be destroyed by the Syrian Greeks.

Once more the *shofar* was sounded in Judea. Loyal men and women answered the call and gathered behind the banner of Mattathias.

Finding one of the caves the Syrian Greeks attacked on the Sabbath. They easily overcame the Jews in this cave who did not want to violate the Sabbath by fighting on the day of rest.

Mattathias shook his head sadly when he heard the news.

"If we do not defend ourselves we will all be destroyed," said Mattathias. "Even on the Sabbath we are allowed to fight to save our lives."

His followers agreed and thereafter fought back whenever attacked by the Syrians.

Aided by the wise counsel of his sons Mattathias planned his strategy. First he attacked the small garrisons of Syrians in the villages. Mattathias would overpower the enemy before aid could be sent to the soldiers. Altars to Jupiter were quickly destroyed.

Sometimes Mattathias would trap Syrian Greek soldiers

traveling along the mountain roads. Soon the Syrian generals gave orders that troops must travel in large numbers out of fear of surprise attacks.

Thousands of Jews now joined Mattathias. He was able to supply a few with swords taken from prisoners, but most of his soldiers remained unarmed.

Unfortunately, aged Mattathias became ill a year after the rebellion had started.

Calling his sons and followers to him, Mattathias said: "I know that I shall soon die. Continue to fight against the enemy until the Hebrew nation has won its freedom. Let brave Judah be your general to lead you into battle. Follow the advice of Simon who is wise in counsel. Be true to the Torah, and fight for God and your country."

When Mattathias died the people mourned their loss. His sons silently carried his body over the mountain roads to Modin and buried him in his native city alongside his fathers.

They vowed never to lay down the sword until they had finished the struggle which Mattathias had begun.

3. JUDAH THE MACCABEE

Mattathias had chosen well when he picked Judah as general. Judah fought like a lion in battle inspiring his men to deeds of courage.

Judah was called by his followers "The Maccabee" which means "hammerer," for Judah crushed the enemy with blows like those of a hammer.

Knowing that he could not meet the enemy in open battle Judah depended on surprise attacks. As if from nowhere his men would suddenly swoop down from their mountain dens on the Syrians.

Soon all of Judea had been freed by Judah except for Jerusalem. Antiochus quickly sent word to the Syrian general in Samaria to attack Judah.

The general, who was named Apollonius, marched southward to Judea to do battle with Judah the Maccabee. Many Samaritans joined the forces of Apollonius, eager to destroy their Jewish neighbors.

"How can we fight against such superior forces?" asked Judah's followers in dismay.

"God will fight for us," replied Judah. "We will slay the enemy the way David slew Goliath!"

Cautiously choosing a mountain road Judah and his men silently stole behind Apollonius. Judah decided to attack at night.

"Forward! For God and our Torah!" shouted Judah.

Completely taken by surprise Apollonius and his army of Syrians and Samaritans were badly defeated. The soldiers fled in fear.

"Stop!" pleaded Apollonius. "Do not run away!"

Only a few obeyed the general's command. When Apollonius looked up, he saw to his amazement Judah the Maccabee standing before him.

Drawing his great sword Apollonius tried to defend himself. With the strength of a lion, sword in hand, Judah bore down upon the general and slew him.

Judah picked up the Syrian's fallen sword. Admiring its polished steel Judah fastened the great sword to his belt and proudly wore it in all his battles.

4. A GLORIOUS VICTORY

Dismayed by the defeat of his soldiers Antiochus resolved to take desperate measures.

Hiring thousands of soldiers from other lands Antiochus paid them a year's wages in advance.

"It is not enough to force upon the Jews the worship of Jupiter," said Antiochus to Lysias, his closest adviser. "We must destroy them all. We will bring other races to inherit their land. Let there not remain even the memory of the Jewish nation!"

Antiochus soon saw that he could not long support this costly war against Judah the Maccabee. Other lands in the East, aroused by the king's decree to worship Jupiter, had refused to pay taxes. The money he had inherited from his father he had long since squandered.

Worst of all, Rome had insisted on the payment by Antiochus of 20 talents as tribute. This was a huge sum of money. "I will go to Persia and Babylon to collect the taxes due to me," said Antiochus to Lysias. "I place you in charge of Syria and of my son. As soon as the winter is over send your army into Judea to destroy every trace of Judah and his followers."

Lysias appointed General Nicanor to lead the army against Judah. Nicanor marched with 40,000 infantry and 7000 cavalry. Each soldier was well equipped with armor, spear and sword. How could Judah and his followers resist such a large army?

Nicanor sent word to the slave merchants of Syria to follow the army.

"You may purchase 90 slaves for a talent of silver," said Nicanor. "You can then resell the Jewish slaves on the open market and make a great profit."

Nicanor hoped in this way to collect at least 20 talents which could be sent to Rome in payment of tribute.

The Syrians set up camp near a village in Judea called Emmaus.

Nicanor decided to use the same tactics as Judah. He planned a surprise, night attack.

Choosing his finest general, Gorgias, he said, "Take part of the army with you and lead a surprise attack against Judah. I shall remain here at Emmaus with the rest of the army."

"How shall I find my way through the mountains?" asked Gorgias.

"Menelaus has sent us some of his followers to serve as guides."

Gorgias and his soldiers, led by traitors, marched along the narrow mountain paths.

But Judah's scouts soon brought word of the surprise attack. This was the opportunity for which Judah had waited. Now that the Syrians had divided their forces he could defeat each group separately.

He heaped fuel on the campfires. The flames shot high into the heavens serving as a beacon light to guide the attacking Syrians under Gorgias.

Judah the Maccabee and his men quickly left the camp and escaped by way of the mountain roads.

Gorgias and his soldiers crept nearer and nearer to the camp. At a given signal they attacked. They had been tricked—the camp was empty. The campfires were still burning but there was no trace of Judah and his followers.

Meanwhile Judah had retraced his steps through the mountains that he knew so well. At dawn he and his men reached Emmaus where Nicanor slept, unaware of danger.

Judah divided his small army into four groups. He and Eleazar led the first; Simon led the second, Jonathan the third and John the fourth.

Eleazar read to the men from a scroll of the law.

"Let us fight for our freedom and for our Torah!" shouted Judah.

Hurling large rocks before them as they descended the mountain-side, the Jews attacked the Syrians who were just waking from their sleep.

Aroused by the sound of the trumpet or *shofar*, Nicanor tried to organize a defense. It was hopeless. The surprise had been complete. Nicanor gave the order to retreat.

Judah and his men followed in hot pursuit. They quickly overtook the surprised slave-merchants who were still busily calculating the profits they would make by selling Jewish slaves. Thousands of Syrians fell by the wayside.

Judah warned his men not to touch the spoil for he still had to contend with Gorgias.

Disapppointed that he had not found Judah, Gorgias returned to Emmaus. To his amazement the entire Syrian camp was in flames.

At that moment Judah and his soldiers returned from their pursuit.

The soldiers of Gorgias, fatigued by their long and fruitless march over the mountains, were dismayed. They learned with horror that Nicanor's army had been destroyed by Judah. In panic they fled for their lives.

Judah the Maccabee had won the most glorious victory since the days of King David!

5. CHANUKAH

King Antiochus arrived in Persia. When he tried to rob one of the temples the people rose up in anger and drove him and his soldiers away.

Word reached Antiochus of Judah's victories. Distressed by his defeat on all sides, Antiochus suffered a stroke. Feeling intense pain the king tried to stand in his on-rushing chariot. The wild motion of the horses threw Antiochus from the chariot to the ground.

A short while thereafter the king died. Thus ended the career of the madman who tried to destroy the Jewish people and the Torah.

Judah and his followers now entered Jerusalem. They wept when they saw what the Syrians had done to the Temple.

Judah and his men quickly destroyed the statue of Jupiter. They built a new altar and *menorah* and replaced the gates that had been burnt. After three weeks they were ready to dedicate the Temple once more.

"When Solomon dedicated the First Temple he and Israel celebrated for eight days," said Judah. "Also when the Second

Temple was dedicated, Zerubbabel and Jeshua celebrated for eight days. We too will rejoice for eight days and give thanks to God that the Temple has been cleansed and restored."

For eight days the *menorah* was lit with pure oil. The light illuminated the Temple and brought joy to the hearts of the people.

There is a beautiful legend that Judah and the *Kohanim* could find enough pure oil to last only one day. But a miracle occurred and the oil lasted for eight days!

The *Kohanim* blew the trumpets and the Levites sang:

"In distress I called upon the Lord,
He answered me by setting me free."

The day on which the Temple was re-dedicated was the 25th day of *Kislev*. Exactly three years had passed since Antiochus had set up a statue of Jupiter in the Temple.

Judah the Maccabee had saved not only the Temple but the Jewish people and their religion.

For the past 2000 years we have continued to celebrate this glorious holiday of lights. We call the festival Chanukah which means "dedication."

Each year on the 25th day of *Kislev* we gather around the *menorah*. After the blessings are recited we sing joyous songs:

"Rock of Ages, let our song
Praise Thy saving power;
Thou amidst the raging foes
Wast our sheltering tower.

Furious they assailed us,
But Thine arm availed us,
And Thy word
Broke their sword
When our own strength failed us."

Then comes the moment that the children have been waiting for so impatiently—Chanukah gifts. And during the week

REDEDICATING THE TEMPLE

(if we're lucky!) our aunts and uncles bring us Chanukah *gelt*, or money.

Every night for supper there are *latkes*—delicious pancakes. And lots of games especially with the Chanukah *dreidel!*

What do those Hebrew letters on the *dreidel* represent? Oh, yes, they tell us about the great miracle of Chanukah:

Nes Gadol Hayah Sham
(A great miracle happened there.)

Spin merrily, *dreidel*, spin! This is a day for joy and festivity.

And each night an added candle! Two candles on the second night, three on the third night. . . . And eight glowing candles on the last night to remind us of the victory of light over darkness and of freedom over tyranny.

EXERCISES

I. Choose the correct name or phrase. (Review section 1, pages 81 to 83.)

1. People ridiculed Antiochus by calling him (Epimanes, Epiphanes).
2. Menelaus was chosen *Kohen Gadol* by (Antiochus, the Jews).
3. Antiochus could not conquer Egypt because of interference by (Persia, Rome).
4. Antiochus ordered all Jews to (obey the Torah, worship Jupiter).
5. (Hannah, Menelaus) refused to worship idols.

II. Who said to whom? (Review section 2, pages 83 to 85.)

1. "Carry out the command of the king by sacrificing to Jupiter. You will be richly rewarded with silver and gold."
2. "I will not obey the king's command."
3. "In the name of King Antiochus I command you to sacrifice to Jupiter."

THE GLORIOUS MACCABEES

    4. "Let those who are zealous for the Lord—follow me!"
    5. "Let brave Judah be your general to lead you into battle."

III. Arrange these sentences in the order in which the events happened. (Review sections 3 and 4, pages 85 to 89.)

1. Judah allowed the campfires to burn in order to mislead Gorgias.
2. Judah was made general by Mattathias.
3. Judah defeated Nicanor and Gorgias.
4. Antiochus went to Persia to collect taxes.
5. Judah the Maccabee defeated Apollonius and took his sword.
6. Nicanor invited slave-dealers to buy the Jewish captives as slaves.

IV. When is each of the following performed—on Purim or on Chanukah? (Review section 5, pages 89 to 92 and Chapter V, section 4, pages 63 to 65.)

1. We eat *latkes*.
2. We spin the *dreidel*.
3. We make noise with the *grogger*.
4. We light the *menorah*.
5. We read the *megillah*.

V. Questions for discussion:

1. What crimes against the Jewish people were committed by Antiochus?
2. Mattathias had many wonderful qualities. In your opinion, which was his greatest virtue?
3. How did Judah the Maccabee prove that he was a great general?
4. We read the prophecy of Zechariah in the synagogue on Chanukah. Why? (Review Chapter II, section 4, pages 37 to 38.)
5. Why do you like the holiday of Chanukah?

THINGS TO DO

1. *Menorah*—Make a Chanukah *menorah* out of wood or clay. In addition to the eight branches be sure to add a small branch for the *shamash*, the candle used to light the others.

2. *Community Chanukah Celebration*—Invite some of the neighboring families to participate in the ceremony of lighting the candles. Arrange for an appropriate place for the ceremony. The following blessings should be recited:

Ba-ruch a-tah a-do-nai e-lo-he-nu me-lech ha-o-lam a-sher kidd'sha-nu b'mits-vo-tav v'tsi-va-nu l'had-lik ner shel cha-nu-kah.

Ba-ruch a-tah a-do-nai e-lo-he-nu me-lech ha-o-lam she-a-sah nis-sim la-a-vo-te-nu ba-ya-mim ha-hem ba-z'man ha-zeh.

(In placing the candles start from right to left. In lighting the candles start from left to right.)

3. *Latke Party*—Learn how to make *latkes* (potato pancakes). Arrange for a Chanukah party for your friends or classmates at which time the *latkes* will be served.

DREIDEL GAMES

1. *Spin the Dreidel*—The following scale can be used for the various letters on the *dreidel:*

    *N*un—*n*othing
    *G*imel—*g*rab all
    *H*eh—*h*alf to be taken by player
    *S*hin—*s*tack two more on the pile

The players can use tickets, checkers, nuts or other objects as stakes.

2. *Climbing to Jerusalem*—Draw a ladder with 20 rungs. The last rung is marked Jerusalem. The players try to reach Jerusalem.

The following scale can be used for the various letters on the *dreidel:*

    Nun—nothing
    Gimel—one rung
    Heh—two rungs
    Shin—three rungs and take another spin.

CHAPTER VIII

THE MACCABEAN STRUGGLE FOR INDEPENDENCE

1. A PEACE TREATY

THE INHABITANTS of the Greek cities in the Land of Israel had taken advantage of the war to attack their Jewish neighbors.

Judah received letters from the Jews in Gilead in Transjordan whose ancestors had once appealed to King Saul for help.

"Come quickly to our assistance," they wrote. "We are besieged by our enemies. Many Jews have already fallen by the sword."

While Judah and his brothers were considering what to do, messengers arrived from Galilee. Their clothes were torn, their bodies exhausted from fatigue.

"We are from Galilee," they said. "We have been attacked on all sides by hostile neighbors. We need help!"

"We must assist our brothers in trouble," decided Judah. "Simon will relieve those in Galilee and I shall help our brothers in Gilead."

Judah and Jonathan led an expedition across the Jordan River. The hostile tribes were dismayed when they heard the news. Their soldiers immediately gave up the siege of the city in which the Jews lived and fled for their lives.

Simon, too, was successful in Galilee. Many of the Jews, fearing their neighbors would attack again as soon as Simon left, returned with him to Judea.

Judah the Maccabee now ruled over a large stretch of land.

But he knew that the danger was not over. What would the new king of Syria, Antiochus V, and his adviser Lysias do? Would they raise another army and invade Judea again?

The answer soon came. Antiochus V and Lysias raised an army of 100,000 footmen and 20,000 horsemen. In addition they brought with them 32 elephants. Each elephant was attended by 1500 soldiers. On the elephants were skilled archers.

The soldiers would pour juice into the eyes of the elephants and thus goad them into madness. The elephants would rush forward furiously so that nobody could stand before them.

Judah met the enemy at a city south of Jerusalem called Beth-Zur. He knew that he could not defeat such a large force, but he calmly planned an orderly retreat to Jerusalem.

This was made possible by the bravery of his brother, Eleazar. Disregarding danger, Eleazar rushed forward to attack the tallest of the elephants. The elephant was beautifully decorated with royal adornments.

"Surely it is the king who is seated on the elephant," thought Eleazar. "If I destroy him the Syrians will flee in panic."

Eleazar slew many in his path and scattered the rest who guarded the elephant. Then dashing between the legs of the elephant Eleazar smote him with his sword. The elephant sank to the earth, but, alas, carried Eleazar with him. The brave hero was crushed to death.

It was not the king, at all, who was seated on the elephant. But Eleazar's brave deed was not in vain. Judah and his men were able to withdraw in orderly manner to Jerusalem.

Judah prepared for a siege. From time to time Judah and his men would carry out a surprise raid and then quickly return behind the walls of Jerusalem.

The Syrians suffered many losses. Then came word that there was rebellion in Syria.

"Why do we continue this useless war?" said Lysias to the boy king, Antiochus V. "Let us promise the Jews the right to worship their God in peace, and let us return to Syria before the rebellion spreads."

The boy king quickly agreed. Judah was overjoyed. Jews would now have the right to live according to the laws of the Torah without interference. Judea, of course, would remain a province of Syria.

Antiochus V and Lysias were allowed to enter Jerusalem after the treaty was signed. Unlike his father, the new king showed great respect when he came into the Temple. He asked the *Kohanim* to offer a sacrifice to God in his name, and they gladly carried out his request.

The king, however, ordered the walls of Jerusalem to be partly destroyed so that Jerusalem would not be strong enough to withstand another siege.

"Menelaus is to blame for the blood that has been shed," said Lysias. "It was he who advised your father to destroy the Jewish religion. He should pay for his crimes."

"Let Menelaus be put to death," replied the king.

The death of the traitor Menelaus ended the struggle for religious freedom. And there was peace in the land.

Judah the Maccabee had saved the Temple, the Torah and the Jewish people from destruction.

2. THE STRUGGLE IS RESUMED

Judah now married and hoped to live in peace in Modin, his birthplace.

Alas, peace did not last very long. The cousin of Antiochus V attacked the boy king with a large army claiming that the crown had been stolen from him.

Antiochus V was defeated and he and Lysias were put to death by the new king.

The supporters of Menelaus, in mortal fear of Judah the Maccabee, now renewed the struggle.

"Judah the Maccabee plans to rebel against Syria," they

said to the new king. "He wishes to make Judea a free nation and to become king in Jerusalem. But we are your friends. We will remain loyal to Syria and will adopt the customs of the Greeks."

"It is dangerous to allow Judah to become so powerful," thought the new king. "This is a good excuse for me to interfere."

"Try to avoid open warfare," the king commanded his generals. "Pretend you are renewing the peace treaty made by Lysias. Seize Judah when he does not suspect any harm."

The Syrians now came with pledges of friendship.

"Why do you bring an army with you if you wish to renew our treaty of peace?" asked Judah.

Pretending to send his army away, the Syrian general placed a large number of soldiers in ambush. He again asked Judah to arrange a new treaty of peace.

Judah agreed, but suspecting treachery he sent his scouts to find out what had happened to the Syrian army.

No sooner had the conference begun than Judah's scouts brought word of the Syrian ambush.

"You come not for peace but for war," said Judah in anger to the Syrian general. Judah hastily left the conference.

It was not a moment too soon. The general had already given the signal and his soldiers had advanced from their ambush to overpower Judah and his body-guard.

A furious battle followed and again Judah was the victor. For seven long years Judah won one glorious victory after another.

The people, however, were tired of war.

"We are lovers of peace, not of war," said many of the leaders. "The Syrians want to make peace with us. Let us accept their offer. They have sworn not to interfere with our religion."

Judah warned the leaders that they were making a terrible mistake.

They refused to give heed to Judah's warning. Sixty of the prominent leaders brought a message of peace to the Syrian camp. They were cruelly seized and put to death.

Alas, the harm had been done. Many of Judah's soldiers had deserted him under the influence of those who wanted peace at any price.

With a handful of soldiers Judah bravely fought his last fight.

"Never shall it be said that Judah the Maccabee fled like a coward!" vowed the brave leader. "Rather let me die on the field of battle for God and the Torah!"

Judah and his few soldiers fought like lions at bay. Again and again they put the Syrians to rout but the Syrians had an endless supply of men and weapons. It was a hopeless struggle for Judah.

That day Judah the Maccabee fell dead on the field of battle.

3. JONATHAN

Jonathan, John and Simon sadly lifted the body of Judah from the battlefield. They brought the body of their brave brother to Modin and buried Judah next to Mattathias.

And the people mourned:

> "Woe unto us, for our hero has fallen in battle,
> Brave Judah, protector and shield of Israel."

Syria now ruled with a heavy hand. Thousands of Jews who had supported Judah were seized and put to death. Crops were taken from the farmers to feed the Syrian soldiers. There was starvation in the land.

The Temple, however, was not disturbed. No attempt was made to force Jews to worship Jupiter.

In their misery the Jewish people remembered the Maccabees. Turning to Jonathan they said, "You and your brothers must help us. Let us continue to fight for our freedom."

"I am ready to fight for Israel," replied Jonathan.

Jonathan, Simon and John gathered a few hundred men in the caves near the Jordan River above the Dead Sea. Each day they practiced archery and swimming.

John was put in charge of a delegation that brought whatever could be saved to a friendly Arab tribe for safekeeping.

John, however, was ambushed by bandits and cruelly slain. Thus fell the third of the Maccabean brothers.

Jonathan and Simon quickly found the bandits and punished them for their crime.

"Let us attack Jonathan before he can gather a large army," said the Syrians.

One Sabbath day as Jonathan and his men rested, a messenger came running in haste.

"The Syrians are attacking from the north," he shouted.

Immediately thereafter a second messenger arrived. "A Syrian army is approaching from the south."

Jonathan was hemmed in on all sides. To the west was desert, to the east was the Jordan River. The enemy attacked from north and south.

Jonathan skillfully repelled the first attack. Then, before the Syrians could reorganize their ranks, Jonathan gave the signal agreed upon in advance.

"Swim across the Jordan!"

The brave soldiers leaped into the rushing waters and swam to safety.

For two years Jonathan strengthened his army, as Mattathias and Judah had once done. At last he felt ready for battle.

Jonathan won a series of brilliant victories that showed him to be almost as great a general as Judah had been. History was indeed repeating itself.

At last came the day for which Jonathan had waited. A rival appeared to claim the Syrian crown. A furious civil war broke out in Syria.

Both sides pleaded with Jonathan for help. Jonathan helped the side which would be friendly to Judea.

Jonathan now proved to be as great a diplomat as he was a general. He signed several treaties which won many advantages for the Jews. Among these advantages were:

1—Jonathan, who was a *Kohen,* was recognized as High Priest. Jews could observe the Torah without interference.

2—Simon was made governor of the cities along the coast.

3—Samaria, Galilee and Transjordan were added to the regions over which Jonathan ruled.

4—Jonathan was allowed to rebuild the walls of Jerusalem.

5—Jerusalem and the Temple were freed of all taxes.

6—The ½ tax on fruit trees and ⅓ tax on grains no longer had to be paid to Syria.

7—The poll tax for each inhabitant and the salt tax no longer had to be paid to Syria.

8—Jonathan was allowed to fortify many of the cities of Judea.

Jonathan, of course, was still subject to the king of Syria and had to pay a small yearly tax.

Four kings of Syria, who succeeded one another in rapid succession after constant civil wars, proclaimed Jonathan "friend" and clothed him in purple robes.

Judah the Maccabee won religious freedom for his people. Jonathan, his brother, won for them complete self-government.

4. INDEPENDENCE

Jonathan sent messengers to Rome and to Sparta to draw up treaties of friendship with these two great cities. Here too he continued the policy of Judah who had drawn up a friendship treaty with Rome.

Antiochus VI now reigned in Syria. He owed the throne to the support of Jonathan and a Syrian general named Tryphon.

Unknown to Jonathan it was Tryphon's secret ambition to become king.

"I shall never be able to become king as long as Jonathan, the friend of the king, stands in my way," thought Tryphon.

Tryphon marched toward Judea with an army hoping to surprise Jonathan. But Jonathan marched to meet him at the head of a large army.

Tryphon sent word saying, "I come for peace and to renew our friendship."

When Tryphon and Jonathan met face to face, the Syrian general said, "I know that you have often claimed the city of Acre. As a sign of our friendship I shall now give you control of the city. Come with me to Acre where the leaders are ready to accept your rule."

Jonathan was pleased. He little suspected the treachery of Tryphon.

"Of course," added the Syrian general, "it would be unwise for us to appear at the head of large armies. The people of Acre would regard such an action as an unfriendly one. We will enter the city accompanied only by a small group of soldiers as an escort."

Jonathan agreed. He entered the city with a thousand soldiers and was welcomed by the people of Acre. That night the soldiers and supporters of Tryphon, at a given signal, overpowered the Jewish soldiers and took Jonathan prisoner. Later Jonathan was put to death.

Judea was shocked by this act of treachery. Distressed by the loss of their leader they turned to Simon, the last of the sons of Mattathias.

"I shall continue to fight for the freedom of our nation as my brothers and father have done before me," pledged Simon.

It was Tryphon's purpose to attack Jerusalem before Simon could organize an army to defend it. Choosing his cavalry to lead the way he planned to ride quickly to Jerusalem and destroy it.

Would his plan succeed? It might have succeeded except for one thing—that day it snowed.

This is a rare thing in Judea where snow falls only once or twice in many years. The paths turned to mud. The roads were blocked and Tryphon's cavalry could not reach the city of Jerusalem in time for a surprise attack.

Simon was declared governor and High Priest. One of his first acts was to recover the body of Jonathan and to bury him in Modin next to Mattathias and Judah.

Tryphon succeeded in becoming king of Syria for a while. But he was soon defeated by the real king with the help of Simon.

As a reward for Simon's help, Judea was given full freedom. Later the king of Syria, like Pharaoh of old, hardened his heart.

"I shall enslave Israel again," said the king.

But Simon fought hard against the Syrian army and successfully defended Israel's newly-won freedom.

For the first time in almost 450 years, Judea was completely free.

The Maccabean brothers had fought for 25 years to achieve this goal. Judah had won religious freedom. Jonathan had won the right to self-government. Simon had now won complete independence.

Thanks to Mattathias and his valiant sons Judea was now a free nation.

EXERCISES

I. Fill in the correct name. (Review, section 1, pages 95 to 97.)

Antiochus V, Eleazar, Judah, Lysias, Menelaus, Simon

1. _____ helped free the Jews of Galilee from hostile tribes.
2. _____ was crushed in battle by an elephant.

3. _____ was a Syrian general who proposed that religious freedom be granted to the Jews.
4. _____, king of Syria, showed respect to God when he visited the Temple.
5. _____ succeeded in winning a peace treaty in which the Jews were granted religious freedom.
6. The traitor _____ was slain because he had persuaded the king to try to destroy the Jewish religion.

II. True or false? (Review section 2, pages 97 to 99.)

1. Antiochus V was killed during a Syrian civil war.
2. The new king of Syria really wanted to renew the treaty of peace with Judah.
3. The Syrian general tried to seize Judah by treachery.
4. Some of the Jewish leaders failed to support Judah because they thought they could make peace with Syria.
5. Judah died in Modin of old age.

III. Answer each question in a complete sentence. (Review sections 3 and 4, pages 99 to 103.)

1. Why did the people ask Jonathan to renew the rebellion against Syria?
2. How did Jonathan save the army near the Jordan?
3. What privileges did Jonathan win for Judea?
4. How was Jonathan taken prisoner?
5. Why did Tryphon's cavalry attack against Jerusalem fail?
6. Who won complete independence for Judea?

IV. Questions for discussion:

1. Why is Judah the Maccabee regarded as one of the greatest heroes in Jewish history?
2. What were the achievements of Jonathan and Simon?
3. "Syrian civil war led to Jewish independence." Show how this is true.

REVIEW QUESTIONS

for Units One and Two (pages 17 to 104)

1. Summarize one prophecy of each of the following prophets: Jeremiah, Ezekiel, Zechariah.
2. What part did each of the following play in the rebuilding of Jerusalem: Zerubbabel, Jeshua, Ezra, Nehemiah?
3. What was the attitude of each of the following kings to the Jewish people: Cyrus, Darius, Alexander, Philadelphus, Antiochus IV?
4. What was the greatest achievement of each of the following: Mattathias, Judah, Jonathan, Simon?
5. Why do we celebrate Purim? Why do we celebrate Chanukah?
6. Identify: Baruch, Daniel, Belshazzar, Bel, Samaritans, *Knesset Ha-g'dolah*, Mordecai, Esther, Haman, Ahasuerus, Simon the Just, Menelaus, Nicanor, Lysias, Eleazar, John.

TEST

on Units One and Two

I. Name the prophet: (12 points)
 1. In my vision God told Rachel that her children would some day return to Israel.
 2. I saw the dead bones restored to life. So too the Hebrew nation would be restored to life.
 3. I saw a beautiful *menorah* illuminating the Temple. Just as the *menorah* draws its light from an unseen source so too Israel will draw its strength from God.

II. Complete: (16 points)
 1. _____ led the exiles back to Jerusalem and built the Second Temple.
 2. _____ was the first to serve as *Kohen Gadol* after the Jews returned from Babylon.
 3. _____ the scribe helped the *Knesset Ha-g'dolah* to arrange the Bible.

4. _____ prevented the Samaritans from interfering with the rebuilding of the wall of Jerusalem.

III. Match: (20 points)

Column A   *Column B*
Alexander   1. Allowed Jews to complete the Temple
Antiochus IV   2. Brought Jews under Greek rule
Cyrus   3. Invited scholars to translate Bible
Darius   4. Allowed Jews to return from exile
Philadelphus   5. Tried to destroy the Jewish religion

IV. Choose the correct name or phrase: (28 points)
1. Purim took place while the Jews were under (Greek, Persian) rule.
2. Mordecai helped save the life of (Ahasuerus, Antiochus).
3. On Purim we eat (*hamentashen, latkes*).
4. (Chanukah, Purim) is the festival of lights.
5. The leader of the Jews, after the death of Mattathias was (Jonathan, Judah).
6. Judah won (complete independence, religious freedom) for the Jews.
7. On Chanukah we spin the (*dreidel, grogger*).

V. Who am I? (24 points)
1. I was one of the Jews exiled to Babylon. I explained the meaning of the handwriting on the wall to Belshazzar. I refused to worship the king. I came out of the den of lions unharmed.
2. I was queen of Persia. I saved my people from death at the hands of the wicked Haman.
3. I was *Kohen Gadol* in Jerusalem. I welcomed Alexander. My favorite saying was: "The world depends on three things: on Torah, on worship and on kindness to one's fellow-man."
4. I was the father of five brave sons. I rebelled against Syria because it would not allow Jews to practise the Jewish religion.

5. I was the first of five brothers to die. I was crushed by an elephant during the struggle against Syrian tyranny.
6. I was leader of the Jewish people after my father and my four brothers gave their lives in defence of their people. I won complete independence for Judea.

UNIT THREE

Rome and Jerusalem

CHAPTER IX

UNDER ROMAN RULE

1. THE REIGN OF QUEEN SALOME

SIMON'S son ruled after him as *Kohen Gadol* and as governor. Simon's grandson assumed the title "king." The Maccabean kings were great warriors and organized large and powerful armies. Judea expanded in all directions, especially under the rule of King Alexander Jannai and Queen Salome Alexandra.

Greatest of the rulers was good Queen Salome Alexandra. When King Alexander Jannai died his wife, Salome, reigned as queen of Israel.

Salome tried to live up to her name which means peace. Her army was so strong that no foreign country dared invade Judea. Within the nation too there were few conflicts and men lived with each other in peace.

The laws of the land were controlled by the Sanhedrin. This was a supreme court of 71 judges. It also served as the senate and made new laws.

At the head of the Sanhedrin was Salome's brother, Simon ben Shetah. Simon's followers were known as Pharisees. They led righteous lives and tried to apply the laws of the Torah with mercy and kindness.

Their motto in judgment was, "Try to judge each man favorably."

Witnesses were questioned very carefully so that no innocent man would be condemned to death. Capital punishment was rare.

The Pharisees believed that, in addition to the written law

which is found in the Bible, there is an oral law handed down from generation to generation. Without the oral law one cannot really understand the written law.

Some people, for example, took the saying "an eye for an eye" literally.

"The oral law," said the Pharisees, "teaches us the correct interpretation of this law. 'An eye for an eye' means that we must be strict in compensating the victim by paying him damages. The Torah wants us to be merciful and does not command us to inflict cruel punishments."

Judaism accepts the teachings of the Pharisees. The Jewish religion teaches that all people must be judged with mercy and kindness.

Simon said to the Sanhedrin, "The Torah warns us to teach our laws to our children. Let us set up schools in each city so that our young men can learn the teachings of the Torah."

The members of the Sanhedrin thought that this was a good plan. A law was adopted that each city must set up schools so that young men about 16 or 17 years old could study the Torah. Later schools for young children were made compulsory.

This was the first time in history that a compulsory education law was passed. Throughout the Land of Israel children and young men studied the Torah and its wise laws.

We gain some idea of Simon's fine character from the following story.

Simon ben Shetah received no pay as head of the Sanhedrin. He earned a living by cleaning flax. Since he was too poor to buy a donkey his pupils decided to present him with one as a gift.

The pupils bought a donkey from an Arab and found a precious pearl in a bag tied to the donkey.

"You are a rich man," said one of the pupils to Simon. "We have found a precious pearl in a bag tied to the donkey."

"Did the Arab know about the pearl?" asked Simon.

"Of course not," replied the pupil.

"You purchased a donkey not a pearl," said Simon, "Return the pearl to its owner."

The Arab rejoiced when the pearl was returned.

"Blessed be Simon ben Shetah and the God of Simon ben Shetah," said the Arab.

The people admired Simon and the Pharisees because of their honesty, their kindness, their wisdom and their loyalty to the Torah.

Queen Salome reigned for nine years. With the help of her brother, Simon, she made this one of the happiest periods in Jewish history.

2. CIVIL WAR

Although the Maccabean kings helped the Jewish people they also made many mistakes. One of their greatest mistakes was to force the Edomites, who lived in the southern part of the land, to accept the Jewish religion. This was the only time in Jewish history that people were forced to become Jews.

The Jewish people were unhappy because there were so many disputes about who should be king. They also remembered the warning of Samuel that kings would act like tyrants and be cruel.

The worst fears of the people came true after the death of good Queen Salome Alexandra.

The queen had two sons named Hyrcanus and Aristobulus. The older son, Hyrcanus, served as *Kohen Gadol* during his mother's reign. Hyrcanus was kind and gentle but very weak as a leader.

Shortly before her death Queen Salome Alexandra said, "Hyrcanus will rule as king after my death since he is my older son."

Jealous of his brother, Aristobulus tried to seize the throne from Hyrcanus. A furious civil war broke out which led to disaster for the Jewish people.

Aristobulus proved to be the stronger and gained control of Jerusalem. He pardoned Hyrcanus and allowed him to remain in Jerusalem. Goaded on by his friends, the older brother fled from Jerusalem and renewed the civil war.

About this time the great Roman general, Pompey, invaded Asia. City after city fell before the powerful Romans.

Both Aristobulus and Hyrcanus decided to appeal to Pompey for help in the civil war. This was a sad mistake, for the selfish Romans were only too happy to interfere.

"The prize will be given neither to one side nor to the other," thought the Romans, "but to us."

At first the Romans sided with Aristobulus especially since he was stronger and richer. Aristobulus promised the Romans a rich gift, and later sent a beautiful golden vine worth a large sum of money which he took from the Temple treasury.

Pompey soon found an excuse for removing Aristobulus from his kingship. When Aristobulus tried to resist, Pompey imprisoned him and sent an army against Jerusalem.

Aided by Hyrcanus, the Romans entered Jerusalem without bloodshed. The soldiers of Aristobulus hid behind the Temple walls and tried to fight off the Romans.

After a short siege Pompey conquered the Temple. Out of curiosity Pompey entered the Holy of Holies which only the *Kohen Gadol* was allowed to enter on Yom Kippur. Pompey was amazed to discover that the Holy of Holies contained no idols. It was hard for him to understand that the Jews worshiped an unseen God.

Many of the soldiers of Aristobulus were slain during the siege. Pompey, however, was not a cruel master. He did not touch the *menorah* or golden vessels which he found in the Temple. He ordered the soldiers to cleanse the Temple so that the Jews could continue with their sacrifices.

Hyrcanus was made *Kohen Gadol*. Judea was declared a Roman province.

Only 100 years before, the Maccabees had sacrificed their

lives to win independence for Judea. The Jews lost their political freedom after less than a century of independence.

The civil war had ended in Roman conquest.

3. JULIUS CAESAR

Aristobulus and his sons were brought as prisoners to Rome where they were forced to march in Pompey's victory parade.

Aristobulus succeeded in escaping from prison. He returned to Judea where many Jews joined his ranks in hopes of winning back independence.

However, without the united support of the nation Aristobulus could not hope to defeat the Romans. He was badly wounded in battle and was brought back once more in chains to Rome.

Soon Rome itself was torn asunder by civil war as Julius Caesar and Pompey fought each other for power. Caesar freed Aristobulus hoping that he could stir up trouble for Pompey in Judea.

Aristobulus did not get very far, however, for he was poisoned by the followers of Pompey.

Julius Caesar was victorious and Pompey was slain 15 years after he had conquered Jerusalem.

Caesar was very friendly to the Jewish people. He allowed Hyrcanus to remain *Kohen Gadol*, and gave the Jews many privileges.

Jews were given the right to worship God without interference. Taxes on farmers were canceled during the sabbatical year when no new crops were planted. Jerusalem was allowed to repair the wall around the city. The port city of Jaffa was made part of Judea again.

Once the Jews on one of the Greek islands complained to Julius Caesar that the Roman officers interfered with religious services.

Julius Caesar wrote to the Roman officers, "It does not

please me to hear that our friends, the Jews, are not allowed to follow the customs of their fathers."

The Roman officers replied that a law had been passed by Rome preventing the drunken feasts in honor of Bacchus, god of wine. They thought, therefore, that Jews too should not be allowed to gather for their festivals.

Caesar ordered the officers not to interfere again with Jewish worship since Jews had nothing to do with the riotous, drunken feasts in honor of Bacchus.

The High Priest was given the right to appear with any request before the senate. He was to be introduced by Caesar or by one of the generals, and was promised a reply within ten days.

"It is also granted to Hyrcanus and to his sons and ambassadors," wrote Caesar, "that in the fights between gladiators and in those with beasts, they shall sit among the senators to see those shows."

In the Roman campaign against Egypt, the Jews were of great help to Julius Caesar. Money and food were provided for the soldiers passing through Judea. Many Jews joined the Roman forces and fought with bravery.

After one battle the Roman general wrote, "We would have been defeated were it not for the bravery of the Jewish soldiers."

Caesar confirmed the citizenship rights of the Jews of Alexandria in Egypt. This decree was written on a brass tablet in Latin and in Greek, and was posted in the market-place.

When Julius Caesar was murdered the Jews mourned because they had lost a good friend.

EXERCISES

I. Write a sentence about each of the following. (Review section 1, pages 111 to 113.)

1. Queen Salome Alexandra
2. The Sanhedrin

3. Simon ben Shetah
4. Pharisees
5. The oral law

II. Who? (Review section 2, pages 113 to 115.)
1. Who forced the Edomites to become Jews?
2. Who was loved by the people because she was a good queen?
3. Who served as *Kohen Gadol* during the reign of his mother?
4. Who rebelled against his older brother?
5. Who led a Roman army into Jerusalem?

III. Pompey or Julius Caesar? (Review section 3, pages 115 to 116.)
1. _____ put an end to Jewish political independence.
2. _____ gave Jews of Alexandria full citizenship rights.
3. _____ made Aristobulus march as prisoner in a victory parade in Rome.
4. _____ canceled Jewish taxes during the sabbatical year.
5. _____ gave Jews the right to present requests to the senate of Rome.

IV. Questions for discussion:
1. Why did the people admire the Pharisees?
2. What advantages did the Maccabean kings bring to the Jewish people? What disadvantages?
3. What were the causes of the loss of Jewish political independence?
4. How did Pompey and Julius Caesar treat the Jews?

THINGS TO DO

1. *Sanhedrin*—Pretend you are members of the Sanhedrin. Discuss the question, "Should the Sanhedrin rebuke the king for forcing the Edomites to accept Judaism at the point of the sword?"
2. *Dioramas*—A diorama is an exhibit which resembles the setting of a stage. A box is used for the stage. The scenery is made

of paper and clay. Landscapes can be printed on cardboard. Suggested subjects:

    a—The Sanhedrin trying a defendant
    b—The Temple
    c—Jerusalem
    d—Studying the Torah
    e—Jewish farmers planting vines and olive trees
    f—Queen Salome Alexandra and her court

HOW OLD WAS THE QUEEN?

It isn't polite to ask a woman's age. We know from history, however, the exact age of Salome Alexandra.

Take the number of judges in the great Sanhedrin. Deduct the number of years it took Zerubbabel to build the Second Temple. Add the number of days that we celebrate Chanukah. Add the number of sons of Mattathias.

The answer is the age of Queen Salome, at the time of her husband's death, when she was sole ruler in Jerusalem.

CHAPTER X

IN THE DAYS OF KING HEROD

1. HEROD—FRIEND OF ROME

ROME put an end to Judea's political independence but allowed a member of the Maccabean family to rule as governor and as High Priest. An Edomite Jew named Herod put an end entirely to Maccabean rule.

Herod's ancestors were forced to accept Judaism by the Maccabean kings. His father was chief adviser to Hyrcanus and a close friend of Rome.

Herod, as a young man, was made governor of Galilee by his father with the consent of Hyrcanus. He soon showed his two chief qualities, courage and cruelty.

With courage Herod fought against the many outlaws in the hills of Galilee. With cruelty he put to death every prisoner without even a trial. Rome was pleased. The Jews of Galilee hurried to Jerusalem seeking justice.

"Herod has committed murder," they cried. "He put to death without a trial men who were not outlaws but who were innocent."

Many of those put to death were really patriots who hoped some day to fight for freedom against Rome.

The Sanhedrin, in great anger, ordered Herod to come to Jerusalem to stand trial. Herod came to Jerusalem escorted by many soldiers. Dressed in princely clothing he entered the courtroom accompanied by armed soldiers.

Hyrcanus, the High Priest, and the members of the Sanhedrin were too frightened to utter a word.

Shemaya, one of the leaders of the Pharisees, then stood up and said, "Never have I witnessed such a scene before. All who are accused come before us in black clothes, as a sign of mourning. They plead for our mercy. But Herod appears as a prince and threatens to slay us. Hear my warning. Even if you free him, Herod will try to destroy us. It is our duty to render justice without fear!"

Fearing that the Sanhedrin would condemn Herod, the High Priest Hyrcanus quickly postponed the trial. Hyrcanus had received a letter from the Roman governor in Syria ordering him to free Herod.

Hyrcanus warned Herod, "You will be declared guilty. Flee before it is too late."

Herod escaped to Syria and then returned with a large army.

Herod was now the real master of Judea!

When Julius Caesar died, Herod succeeded in winning the friendship of Mark Antony through large bribes. To increase his power Herod married Mariamne, granddaughter of Hyrcanus and a descendant of the Maccabees.

Outraged by the cruelty of Herod, the Jews sent a delegation to Mark Antony asking that Herod be removed as governor.

Selfish Mark Antony cared only about wealth and power. Herod had given him rich bribes.

"Are these accusations true?" asked Mark Antony turning to the ambassadors of Hyrcanus, knowing full well that Hyrcanus would favor the man who had married into his family.

"They are not," replied the ambassadors of Hyrcanus.

Annoyed by the persistent complaints of the Jews, Antony ordered that the delegates be put to death.

There was civil war for several years throughout the Roman empire. The son of Aristobulus entered Judea during this period of unrest. He was warmly welcomed by all who prayed for freedom from Rome.

This was the opportunity for which Herod had waited. Sailing to Rome, he appeared before Mark Antony and the senate.

"Make me king of Judea," pleaded Herod, "and I will destroy the rebels. Rome can count on me as its true friend!"

Herod was declared king. With the help of a Roman army Herod laid siege to Jerusalem. After a long siege Herod and the Roman army conquered the city.

The Romans butchered men, women and children without mercy.

Even wicked Herod pleaded for the slaughter to stop. "I shall be king of a land without a people if the slaughter continues," he said.

Finally the bloodshed came to an end.

One of Herod's first acts was to destroy all members of the Sanhedrin before whom he had once stood trial. Shemaya's warning had come true. Shemaya himself was spared because Herod respected his wisdom, and because Shemaya had pleaded with the Jews to admit Herod when he saw that resistance was hopeless.

Herod, friend and servant of Rome, was now king in Jerusalem.

2. HEROD THE TYRANT

Herod's policy was to show that he was more Roman than the Romans. He succeeded in making himself the most hated king in Jewish history.

Herod was eager to please Mariamne, his wife, who was even more beautiful than Cleopatra. He made her younger brother High Priest.

When Sukkot came thousands of Jews crowded into Jerusalem to celebrate the festival. They showed their great pleasure when they saw Mariamne's brother serve as High Priest.

They remembered the family from which this young man came and yearned for the days of the Maccabees.

"Soon they will rebel and place the Maccabees on the throne," thought Herod.

Shortly after the holiday Herod's servants went swimming with the young High Priest in the Dead Sea. He was drowned by "accident"—at Herod's command.

Next came the turn of aged Hyrcanus, now 80 years old, who was accused of plotting against the king. Even beautiful Mariamne did not escape. In a fit of jealousy Herod ordered the death of the beloved queen. Later their two sons were accused of seeking to avenge Mariamne's death and were slain by Herod.

Rome approved Herod's crimes as long as he paid heavy taxes which he took from the people.

To please Rome, Herod built an arena in which captives were thrown to the beasts. The Jews were shocked by such cruelty.

Herod tried to make the people forget their hatred for him. In a year of famine he generously fed the people by selling all of his treasures to obtain money for food. He believed in "bread and circuses." This was an old Roman trick for keeping the people quiet.

Herod was a great general and won victories over all hostile tribes. Throughout most of his reign there was peace. He built many cities and great buildings.

Herod called the leaders of the Pharisees and said, "The Temple in which we worship is not as large as it should be. Solomon's Temple was larger. It is my hope to rebuild and to enlarge the Temple."

Fearing that Herod planned to destroy the Temple, the leaders at first refused to give their consent. Herod promised that the Temple would be rebuilt one section at a time. Thus the old would stand until the new was finished.

At last the great task began. For many years Herod's workers labored until the work was completed. So beautiful was the new Temple that the whole world marveled.

But even in building the Temple, Herod tried to please the Romans. He placed a large golden eagle, emblem of Rome, over the great gate of the Temple. Herod knew that the people regarded all images as idols.

Brave young students tried to remove the golden eagle. They were cruelly put to death by Herod.

After having reigned for 34 years Herod became violently ill. Knowing that death was approaching he ordered his sister and servants to place all the leaders of the Jewish people in the arena in Jericho.

"As soon as I die," ordered Herod, "put these men to death. I know that the people will rejoice when I die. But when I die their rejoicing will be turned to mourning when they hear of the death of their leaders."

Fortunately his sister dismissed the leaders from the arena when Herod passed away.

Thus died the cruel tyrant hated by all his subjects.

3. THE HOPE FOR A MESSIAH

In their distress the people turned to the Torah for comfort.

Let us spend a few moments, for example, with a typical Jew living in Jerusalem. We will call him Jacob the sandal-maker.

Jacob earns a living by the sweat of his brow. All week long he is bent over his tools as he squats on a mat in the market-place. Much of what he earns he must pay to the king as taxes. He and his wife and children live on a diet of bread, olives, dates and cheese. It is hardly enough to keep them alive.

Jacob sells sandals to rich merchants. He and his family go barefoot for he cannot afford to pay for the leather needed for shoes.

On Friday there are special preparations for the Sabbath. Jacob walks to the street where meat is sold.

"Give me some calf's meat," said Jacob to the merchant as he put down a few coins.

"Ah, you have found customers this week," said the merchant.

"God has been good. Some of the king's officers gave me a special order for sandals," replied Jacob with a smile.

Late that afternoon the *shofar* was blown as a sign that soon the Sabbath would begin. Jacob hurried home.

Jacob poured a little oil into a clay lamp and placed a wick in the lamp. His wife lit the lamp and recited a blessing.

"Blessed art Thou, O Lord our God, King of the world, who made us holy with His commandments and commanded us to kindle the Sabbath light."

Jacob and his sons joined in prayer with some neighbors in a nearby synagogue. When Jacob returned he raised a cup of wine and chanted a blessing thanking God for the joy and rest of the Sabbath day.

The next day after the morning prayer Jacob and his wife sat down for their Sabbath meal.

"God has indeed been good," said Jacob. "It is not often we can afford such good food."

Several of Jacob's neighbors were sitting in the courtyard. Nearby was a cistern from which they drew water. Each roof had a small dome so that the rain-water trickled down from the roof to the cistern in which the water was stored.

"What news of Mariamne's sons?" asked one of the neighbors named Samuel.

"The king has ordered them to be executed," replied another neighbor.

"Surely they are innocent," said Jacob in anger.

"Quiet! The walls have ears," warned Samuel looking around in fear. Herod's spies were everywhere.

"When will these crimes end?" Jacob wondered.

Soon it was time for the afternoon service. The sandal-maker wandered to the splendid Temple. There in a side chamber a learned scholar lectured on the story of Jacob and Esau.

"In the future Jacob will rule over Esau," said the scholar.

The sandal-maker understood that by Esau the speaker meant Rome.

"Our prophets have taught us never to lose hope," continued the scholar. "Some day Elijah the prophet will return to earth to announce that the Messiah, the anointed prince of God will soon appear. Three days later a descendant of King David will usher in a perfect world. A trumpet will blow and Israel will welcome the prince of God whom we call Messiah because he is anointed by God, just as David was once anointed by Samuel, God's prophet.

"All evil rulers will be destroyed," continued the speaker. "A great light will shine throughout the world. Nations will be guided by this light to come to Zion to learn peace and justice. And Israel and mankind will enjoy perfect happiness on earth."

The sandal-maker sighed. He knew that the speaker meant kings like Herod when he spoke of "evil rulers." Some day a righteous prince, Messiah of the house of David, would rule wisely and justly. All Israel would then enjoy God's blessings. And Jacob was comforted.

The hope that some day we might build a better world is one of the most beautiful ideals of Judaism.

EXERCISES

I. Arrange these sentences in the order in which the events happened. (Review section 1, pages 119 to 121.)
   1. Herod won the friendship of Mark Antony through large bribes.
   2. Herod was made king of Judea in order to put down the rebellion.
   3. Herod's ancestors were forced to accept the Jewish religion.

4. Herod tried to frighten the Sanhedrin with armed force when ordered to stand trial.
5. Herod as governor of Galilee put many men to death without a trial.
6. Hyrcanus the High Priest helped Herod flee when the Sanhedrin was about to convict him.

II. True or false? (Review section 2, pages 121 to 123.)

1. Herod tried to show that he was more Roman than the Romans.
2. Herod was kind to the members of his family.
3. Rome was angry because of Herod's crimes.
4. Herod refused to help in time of famine.
5. Herod helped enlarge and beautify the Temple.

III. Choose the correct name or phrase. (Review section 3, pages 123 to 125.)

1. The people turned for comfort to (amusements, the Torah).
2. Jacob's daily diet consisted of (bread and olives, meat).
3. The *shofar* was blown to announce the beginning of (the Sabbath, work).
4. Esau meant (Israel, Rome).
5. Messiah means (anointed, prophet).
6. "The Messiah," said the scholar, "will be descended from (David, Judah the Maccabee)."
7. The belief in the Messiah gave (Jews, Romans) new hope for a better world.

IV. Questions for discussion:

1. How did Herod show that he was a friend of Rome?
2. Why was Herod hated by his people?
3. Mention some ways in which the life of Jacob the sandal-maker was different from the life of a worker today.
4. How did the Jews find comfort in the Torah?

THINGS TO DO

1. *Original Story*—Write a story about a Jewish prisoner who was forced to fight wild beasts in the arena.

2. *Jewish Library*—Visit a Jewish library in your synagogue or community center. Find a legend, story, poem or prayer dealing with the Messiah. Tell your class about what you read.

Take out a book dealing with some aspect of Jewish history.

A WORD GAME

How many words can you form out of the letters in the word "Sanhedrin"?

CHAPTER XI

HILLEL—TEACHER OF THE GOLDEN RULE

1. THE SCHOLAR

HILLEL was born in Babylon. There he studied the Torah for many years. Travelers brought word of two great teachers in Jerusalem named Shemaya and Avtalyon. Hyrcanus was then High Priest under Roman rule and there was peace in the land.

"I shall go to Jerusalem where I can study in the academy of these two great scholars," decided Hillel.

Arrived in Jerusalem, Hillel worked hard as a wood-cutter and as a day laborer. He performed odd jobs for which he was paid a few cents. In the afternoon he visited the academy of Shemaya and Avtalyon.

Hillel would buy food for his family with the money he had earned. But he would always leave over a few cents which he paid to the usher at the door of the academy. This fee was collected from each student as he entered for the upkeep of the academy.

One Friday Hillel earned no money. He was very eager to attend the lecture of Shemaya and Avtalyon, but was ashamed to ask permission to enter without paying the fee.

Hillel mounted the roof by means of the ladder attached to the side of the building. Through the skylight he listened carefully to the lecture delivered by the two scholars.

It was a cold winter's day. Exhausted and cold Hillel fell asleep on the roof. That night snow fell on the rooftops of Jerusalem.

Early the next morning Shemaya and Avtalyon and their students gathered for the Sabbath prayers.

"Why is it so dark here?" asked Shemaya. "The sun has already risen."

They glanced at the skylight and saw a man's form. Quickly they climbed to the roof where they found Hillel covered with snow.

A fire was kindled, even though it was the Sabbath, and Hillel was warmed by the heat of the flames. Soon he revived.

Shemaya and Avtalyon then ordered the usher to admit Hillel whether or not he could pay the fee.

For many years Hillel, thirsting for knowledge, studied in the academy. At last he was forced to return to Babylon, perhaps because of Herod's wars. In Babylon, Hillel taught what he had learned in Jerusalem.

Several years after the death of Shemaya and Avtalyon, Hillel went up to Jerusalem once more.

These were sad days, for many of Judea's greatest scholars had been killed by Herod.

That year the Passover fell on a Sabbath. In great confusion the *Kohanim* turned to the Sanhedrin for help.

"What are the rules for such a Passover?" they asked. "Are we allowed to make the Passover sacrifices on a Sabbath?"

The members of the Sanhedrin argued the matter but could come to no decision.

"Let us ask Hillel the Babylonian," said one member of the Sanhedrin. "For many years Hillel studied with Shemaya and Avtalyon. He will surely know the correct answer."

"The sacrifices must be brought even on the Sabbath," replied Hillel.

Hillel told them the laws of Passover. In amazement the members of the Sanhedrin listened as Hillel repeated word for word the many rules he had studied in the academy of Shemaya and Avtalyon.

No matter what the question, the members of the Sanhedrin turned to Hillel for instruction. At last the day came when the head of the Sanhedrin resigned his post.

"Let Hillel be our *Nasi* (president)," he said. "He is worthier than I."

Thus Hillel the Babylonian became the *Nasi* of the Sanhedrin.

2. HEAD OF THE SANHEDRIN

Was Hillel among the leaders placed in the arena at the command of Herod before his death? We do not know.

Hillel tried not to meddle in politics. He followed the advice of his teacher, Shemaya, who said, "Love work; be not eager to rule over others; do not be too close to those who govern." This was excellent advice when tyrants like Herod ruled.

Hillel was surely among those who advised Herod about beautifying the Temple. Nothing gave Hillel more joy than to be present at the great festivals of Passover, Shavuot and Sukkot when thousands of Jews from all over the world streamed to the Temple.

Hillel believed that the oral law was necessary in order to understand the true meaning of the Torah. The oral law meant all traditions not found in the written Bible. These traditions were called oral law because they were handed down orally from father to son and from teacher to pupil.

But which explanations of the Bible were true and which were false? Hillel drew up seven rules to help those who taught the oral law.

Here is an example of how a regulation, based on the oral law, helped the people.

The Bible tells us that all debts must be canceled in the seventh year. When a man is hungry his neighbor must help without thought of repayment.

That is why Nehemiah told the princes in time of famine, "Feed the hungry. Cancel all debts!"

If a farmer's crop was spoiled he could get help from his neighbor. If he could not repay, his debts were canceled in the seventh year. This was an excellent law.

Hillel saw, however, that the merchant's needs were different from a farmer's.

Sometimes a merchant needed money to buy merchandise.

"Lend me money," the merchant might say to a rich neighbor. "I shall buy merchandise, make a profit and then repay the money."

"Why should I lend you money?" the neighbor might reply. "Soon the sabbatical year will come and then you do not have to pay back."

To help the merchants Hillel asked the Sanhedrin to adopt an excellent rule.

The Torah tells us that a person cannot ask to be repaid in the seventh year. A court, however, is different from a man. A debtor could say to the court, "When the seventh year comes let the court collect the money that I am now lending." This statement was then put in writing and the court would collect the debt during the seventh year.

The Sanhedrin agreed with Hillel that this was an excellent rule. In this way merchants were able to borrow money when they needed it. The lender knew the money would be repaid.

The statement signed by the lender was called "prosbul." This means "transfer." It was called "transfer" because the lender transferred to the court the duty to collect the debt.

The Torah also tells us that a man who sells a house in a city like Jerusalem can buy the house back within one year. Houses were handed down from father to son. If a man sold his house he was usually in great need of help. The Bible therefore gives him the right to redeem the house for his family.

Sometimes the buyer purposely left Jerusalem as the year drew to a close.

"If the seller can't find me," thought the buyer, "he can't pay me back. Soon the year will be over. After that he no longer has the right to redeem the house."

Hillel was very angry when he heard of this unfair practice of buyers.

"Let the seller come to court and pay the court. The court will enter the house and return it to its rightful owner."

These regulations by Hillel were part of the oral law. Through the oral law Hillel showed how the Torah could help the people even though times had changed. The oral law became a very important part of the Jewish religion.

3. THE GOLDEN RULE

Hillel was called Rabbi by the pupils as a sign of love and respect. Rabbi means "teacher" or "master."

Many strangers heard of the wonderful teachings of Rabbi Hillel and the other Rabbis.

"We cannot believe in idols," said many of these strangers. "We will accept the religion of the Jews who believe in one God."

The Rabbis believed that it was wrong to force people of other religions to accept our religion. "Righteous people of all nations have a share in the world to come," taught the Rabbis.

When non-Jews came of their own free will, however, the Rabbis patiently taught them the laws of Judaism.

Once a non-Jew came to Shammai, the vice-president of the Sanhedrin.

"I should like to become a Jew," said the stranger, "but I have one condition."

"What is that?" asked Shammai.

"Teach me the entire Torah while I stand on one foot."

"Surely this man is trying to mock me," thought Shammai. Shammai turned away abruptly.

"You do not really want to learn the Torah. Please don't bother me," he said.

The non-Jew then went to Hillel and repeated his strange request.

"Rabbi Hillel, teach me the entire Torah while I stand on one foot."

Hillel understood that the stranger really wanted to learn, in a few moments, the basic principle of Judaism.

Hillel smiled and replied, "Do not do unto others what you do not want others to do unto you. That is the entire Torah. The rest is only an explanation of this rule. Go, study it!"

The stranger was greatly pleased when he heard Hillel's reply, and he accepted the Jewish religion.

Hillel, of course, referred to the words of Moses, "Love your neighbor as yourself." The laws of the Torah teach us to be kind and fair to our fellow-man.

Hillel's words, slightly changed, were later widely accepted as the golden rule.

4. "AS PATIENT AS HILLEL"

The people loved Hillel because of his great wisdom and his wonderful character. They admired him because he was so patient and kind.

Two men once made a wager concerning Hillel.

"Hillel never loses his temper," said the first man.

"I'll wager 400 *zuzim* that I can make him lose his temper," replied the second man. (A *zuz* was a small, silver coin worth about 25 cents.)

"Agreed," said the first. "You will never succeed in making him angry."

The stranger went to Hillel's house and called, "Hillel! Hillel! Where is Hillel?"

Hillel was then preparing for the Sabbath. He wrapped himself in a cloak and went to the door.

"What do you want?" asked Hillel.

"Why do the Babylonians have round heads?" asked the stranger.

Even though Hillel himself was a Babylonian he did not become angry.

"Their nurses are not experienced in taking care of babies," replied Hillel.

Hillel returned to his Sabbath preparations. Hardly had he closed the door when again he heard the same voice, "Hillel! Hillel! I want to speak to Hillel!"

Hillel patiently wrapped himself again in his cloak.

"What is it?" he asked without a trace of anger in his voice.

"I have an important question to ask. Why do the Arabs have red eyelids?"

"They live in sandy country. The sand causes irritations when it flies into their eyes."

By this time the stranger was growing impatient. Surely Hillel would rebuke him for his impudence if he tried again!

The stranger waited a few moments, and then knocked loudly on the door.

"I must speak to Hillel! I want Hillel!" he shouted.

Hillel was amazed to see the stranger again.

"What is it, Son?" asked Hillel.

"Why do Africans have broad feet?" asked the stranger.

"They live in marshes," replied Hillel in a quiet voice. "That is the way they adjust to walking through marshes and swamps."

"Are you really Hillel, whom people call 'Prince of Israel' "? asked the stranger.

"Hillel is my name," was the reply.

"May there not be many more like you in Israel," said the stranger impudently. "Because of you I lost 400 *zuzim* to a man who wagered I could not make you lose your temper."

"That was a foolish wager," replied Hillel smiling. "It is better that you lose your wager than that I lose my temper because of a few silly questions."

"Let a man be always as humble and patient as Hillel," became a proverb among the Jewish people.

5. THE SAYINGS OF HILLEL

Many of Hillel's sayings have become proverbs.

Hillel believed that we must always rely on ourselves. "If I am not for myself, who will be for me?" said Hillel.

This became the motto of the pioneers of Israel in our day, for they knew that Jews must rebuild with their own efforts if they wish to be free.

Even though we rely on ourselves, we need the cooperation of others. "And when I am for myself, what am I?" taught the great teacher.

Even self-reliance and cooperation with others are not enough. We must not delay. "And if not now—when then?" added Hillel.

Hillel believed that cleanliness is part of godliness. "Cleanliness," he taught, "is a holy duty."

Hillel urged his listeners to be as peace-loving as Aaron, the first *Kohen Gadol*.

"Be one of the followers of Aaron," he said; "love and pursue peace, love your fellow-men and draw them close to the Torah."

Perhaps Hillel was thinking of Herod and his officers when he taught, "He who tries to make a name for himself often loses his good name."

Hillel knew that one must never stop learning. "Unless you add to your knowledge, your knowledge will decrease," he taught. One's education cannot remain at a standstill. Either you go ahead or slip back.

Many people wanted to study Torah but always found some excuse for not studying. Hillel's warning to them was: "Say not, 'When I shall have leisure I shall study,' for you may never have leisure."

Hillel believed that the Jewish religion is based on education. "An ignorant person cannot be truly pious," he taught.

What should be one's goal in life—riches or wisdom? Hillel's answer was: "The more property, the more worries; the more Torah, the more life."

Hillel had excellent advice for pupils and teachers. In order to be a good student one must have curiosity, ask questions and look for solutions. A good teacher must patiently guide the pupil in searching for the answers to problems. That is why Hillel said, "A bashful person cannot learn, nor can an irritable person teach."

One must cooperate fully with others. "Do not separate yourself from the community," wrote Rabbi Hillel.

When others, however, refuse to show manly courage one should not follow their bad example. "In a place where there are no men, try to be a man," taught Hillel.

Have you ever criticized another person only to discover later that the criticism was unfair? Hillel urged his students to be tolerant. "Do not pass judgment on your fellow-man until you have been in his place," was his motto.

Hillel believed that evil deeds are always punished. Once when he saw a skull floating on the water he said, "Because you have drowned others, others have drowned you; and those who have drowned you shall themselves be drowned." Perhaps he was thinking of the misdeeds of Herod and the Romans.

Hillel taught that peace comes as the result of doing what is right. "The more righteousness, the more peace," he said.

Hillel was praised as the greatest teacher of the Torah since Ezra. He came to be known as "the pious and gentle follower of Ezra."

When the peace-loving Hillel died the people mourned:

> "Woe, pious Hillel!
> Woe, gentle Hillel!
> Woe, O follower of Ezra!"

EXERCISES

I. Choose the correct name. (Review section 1, pages 128 to 130.)

Avtalyon, Herod, Hillel, Passover, Sanhedrin

1. _____ came from Babylon to Jerusalem to study Torah.
2. The academy was headed by Shemaya and _____.
3. Many scholars were slain by _____.
4. The *Kohanim* wanted to know the rules of sacrifices when _____ falls on a Sabbath.
5. Because of his knowledge and wisdom Hillel became *Nasi* of the _____.

II. Answer each question in a complete sentence. (Review section 2, pages 130 to 132.)

1. What is meant by oral law?
2. When were debts canceled?
3. What is a *prosbul*?
4. How long does the seller of a house have the right to buy the house back?
5. How did Hillel help those who wanted to redeem their houses?

III. Who said to whom? (Review sections 3 and 4, pages 132 to 135.)

1. "Teach me the entire Torah while I stand on one foot."
2. "You do not really want to learn the Torah. Please don't bother me."
3. "Do not do unto others what you do not want others to do unto you."
4. "Why do the Babylonians have round heads?"
5. "It is better that you lose your wager than that I lose my temper."

IV. Complete each of Hillel's sayings. (Review section 5, pages 135 to 136.)

1. "If I am not for myself _____."

2. "And when I am for myself _____."
3. "And if not now _____."
4. "Say not, 'When I shall have leisure I shall study,' for _____."
5. "An ignorant person cannot _____."
6. "The more property _____."
7. "The more Torah _____."
8. "A bashful person _____."
9. "Do not separate yourself from _____."
10. "In a place where there are no men _____."

V. Questions for discussion:
1. Why is the oral law important in Jewish life?
2. Why was Hillel loved by the people?
3. Relate an incident that shows how people lived up to (or failed to live up to) each of the following sayings:

a—The golden rule
b—"If I am not for myself who will be for me?"
c—"He who tries to make a name for himself often loses his good name."
d—"Unless you add to your knowledge, your knowledge will decrease."
e—"The more property, the more worries."

THINGS TO DO

1. *Proverbs*—Make up a list of proverbs in English or in other languages that express the same thoughts as the sayings of Hillel.
2. *Memory Gems*—Memorize at least five of Hillel's sayings.
3. *Dramatization*—Dramatize the following scenes:
a—Hillel on the roof-top
b—Teaching the Torah on one foot
c—Patient Hillel

CHARADES

Act out charades based on sayings by Hillel or other proverbs learned during the study of Jewish history.

CHAPTER XII

THE GATHERING STORM

1. THE SPREAD OF JUDAISM

MANY GENTILES began to learn about the teachings of Rabbi Hillel and the Jewish religion. In Syria, Egypt, Rome, Babylon and throughout the world Gentiles asked to be admitted to the Jewish religion.

The Rabbis prepared manuals to guide these new Jews. The manuals contained the following:

a—The *Shma Yisrael* declaring that God is one and that man must love God with all his heart and with all his soul.

b—The golden rule, "Love your neighbor as yourself" and Hillel's interpretation, "Do not do unto others what you do not want others to do unto you."

c—The ten commandments.

d—The way of life based on the commandments of the Torah and the way of death resulting from sins such as greed, envy and hatred.

The great influence of the Jewish religion may be seen from the history of Queen Helena and her son.

Queen Helena ruled over a kingdom in the east called Adiabene. This country included cities such as Nineveh, once the greatest city in the world.

Queen Helena learned about the Jewish religion from a merchant of Jerusalem who visited Adiabene. The good queen began to believe in one God and refused to worship idols.

When Helena's husband died there was a dispute among the sons about who should be king. The people chose Izates in accordance with the wishes of the former king.

Izates, like his mother, had begun to believe in the Jewish religion.

"Your brothers will rebel against you," Izates was told. "Put them to death or your life is not safe."

"I believe in a God who has commanded us not to kill," replied Izates.

"At least place them in prison," advised his counselors.

"That too would be cruel. I shall allow them to settle in Rome where they can live in peace. In this way they will not be able to stir up the people against me."

Izates now invited Jewish teachers to instruct him in the Torah. One of his brothers and many of his subjects followed his example and entered the Jewish religion.

King Izates ruled his people with justice and kindness in keeping with the teachings of Judaism.

Some of his subjects who still worshiped idols rebelled against him. They urged the powerful king of the Parthians to attack Izates.

The kingdom of Adiabene was now in great danger. Just as the king of Parthia was prepared to march into Adiabene, word came that there was a rebellion in Parthia. The enemy quickly returned to Parthia without harming Izates or his country.

Queen Helena now resolved to visit Jerusalem and to worship God in the Temple. She took with her the sons of King Izates who were eager to learn Hebrew and the Torah.

At this time there was a severe famine in Judea. When Queen Helena arrived she gave large sums of money to the poor so that they might buy bread.

The people blessed the good queen who devoted her entire life to charity and to good deeds.

When Helena and Izates died they were buried near Jerusalem. The children of the king and many of his subjects remained faithful Jews.

We are told that one of their customs was to place a *mezuzah* on a staff which they carried with them in all their travels.

The conversion of Queen Helena and her son is an example of how the teachings of the Jewish religion began to spread to all corners of the world.

Judaism had become a world religion.

2. ROMAN CRUELTY

After the death of Herod, Rome divided the Land of Israel into three parts. Herod's three sons ruled as dukes. Herod's son in Jerusalem was guilty of so many crimes that he was finally banished by Rome.

Jerusalem now came under the rule of Roman governors whose cruelty knew no limits.

One of the governors was named Pontius Pilate. He cruelly put to death all whom he suspected of being unfriendly to Rome.

Once he plundered the money in the Temple to build a viaduct to bring water to Jerusalem. The Jews protested, since Temple money could be used for holy purposes only.

A large crowd gathered and demanded that Pilate restore the money. Pilate ordered his soldiers to disguise themselves in civilian clothes and to hide daggers under their cloaks.

"We will protest to Rome that you have stolen Temple money!" shouted the angry crowds.

"Disperse or you will be punished as rebels," replied Pilate.

"Restore the stolen money!" the Jews cried out in anger.

Pilate gave the signal and his soldiers fell upon the defenceless crowd. Rivers of blood flowed in the streets of Jerusalem before Pilate ordered an end to the slaughter.

The Samaritans in Samaria were treated in the same brutal manner. Jews and Samaritans sent angry protests to Rome. At last after ten years wicked Pontius Pilate was removed and forced to return to Rome because of his crimes.

3. A NEW RELIGION

More and more the people yearned for the Messiah, the anointed prince of God.

"When will our persecution end?" they asked. "When will God send the Messiah to put an end to our suffering?"

From time to time men arose who called themselves Messiah. But always the hopes of the people were doomed to disappointment.

At this time there appeared a new sect which taught that the Messiah had already come. Followers of this religion were called Christians.

Many of their beliefs were taken from Judaism. Members of the new sect accepted the belief in one God, the 10 commandments, the teachings of the prophets and Hillel's golden rule.

Some of the beliefs and customs of the new religion, however, were different from those of Judaism.

Rabbi Gamaliel, grandson of gentle Hillel, taught the Jewish people to treat members of the new sect with kindness even though their beliefs were different.

Pontius Pilate, however, was as cruel to the Christians as he had been to the Jews and Samaritans.

At first the new sect was persecuted by Rome. After 300 years, however, a Roman emperor was converted to the Christian religion which now gained great power.

A sad thing then happened. The new religion began to persecute Judaism, the mother religion from which it had taken most of its beliefs.

Jews, however, stood firm.

With great courage Jews said, "Nobody can force us to change our religion!"

At last after hundreds and hundreds of years the world is beginning to learn the meaning of religious freedom.

Christians and Jews now live next to one another in peace. Good neighbors know that we must respect the right to be different. Every person may worship God as he pleases.

The world too has begun to recognize how Judaism, the mother religion, has enriched mankind.

4. THE BEGINNING OF THE REBELLION

The Roman governors of Jerusalem grew more and more cruel. They had only one purpose—to gain as much riches as they could through taxes and bribes.

Perhaps the worst governor of all was a Roman named Florus who was appointed by the emperor Nero. Florus openly boasted of his crimes.

Florus greedily robbed as much as he could in every city of the Land of Israel. The Jewish people protested but Rome was deaf to all complaints.

At last Florus sent messengers to rob the Temple in Jerusalem.

On all sides were heard cries, "Let us resist! Let us fight for independence!"

Several young men took baskets and mocked Florus saying, "Help a poor beggar named Florus! Throw some money into our basket for poor, starving Florus!"

In great anger Florus came to Jerusalem to punish those who had mocked him.

"Give me the names of those who are the rebels," said Florus, "or I shall punish all of Jerusalem."

The people were silent.

"Is it not better to forgive than to stir up a rebellion?" pleaded some of the leaders.

"Destroy the upper market!" Florus commanded his soldiers.

Thousands of people in the upper market were cruelly slain by the Romans.

A group of patriots known as Zealots now urged open rebellion. They called themselves by this name from the words of Mattathias, "Let those who are zealous for the Lord—follow me."

The Pharisees pleaded with the people to be calm. A delegation came to Florus begging that he prevent further bloodshed.

"As proof that you plan no rebellion, let the people welcome the soldiers who are coming today to reinforce my army," said Florus.

The leaders agreed. The *Kohanim* appeared in their special robes, followed by the citizens of Jerusalem.

They loudly welcomed the Roman soldiers. The response of the soldiers was a stony and insulting silence.

"This is an insult!" murmured some of the Zealots. "It is a trick by Florus!"

"Destroy the rebels!" commanded the Roman officers. Again there was wholesale slaughter.

Florus finally withdrew from Jerusalem to his palace near the coast. He left a garrison of Roman soldiers in Jerusalem.

At the same time came word that in many of the mixed cities the Romans had permitted the inhabitants to slay their Jewish neighbors.

The Zealots seized control of Jerusalem.

"We defy Rome!" they cried. "We will fight for our freedom!"

The rebellion had begun.

EXERCISES

I. Match. (Review sections 1 and 2, pages 139 to 142.)

Column A	Column B
Adiabene	1. Cruel Roman governor
Helena	2. Author of golden rule
Hillel	3. King who converted to Judaism
Izates	4. Queen who fed Jews during famine
Pontius Pilate	5. Country over which a Jewish king ruled

II. Mention some beliefs or teachings which Christian religion borrowed from Judaism. (Review section 3, pages 142 to 143.)
III. True or false? (Review section 4, pages 143 to 144.)
   1. The Roman governors ruled with kindness and mercy.
   2. The Jews were angry because Florus tried to rob the Temple.
   3. Some Jews mocked Florus with a beggar's basket.
   4. Florus forgave those who criticized him.
   5. The Zealots led the rebellion.
IV. Questions for discussion:
   1. Why did so many Gentiles convert to Judaism?
   2. Why is Judaism called a "mother religion?"
   3. How can we encourage young people to observe Chanukah instead of Christmas?
   4. Why is freedom of religion important?
   5. What were the causes of the rebellion against Rome?

THINGS TO DO

1. *Film*—Show a film or film-strip dealing with some phase of religious freedom, good-will or fighting against prejudice.

2. *Brotherhood Observance*—Arrange an appropriate observance for Brotherhood Week in your club or school. Discuss the subject, "How can we combat religious prejudice?"

3. *Trial*—Pretend you are members of the Roman Senate. Bring up Florus on trial on charges of cruel treatment of the Jews.

HISTORY CONTEST

Each class selects five representatives. Contestants pick questions placed on separate pieces of paper in a hat or box. The class with the highest number of correct answers wins. The questions may be based on any aspect of Jewish history studied in class.

CHAPTER XIII

WAR AGAINST ROME

1. THE WAR IN GALILEE

FLORUS and the Romans attacked Jerusalem. The Zealots showed such great courage that the Romans were forced to flee.

The people, proud of their victory, rejoiced. "Perhaps the days of Judah the Maccabee are returning," they thought.

Soon the entire Land of Israel was controlled by Jewish soldiers. The Zealots made careful plans to defend the country against Roman attack.

The command in the north, in Galilee, was given to Josephus, a man noted for his good judgment and learning.

Josephus had recently gone to Rome to plead for several Jews who had been unjustly thrown into prison. During the journey the boat on which Josephus sailed was shipwrecked. Josephus and a few others swam for many hours until they were sighted by a passing boat. In Rome, Josephus appeared before Nero who granted the request of Josephus and freed those who had been imprisoned.

Josephus was not really in favor of the war against Rome since he felt that Rome was too powerful to be defeated. Once the rebellion started, however, Josephus decided to fight with the Zealots.

Josephus knew that the Romans would invade Galilee first.

"We must be prepared to resist a strong army," Josephus warned.

With great skill he organized his soldiers and strengthened the walls of each city.

Josephus was a master of strategy. When he heard that the city of Tiberias on the Sea of *Kinneret* had rebelled against him, he sailed with a fleet of fishing ships to Tiberias. The city leaders quickly surrendered to Josephus, not knowing that the ships were almost empty and that Josephus had only a few soldiers with him.

Nero, emperor of Rome, was greatly angered when he heard that his troops had been beaten in battle. He chose Vespasian, the general who had conquered Britain, to put down the rebellion.

Vespasian defeated one city after another. Josephus, of course, could not risk an open battle. He wrote to Jerusalem suggesting that he come to terms with Vespasian. The Zealots ordered resistance to the very end.

Josephus and his army took refuge in the mountain city of Jotapata. The Romans began to besiege the city but suffered many losses from raids by the brave Jewish soldiers. Vespasian himself was wounded during the fighting.

The Romans built an embankment high enough for them to shoot their stones and arrows into Jotapata. Hundreds of engines poured ammunition into the besieged city.

"Let us build our wall higher," ordered Josephus.

Under the protection of animal skins which were placed above the wall, Josephus and his soldiers built the wall higher and higher. For the time being Josephus had saved the city from defeat.

Water and supplies were growing scarce. Through a secret exit leading to the mountains Josephus would send his soldiers to obtain supplies. The soldiers were camouflaged in sheepskins.

The Romans finally placed their battering-rams in position. Josephus put sacks of wheat in front of the wall to soften the blows of the battering-rams.

"We must destroy the battering-rams before the walls crumble," said Josephus.

The Jewish soldiers made a surprise attack and set fire to the battering-rams. For many days the battle continued.

The Jewish defenders, however, were growing weaker and weaker because of fatigue and lack of water. After 47 days a deserter escaped from the city to the Romans.

"I have just escaped from the city at a point where the guards have fallen asleep," said the deserter to Vespasian. "If you send your soldiers to this point in the wall you can enter the city without resistance."

Vespasian quickly sent troops to the unguarded section of the wall. The Romans quietly entered the city and overpowered the sleeping guard.

In a short while the invaders conquered the city.

Galilee's strongest city had fallen!

2. JOSEPHUS AND VESPASIAN

When the city fell Josephus and 40 soldiers hid in a deep cave.

"The Romans shall never capture us," swore the soldiers. "It is better for us to die by our own swords than to be taken prisoner!"

"Why do you wish to take your own lives?" asked Josephus. "During a battle death is better than cowardice. But now that the battle is over let us surrender to the Romans."

From all sides the soldiers rushed upon Josephus.

"Death to the coward!" they shouted.

"I am no coward," replied Josephus. "If you are resolved to die, I will die with you. Let us draw lots. Each will slay the other according to lot. The last one must take his own life."

The soldiers agreed. As luck would have it Josephus and another soldier drew lots to be the last two slain.

Soon only Josephus and the soldier were left alive.

"Why should we die in this manner?" argued Josephus. "Is not suicide contrary to the Jewish law?"

"You are right," said the soldier. "Let us surrender to the Romans."

Josephus and the soldier left the cave and were taken prisoner.

Vespasian was overjoyed when the capture of Josephus was reported to him.

"Bring Josephus to me immediately," commanded Vespasian.

When Josephus was brought before Vespasian he said, "Hail, O Emperor!"

"How dare you call me by that name?" demanded Vespasian in anger. "Emperor Nero lives in Rome and to him I owe loyalty."

"Nero will soon die and you will be chosen emperor in his place," replied Josephus.

This was a shrewd trick to save his own life. Josephus knew that Vespasian's greatest ambition was to become emperor of Rome.

Vespasian, pleased by the prediction of Josephus, ordered his soldiers to treat the Jewish general kindly.

Soon came word that Nero's soldiers had rebelled against him. Nero, who had devoted much of his time to amusing the public by playing music and singing, was shocked to hear of the rebellion. He committed suicide.

Nero had not been cruel to the Jewish people. In fact, his wife Poppea had begun to believe in one God and observed some Jewish customs. On several occasions Poppea influenced Nero to grant favors to the Jews. Nero never interfered, however, with the wicked Roman governors of Jerusalem who had forced the Jews to rebel.

Vespasian's soldiers proclaimed their general emperor after a brief civil war.

Josephus had guessed right. His chains were cut to pieces as a sign that he was now a free man.

Josephus agreed to accompany the Romans to Jerusalem to try to persuade the Zealots to end the rebellion.

Was Josephus a traitor? History has never really decided. Josephus claims that he fought bravely until resistance was useless. Others claim that he was more concerned about his own safety than about Jewish freedom.

3. THE SIEGE OF JERUSALEM

Vespasian appointed his son Titus to lead the Romans against Jerusalem.

The leading Jewish general in Jerusalem was a youth named Simon Bar Giora. Although only 20 or 21 years old, Bar Giora had proved his heroism in the war against Rome.

Again the Romans were amazed by the courage shown by the Jews. No sooner did the Romans set up embankments than the Jews attacked and burnt what had been built.

Once the Jews dug a deep tunnel under the Roman embankment. The ground gave way and the Roman embankment fell into the ditch.

Josephus approached the wall on horseback.

"Why do you continue this hopeless struggle?" shouted Josephus. "Surrender before it is too late and your lives will be spared. But if you fight on, you will bring destruction on yourselves and on Jerusalem!"

"Death to the traitor!" was the reply of the defenders as they aimed their arrows at Josephus who quickly withdrew.

Titus now held a council of war with his officers.

"What is the best plan of attack? Shall we build more embankments or shall we try to storm the walls?" asked Titus.

"Neither plan can succeed against the brave defenders," replied the officers.

"Then we will starve them out," said Titus. "To close up

all secret exits we will build a wall shutting them in completely. Famine will do the rest."

The Romans built a wall surrounding Jerusalem. When the work was finished the Jewish soldiers were completely shut off from the rest of the country.

It is possible that if the Jews were all united under the command of Bar Giora they might have defeated the Romans. There were many disunited groups, however, within Jerusalem. Their disagreements weakened their defense.

The war dragged on for four long years. At last the defenders were so weak from hunger that they began to yield.

One by one the walls of Jerusalem fell. The Jews made their last defense in the court surrounding the Temple. After fierce fighting the Romans succeeded in setting fire to the glorious Temple.

The Second Temple was destroyed on the ninth day in the month of Av (*Tisha B'Av*) in the year 70 of the Common Era. 600 years had passed since the Temple had been rebuilt by Zerubbabel.

The ninth of Av was the very day on which the First Temple too had been destroyed. *Tisha B'Av* became the saddest day in Jewish history. Each year on this day Jews wept and fasted as they remembered the sad fate of Jerusalem and the Temple.

4. THE END OF THE WAR

Brave Bar Giora refused to surrender. He and his soldiers retired to the section of Jerusalem called the Upper City.

"Allow us to go free and we will lay down our arms," said Bar Giora to the Romans.

Titus refused. After another month all resistance in Jerusalem had ended. Bar Giora hid in a secret tunnel.

Lacking food Bar Giora was forced to leave the tunnel. He was soon seized by Roman soldiers who took him to Titus.

Josephus pleaded for the lives of several hundred women and children who were found in the Temple. Titus granted his wish. Josephus also saved many holy books.

The others who were taken captive were sold as slaves. 700 of the finest soldiers, led by Bar Giora, were forced to march through the streets of Rome.

The crowds in Rome thundered their applause as Vespasian and Titus marched by in the victory parade. Behind the emperor and his son, Roman soldiers carried the golden *menorah*, the musical instruments and the decorations which once stood in the Temple.

Simon Bar Giora was taken to the Tarpeian rock from which he was hurled to his death.

At the point where the procession entered the city the Romans built a victory arch. They called it the Arch of Titus. On it they showed the golden *menorah* and the instruments taken from the Temple. The arch still stands.

Vespasian struck a coin showing Judea in mourning beneath a palm tree. Under the picture were the words, "Judea has been taken captive."

Josephus continued to live in Rome where he was honored by the emperor. To show the courage of the Jewish people Josephus decided to write the story of the rebellion. He also wrote a history of the Jews so that the world would know about the glorious past of his nation.

Josephus was a great historian. His books have helped to preserve a full record of the wonderful history of the Jewish people. Josephus had failed with the sword, but he succeeded with the pen.

5. THE WAILING WALL

Jerusalem was in ruins.

The Temple had been burnt to the ground.

Only one wall of the Temple was not destroyed by fire. This was a section of the Western Wall of the Temple.

Many beautiful legends were told about this wall. It was said that when Solomon's Temple was destroyed the Western Wall escaped destruction because it had been built from the gifts brought by the poor.

The Western Wall, according to the legend, rests on seven stones that can never be destroyed. The first stone was placed on the site of the Temple by Adam, father of mankind. Abraham, Isaac and Jacob, fathers of the Hebrew people, laid the next three stones. Joseph placed the fifth stone in position, David the sixth and Solomon the seventh.

When the Romans destroyed Jerusalem they tried to set fire to this wall, but in vain. The soldiers who stormed the wall were thrown to the ground.

At last, according to the legend, Titus himself approached the wall.

A heavenly voice was then heard, "Wicked Titus, turn back! I have allowed you to destroy three of the Temple walls, but the Western Wall will stand forever!"

Titus, mocking the voice, leveled the battering-ram to destroy the Western Wall. Immediately his hand withered.

At that moment six angels descended from heaven and wept as they rested on the wall. The tears fell upon the stones of the wall and mingled with the mortar, making the Western Wall eternal.

As the years went by the rulers of the land gave the Jews permission to visit the Western Wall on *Tisha B'Av* and on other holy days.

The Jews descended the steps on which the old city of Jerusalem is built until they came to the Western Wall. They crowded into the narrow courtyard in front of the wall.

Beating their breasts in sorrow, the pilgrims wept as they raised their voices in prayer. They pressed their lips against the stones already worn smooth by the kisses of generations of worshipers.

"How long, O Lord? How long?" they cried. "When will

THE WAILING WALL

Jerusalem be rebuilt? When will the exiles be gathered together from the four corners of the earth?"

The tears of the pilgrims mingled with the tears once shed by the angels. Because of the weeping and the wailing of the mourners, the wall came to be known as the Wailing Wall.

The Western Wall became a symbol of Israel itself. Israel, like the Western Wall, can never be destroyed. Israel too is eternal. Israel too will stand forever.

And as the Jews wept they remembered the words of Jeremiah:

> "Refrain thy voice from weeping,
>   And thine eyes from tears;
>   For thy work shall be rewarded, saith the Lord;
>   And they shall come back from the land of the enemy.
>   And there is hope for thy future, saith the Lord;
>   And thy children shall return to their own border."

And the mourners were comforted. Some day Jerusalem would be rebuilt!

EXERCISES

I. Josephus or Vespasian? (Review sections 1 and 2, pages 146 to 148.)

1. _____ was commander of the Roman troops.
2. _____ was commander of the Jewish soldiers in Galilee.
3. _____ obtained supplies by sending soldiers through secret tunnels.
4. A deserter told _____ that the guards had fallen asleep.
5. _____ became emperor of Rome.
6. The chains of _____ were cut as a sign that he was a free man.

II. Choose the correct name or phrase. (Review sections 3 and 4, pages 150 to 152.)

1. The commander of the Jews in Jerusalem was (Bar Giora, Josephus).

2. The Jews called Josephus a (hero, traitor) when he urged them to surrender.
3. Jerusalem was conquered on *Tisha B'Av* by (Titus, Vespasian).
4. The Arch of Titus is in (Jerusalem, Rome).
5. Josephus helped the Jews most as a (general, historian).

III. Answer each question in a complete sentence. (Review section 5, pages 152 to 155.)
1. Which wall of the Temple was not destroyed?
2. According to the legend, what happened when Titus tried to destroy the last wall of the Temple?
3. When did Jewish pilgrims visit the Western Wall?
4. Why is the Western Wall called "Wailing Wall"?
5. What message of hope did the mourners carry away from the Western Wall?

IV. Questions for discussion:
1. In your opinion, was Josephus a traitor?
2. The war against Rome ended in the greatest calamity in Jewish history. Why is this the saddest event in our history?
3. Should *Tisha B'Av* still he observed as a day of mourning now that the State of Israel has been established once more?
4. The Western Wall has been called a symbol of the Jewish people. Why?

THINGS TO DO

1. *Exhibit*—Arrange an exhibit called "From the Pages of Jewish History." Include drawings, dioramas, posters, scrap-books etc. Notes should be prepared to explain each important event.
2. *Tisha B'Av*—The chant used on *Tisha B'Av* has a haunting sadness. Play a recording of this chant, or invite the cantor of your synagogue to sing an excerpt to your class.

THE JOSEPHUS PUZZLE

According to some authors Josephus escaped from the cave by means of a trick. Finding that all except himself and one other man had resolved to kill themselves, Josephus suggested that the

41 soldiers arrange themselves in a circle. "Every third person," said Josephus, "will be killed until but one man is left who must then commit suicide." Josephus then put himself and the other man opposed to suicide in positions where they would be the last chosen.

What positions did Josephus pick for himself and the other man?

(Answer: 16th and 31st positions. Try it out and see whether this is correct.)

UNIT FOUR

The Struggle for Survival

CHAPTER XIV

JOHANAN BEN ZAKKAI—THE MAN WHO SAVED JUDAISM

1. COULD JUDAISM SURVIVE?

THE LONG EXILE had begun. Many Jews fled from the Land of Israel, now almost in ruins. They escaped to Egypt or Babylon. Others were sold as slaves in Syria or in Rome or in the lands of the Mediterranean.

The Jews became wanderers on the face of the earth.

"How can we remain united?" the exiles asked. "Can we who are scattered in so many lands remain one nation? Can Judaism survive?"

It was a pupil of Hillel named Johanan ben Zakkai who, more than anybody else, helped to save Judaism.

"Only the Torah," taught Johanan, "can unite the Jewish people."

2. THE PUPIL OF HILLEL

Johanan had studied at the schools of both Hillel and Shammai in the days when the Temple still stood.

From Shammai he learned many wise rules. Shammai's motto was, "Say little but do much." He also taught his pupils, "Set aside a fixed time for the study of the Torah."

Johanan tried to follow these rules in life. He appreciated most, however, the teachings of kind, patient, gentle Hillel. He accepted as his life's goal the saying of Hillel, "Love and pursue peace; love your fellow-men and draw them close to the Torah."

There were many differences of opinion between Hillel and Shammai. Nearly always Johanan agreed with Hillel. He felt that Shammai was often too strict.

One Yom Kippur, for example, Shammai not only fasted but refused to allow any adult to prepare food for his young son. The other scholars were angry with Shammai because of this.

"Your son is too young to prepare his own food properly," they said. "Even though you are fasting, there is no harm in preparing a child's food on Yom Kippur."

Johanan remembered too how Hillel had taught the golden rule to the stranger whom Shammai had turned away.

"Both Hillel and Shammai are great teachers," thought Johanan, "but Hillel's teachings are closer to the true spirit of the Torah."

Even though Johanan was one of Hillel's youngest pupils, Hillel called him "the father of wisdom" and "the father of coming generations."

Johanan was a merchant, and thus earned money to support his family. Most of his time, however, he devoted to the study of the Torah. It was said that he was always the first to enter the academy.

Some years after Hillel's death, Johanan became the leader of the school of Hillel. He often taught in the open street in the shadow of the holy Temple.

The people loved Johanan ben Zakkai and said that he was as kind and as modest as Hillel. They noticed, for example, that when Johanan met somebody in the market-place he was always the first to say "Shalom!" (peace). Honor and greatness had not made him proud or arrogant.

Pupils flocked to the school of Johanan in great numbers. Johanan also sat in the Sanhedrin where he was one of the greatest judges.

Johanan once said to five of his pupils, "One must know

how to act toward others. In your opinion, what is the most important thing in life?"

The pupils thought about Rabbi Johanan's question. They observed the people around them and then returned with their answers.

"Generosity is most important," replied the first pupil. "One must regard others with a generous eye."

"Be a good friend," replied the second.

"Be a good neighbor," replied the third.

"Know the consequences of your acts," replied the fourth.

"A good heart is the most important thing in life," replied the fifth pupil.

"That is the correct answer," said Johanan. "The man who has a good heart will also be generous, will be a good friend and neighbor and will not do anything before he studies the consequences of his acts."

Johanan, perhaps, thought of Solomon's prayer for a "wise and understanding heart." To him the heart was the seat of both kindness and wisdom.

And who indeed had proved to be kinder and wiser than Johanan ben Zakkai, the beloved teacher of Israel?

3. JOHANAN AND THE WAR AGAINST ROME

To Johanan the Temple was a symbol of peace.

He was very sad when he saw the young men of Israel preparing for war against Rome. He knew how cruel the Romans had been, but he feared that a rebellion would bring ruin upon the Jewish people.

"It is not too late to make peace," pleaded Johanan after the siege of Jerusalem had begun. Simon Bar Giora and his soldiers, however, paid no attention to the advice of Johanan.

Soon famine gripped the city.

"Jerusalem and the Temple are doomed if Bar Giora refuses to make peace with the Romans," said Johanan to his pupils. "We must try to save the Torah!"

Johanan thought of a plan. He would set up a school of learning far from the scene of battle where the scholars could continue their study of the Torah. But how could he escape from Jerusalem? And how could he obtain Roman permission to set up an academy of learning? Legend tells us the following fascinating tale.

"No living person is allowed to leave Jerusalem," Johanan was advised. "Only the dead are brought outside of the walls for burial."

Johanan's pupils spread the rumor that their teacher had died. They placed him in a coffin and brought him to the gate of the city where the soldiers stood guard.

"Open the coffin!" shouted the soldiers. "We will pierce the body to make sure he is dead!"

"Surely you will not show such disrespect for the great Rabbi Johanan ben Zakkai," pleaded the pupils.

The guards permitted the pupils to pass. The coffin was placed in the open field beyond the walls, and the pupils quickly returned to the city.

Later Johanan crept unnoticed from his hiding-place, and crawled to the Roman camp.

There, the legend tells us, he hailed Vespasian as king, just as Josephus had once done. A messenger arrived shortly after that to announce that Vespasian had been declared emperor of Rome.

"What reward shall I grant you?" asked the Roman general.

Johanan knew that he could not ask for Jerusalem and the Temple to be spared as long as the Zealots continued the rebellion.

"Let me set up a school in the village of Jabneh," replied the Rabbi.

The general laughed. This was a small favor to ask for. Little did he realize that this school would help to save Judaism.

"Granted! Anything else?"

Johanan thought for a moment.

"Send a doctor to cure Rabbi Zadok," requested Johanan. "And spare the family of Rabbi Gamaliel."

"Granted!" quickly answered Vespasian. "It shall be done."

Zadok was a great Rabbi who had become ill during the siege. Gamaliel was a young scholar of the family of Hillel.

"If Gamaliel is saved," thought Johanan, "he can revive the Sanhedrin, and serve as its leader for many years. People will accept him as leader because of his learning and because he is of the family of Hillel."

Johanan continued on his way to Jabneh. There in a vineyard he taught the Torah. From all corners of the land scholars came, and joined the new academy.

Johanan's plan had succeeded—he had set up a school where the Rabbis could continue to teach the Torah.

4. THE ACADEMY AT JABNEH

Soon word reached Jabneh that Jerusalem had fallen.

"Woe unto us!" wept Johanan and the scholars. "Jerusalem lies in ruins and the holy Temple has been burnt to the ground!"

"Torah must now take the place of the Temple," taught Johanan. "We will worship God in our synagogues, teach the word of God and devote ourselves to a life of good deeds."

A number of scholars were permitted by the Romans to leave after the capture of Jerusalem, and to come to Jabneh. Among them were Gamaliel and Zadok.

There were many tasks that the academy at Jabneh had to perform. They had to organize a Sanhedrin which would serve as the highest court of the land. They had to set the calendar, arrange for the celebration of the holidays, appoint teachers for young children and fix the order of the prayers.

Since there was no fixed calendar in those days, for example, the Sanhedrin would announce when each new month began. Two witnesses who had sighted the new moon in the heavens would appear before the Sanhedrin to testify.

"We have seen the new moon," the witnesses would declare.

The court would examine the witnesses to see whether they were reliable. Messengers would then be sent to notify the rest of the country that a new month had begun.

Usually the messengers would light fires on the mountain tops. This was a signal to those living at a distance. These people in turn would light a fire, and thus relay the message to communities lying still further away.

In this manner all Jewish communities would learn on which day the new month had begun, and on which days Rosh Ha-Shanah, Yom Kippur, Sukkot, Passover, Shavuot and the other holidays should be celebrated.

The prayers we recite today follow closely the order set by the Rabbis at Jabneh. The words themselves may be as old as Moses, David or Ezra.

Three times a day, morning and afternoon and evening, Jews gathered in the synagogue to recite the *Shma*, the Psalms of David and the 18 Blessings.

What could be more beautiful than the prayer before the *Shma* in which the worshipers expressed their love of Torah and their hope for new freedom?

> Thou hast loved us, O Lord our God, with a great love;
> Thou hast bestowed upon us great and abundant mercy.
> Our Father, our King, for the sake of our ancestors who
>   trusted in Thee
> And to whom thou didst teach the laws of life
> Be gracious unto us and teach us likewise.
> Our Father, our merciful Father who is ever compassionate,
> Have pity on us; and fashion our hearts

> To understand and to know, to perceive, to study and to
>   teach,
> To observe, to do and to fulfill in love all the teachings
>   of Thy Torah.
> Enlighten our eyes in Thy Torah,
> Let our hearts cling to Thy commandments,
> And unite our hearts to love and revere Thee
> So that we may never be put to shame;
> For in Thy holy, great and revered name have we trusted.
> May we rejoice and be glad with Thy Salvation;
> And gather us in peace from the four corners of the
>   earth
> By restoring us with dignity to our land,
> For Thou art God who bringest Salvation.

5. THE LAST DAYS OF JOHANAN

Uppermost in the minds of Johanan and the Rabbis was the precious hope that some day Jerusalem would be rebuilt.

Three times a day they prayed to God:

> "Return in mercy to Jerusalem, Thy city,
>   And dwell in it as Thou hast promised,
>   And rebuild it soon in our days
>   So that it will endure forever."

Once Rabbi Johanan and his greatest pupil, Joshua ben Hananya, rode past the fallen walls of Jerusalem.

When Joshua saw the ruins of the Temple he began to weep.

"Alas, where once the Temple stood there is nothing but a heap of ashes and ruins!"

"Console yourself," replied Johanan. "Did not the prophet say that God wants righteousness rather than sacrifice? The Temple has fallen but the Torah can never be destroyed!"

Johanan lived to a ripe old age. His last words of advice to his pupils were, "Fear God as you fear man."

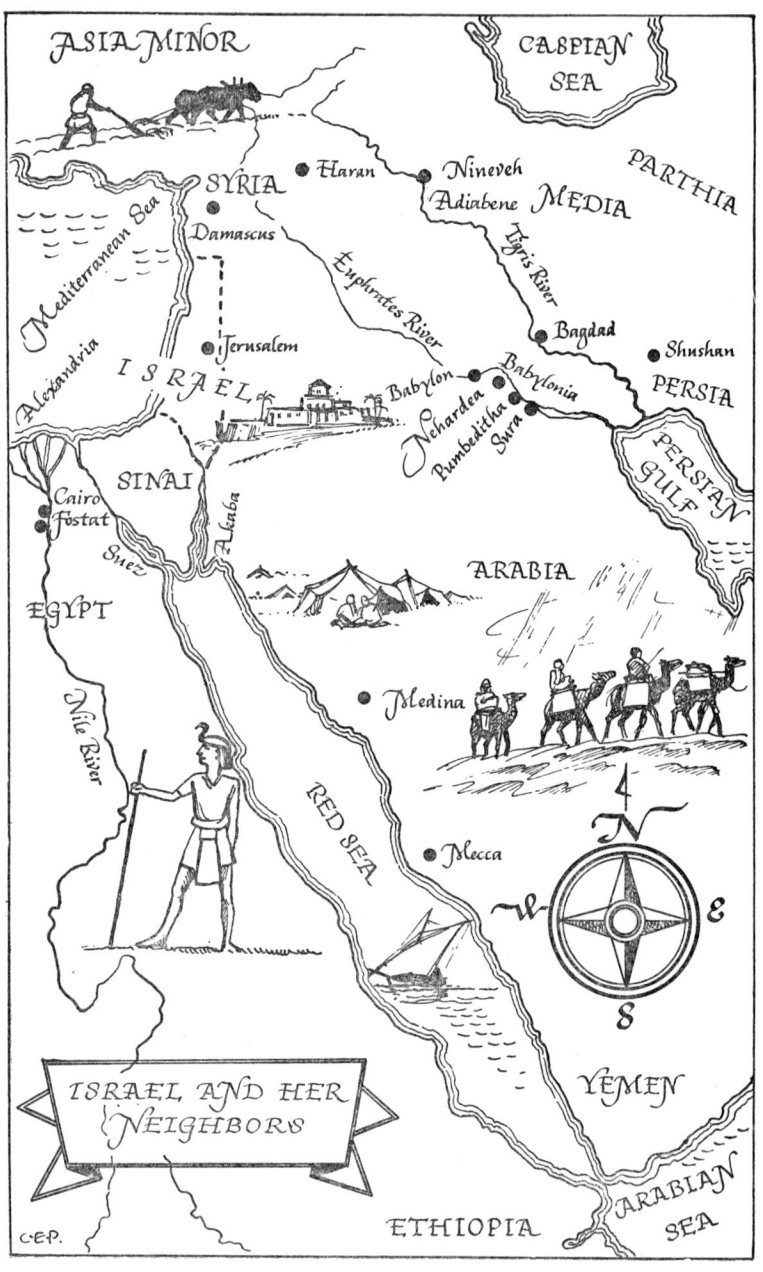

"Surely our fear of God should be greater than our fear of man," said the scholars in wonder.

"A person who knows that another is watching will not commit a wrong," replied Johanan. "Remember that God always watches over us. In this way, our fear of God will keep us free of sin."

After Johanan's death, the academy elected Rabbi Gamaliel to be head of the Sanhedrin. For almost 40 years, with the help of Zadok, Joshua ben Hananya, Akiva and other great scholars, Gamaliel led the Jewish people as president of the Sanhedrin.

Jews in many lands turned to little Jabneh for instruction and guidance. The scattered members of the nation were united by the Torah!

Johanan's dream had come true. The Temple had fallen, but Judaism had been saved!

EXERCISES

I. Choose the correct name. (Review sections 1 and 2, pages 161 to 163.)

Hillel, Johanan, Rome, Shammai, Solomon

1. Many Jews were sold as slaves in Syria and in _____.
2. The motto of _____ was, "Say little but do much."
3. _____ taught, "Love and pursue peace; love your fellow-men and draw them close to the Torah."
4. _____ agreed with his pupil that a good heart is most important.
5. _____ prayed for a "wise and understanding heart."

II. Match. (Review section 3, pages 163 to 165.)

Column A	Column B
Bar Giora	1. Escaped from Jerusalem in a coffin
Gamaliel	2. Village where a great academy was built
Jabneh	3. Leader of Jewish soldiers
Johanan	4. Roman general who became emperor
Vespasian	5. Scholar from the family of Hillel

III. Why? (Review sections 4 and 5, pages 165 to 167.)
  1. Why did witnesses come to testify that they had seen the new moon?
  2. Why did the messengers of the Sanhedrin light fires on the mountain tops?
  3. Why did Joshua ben Hananya weep when he saw Jerusalem?
  4. Why did Johanan believe that the fall of the Temple did not mean the end of Judaism?
  5. Why did Johanan say, "Fear God as you fear man"?

IV. Questions for discussion:
  1. Why is Johanan ben Zakkai called "The man who saved Judaism"?
  2. Compare Johanan and Zerubbabel.
  3. What were the achievements of the academy at Jabneh?
  4. In the prayer "Thou Hast Loved Us" find phrases which prove: a) that the Jews believe that God is a God of love b) that the Jews want to understand and to obey the Torah.
  5. Find prayers in the *Siddur* (prayer-book) in which the Jews pray for: a) freedom b) knowledge c) peace d) rebuilding of Israel.

THINGS TO DO

1. *Hebrew Calendar*—Construct a Hebrew calendar indicating the holidays for each month. The names of the months and the holidays celebrated in each month are as follows:

Tishri—Rosh Ha-Shanah, Yom Kippur, Sukkot
Heshvan—Jewish Book Month
Kislev—Chanukah
Tevet—
Shvat—Tu Bishvat (Israel Arbor Day)
Adar—Purim
Nisan—Passover
Iyar—Israel Independence Day, Lag B'Omer
Sivan—Shavuot

THE STRUGGLE FOR SURVIVAL

Tammuz—
Av—Tisha B' Av
Elul—

2. *Research*—The Roman city of Pompeii, not far from Naples, was destroyed by volcanic eruption in 79 C. E., just nine years after the fall of Jerusalem. Many people believed this was a punishment because of Roman cruelty.

Bring in a report about the ruins of Pompeii. Show pictures of life in Pompeii to the class.

CALENDAR PROBLEMS

1. The Temple was destroyed in 70 C. E. (Common Era). How many years ago did this take place?

2. Zerubbabel began to rebuild the Temple in 536 B. C. E. (Before the Common Era). How old was the Temple when it was destroyed by the Romans?

CHAPTER XV

AKIVA—MASTER OF THE ORAL LAW

1. THE SHEPHERD

AKIVA ben Joseph was one of the greatest Rabbis who ever lived.

Akiva was born about 17 years before the destruction of Jerusalem. His father, Joseph, was poor and uneducated.

As a child Akiva received no education. Instead of attending school the lad helped to support his family by taking care of sheep.

As a young man Akiva was employed as a shepherd by Kalba Savua, one of the richest men in the Land of Israel.

Like David of old, Akiva led the sheep each day over the hills of Judea in search of green pastures.

Kalba Savua had a beautiful daughter named Rachel. One day Rachel went out into the field to inspect her father's sheep.

Akiva the shepherd fell in love with Rachel at first sight. How great was his joy when Rachel returned to the field on the second and third days!

Rachel too fell in love with the handsome shepherd.

At last, after many days, Akiva said, "Rachel, I know that you are the daughter of a rich man and I am only a poor shepherd. But I can no longer remain silent and hide my love!"

When Akiva asked Rachel to become his wife she replied that she would consent provided he studied Torah and acquired an education.

Akiva was sad. How could he attend school now? Was it possible for him to study Torah when he did not know even how to read or write?

One day as Akiva sadly sat beside a brook while tending his sheep, he noticed a large stone with a deep hole in it.

"What formed the hole in the rock?" he wondered.

He looked closely and saw that the constant pressure of the brook's waters had worn away part of the rock.

"If soft drops of water can wear away stone," he thought, "surely the Torah can make an impression on my mind and heart if only I devote myself to constant study."

Akiva promised Rachel that he would try to acquire a knowledge of Torah, and Rachel consented to marry him.

Kalba Savua, in great anger, disinherited his daughter when he heard that she wanted to marry a poor, uneducated shepherd.

Rachel and Akiva were married, but they were very poor indeed. Akiva barely earned a living as a woodchopper.

It seemed impossible for him to take time from his work to attend school. But Rachel never permitted him to forget his promise to study.

At last, when Akiva's first-born son was of school age, father and son attended school together. Akiva's teachers soon discovered that he had great talent for study.

"No sacrifice is too great," said Rachel. "I will support our family while you study at the academy of one of the great Rabbis."

Johanan ben Zakkai was no longer alive. It had become Akiva's dearest ambition to study with one of the Rabbis trained by Johanan.

Akiva attended several schools of learning, and, after many years, became a student of Joshua ben Hananya, the greatest of Johanan's followers.

Akiva's fame now spread throughout the country. The lowly shepherd became one of Israel's most beloved Rabbis.

Kalba Savua regretted his cruel decision and later bestowed much of his wealth on his daughter and on his brilliant son-in-law.

Rachel's sacrifice had been rewarded!

2. THE TEACHER

Rabbi Akiva opened a school in the village of Bnei Brak, not far from Jabneh.

Hundreds and hundreds of pupils came to study with this great teacher. They honored not only Akiva but his beautiful wife, Rachel.

Akiva used to turn to Rachel and say. "Whatever learning my pupils and I have acquired—we owe to her."

Whenever Akiva heard his pupils express a desire for riches he would say, "Who is truly rich—he who has a good wife." Of course, he was thinking of his own beloved Rachel.

One reason the scholars loved Akiva is that he took a personal interest in each pupil. Once when a pupil became ill, Akiva took time from his studies to visit him. Not only did Akiva cheer up the sick pupil, but noticing that the house had not been properly cleaned, he put the house in order.

The pupil, although very ill, was so much encouraged by the visit of the great Rabbi Akiva that he soon got better.

"You have brought me new life," said the pupil gratefully.

Rabbi Akiva taught his pupils that visiting the sick is one of the greatest of the *mitzvot* (commandments).

Like Hillel, Rabbi Akiva was a great master of the oral law. Akiva even extended the seven rules which Hillel had used to explain the Bible.

"There are many hidden meanings in the Bible," taught Akiva. "The Bible doesn't contain a single unnecessary word."

Akiva would search the Bible to find hidden meanings and a basis for the many traditions of the oral law.

"If we hope to preserve the oral law," Akiva explained to his pupils, "we must arrange it in an orderly manner."

Akiva arranged the laws in six divisions: laws of farming, laws concerning the holidays, laws concerning marriage and women, laws of property, laws of holy things in the Temple and laws of purity.

Later the Rabbis compared Akiva to Ezra the editor of the Bible.

"He is like a workman who goes into the fields with his basket," they said. "Whatever he finds he places in his basket —wheat, barley, fruits, vegetables. Later he arranges everything neatly. He places the grains of wheat on one side, the grains of barley on another side; fruits and vegetables are arranged separately etc."

Indeed Akiva helped to preserve the oral law by arranging it in such orderly fashion. No wonder he was called a second Ezra!

3. THE SAYINGS OF RABBI AKIVA

Like Hillel, Rabbi Akiva was a teacher of the golden rule. "Love your neighbor as yourself—that is the most important rule in the Torah," said Akiva.

Akiva taught the people to have faith in God by saying, "Whatever God does is for the best."

He told an interesting anecdote to illustrate what he meant.

Once during his travels he had but 3 things with him in addition to the scroll of the Torah—a lamp by the light of which he would study, a rooster to awaken him early in the morning and the donkey on which he rode.

As the sun sank in the west Akiva came to a village and asked for lodging for the night. The selfish inhabitants drove him away.

Fatigued and downcast, Akiva rode to a nearby forest where he prepared to sleep on the ground. Instead of complaining, however, Akiva thought to himself, "Whatever God does is for the best."

The Rabbi kindled his lamp and began to study the Torah.

A strong gust of wind suddenly blew out the flame. A little while later wild animals came and devoured the rooster and the donkey.

"Whatever God does is for the best," said Akiva.

The next morning Akiva returned to the village. To his amazement he learned that a band of robbers had attacked the village that night and had killed most of the inhabitants.

"How fortunate I was!" exclaimed Akiva. "If the villagers had given me lodging for the night, I too would have been slain by the robbers. Or had they seen the light of my candle, or heard the crowing of the rooster or the braying of the donkey they would have known where I slept and would have attacked me. Now I know indeed that whatever God does is for the best!"

Akiva taught that God is a loving father and that we are called "children of God."

"Beloved is man," said Akiva, "for he was created in the image of God."

Rabbi Akiva taught that God wants man to help himself. "Free will is granted to man," he said. Man must choose between what is right and what is wrong. Man must also work for his own improvement.

A sick man once asked Rabbi Akiva for advice, and Akiva suggested a remedy.

"How dare you interfere with God's will?" asked a laborer who stood nearby. "If it is God's wish that he suffer from a disease, is it right for you to go against God's decision?"

"What is your occupation?" asked Akiva.

"I am a gardener," replied the laborer.

"Why do you interfere with the earth which God has created?"

"If I were not to water the earth and prune the trees they would not produce good fruit," answered the gardener.

"So it is with man," said Akiva. "His body requires careful

attention and tender treatment. God wants man to work for his own betterment."

4. THE LEADER

Just as in the days of Hillel, many non-Jews came to Akiva to learn from him the teachings of Judaism. A famous Roman citizen named Aquila who was a friend of the emperor attended Akiva's academy and became a Jew.

When the emperor rebuked Aquila for converting to Judaism, Aquila replied, "I followed your advice. You advised me to acquire something that stands at a low price now but will rise in value. Today Greeks and Romans worship idols and do not understand the beauty of Judaism, but some day Judaism will rise in value and the whole world will appreciate the greatness of its teachings."

With the help of Akiva and Joshua ben Hananya, Aquila prepared a new Greek translation of the Bible.

The Jews still suffered from wicked Roman rule. Once the Rabbis in the Land of Israel heard that new, harsh laws would be decreed by the Roman emperor.

"Let us send a delegation to Rome to plead for justice," said the leaders of Israel.

Gamaliel, Joshua ben Hananya and Akiva were chosen to head the delegation. They sailed from the Land of Israel to Rome where they were helped by a Roman Senator who had been converted to Judaism. It is possible that Josephus also helped them.

The Rabbis succeeded in their mission and the laws against the Jews were not passed.

We are told that when the Rabbis saw how prosperous the city of Rome was they wept, but Akiva smiled.

"Why do you weep?" asked Akiva.

"Shall we not weep when we see how this city of idol worshipers prospers while Jerusalem is in ruins?" replied the Rabbis.

"That is why I smile," said Akiva. "If this is the reward of those who have done so few good deeds, think of how great will be the reward of those who fully obey God's commandments."

A similar incident occurred near Jerusalem. When the Rabbis saw wild animals crawling among the Temple ruins they wept.

Akiva, however, smiled and said, "The prophet warned us that Jerusalem would be destroyed, but that it would also be rebuilt. Now that the first prophecy of destruction has come true, we can be sure that the second prophecy of rebuilding will also come true."

"Rabbi Akiva," said his companions, "you have consoled us."

Akiva traveled to many far-off places to gather funds for charity, and to bring the Jewish communities his message of hope and of Torah. He traveled in North Africa and in Arabia, in Syria, in Asia Minor and in Babylon.

Once he and Rabbi Gamaliel set sail in two separate boats. A storm came up and, to Gamaliel's horror, the boat in which Akiva sailed was wrecked.

When Gamaliel landed on shore he was amazed to find that Akiva was still alive.

"I held on to one of the boards of the ship," Akiva told Gamaliel, "until I reached the shore in safety."

One of the holidays that Akiva loved to celebrate was Passover. If you look at your Passover *Haggadah*, you will probably find a picture of Akiva and the other Rabbis seated around the *Seder* table telling the story of how the children of Israel gained their freedom from Egypt.

They spent the entire night, we are told, celebrating the Passover. At last their pupils came and said, "Rabbis, the time has come for the recitation of the morning *Shma*."

Akiva taught that the Jews must never forget the Passover ideal of freedom. To fight for freedom became his great am-

AKIVA AND RABBIS AT THE SEDER TABLE

bition. Perhaps that is why he traveled so much—he tried to arouse Jews the world over to strike for their freedom.

Soon Akiva became the leader of a new Jewish struggle for freedom.

EXERCISES

I. True or false? (Review section 1, pages 172 to 174.)
   1. Akiva's father, Joseph, was a great Rabbi.
   2. Rachel promised to marry Akiva if he learned Torah.
   3. Kalba Savua rejoiced because his daughter married a handsome shepherd.
   4. Akiva and his son attended school together.
   5. Akiva studied at the academy of Joshua ben Hananya.

II. Choose the correct name or phrase (Review section 2, pages 174 to 175.)
   1. Akiva opened a school in _____. (Bnei Brak, Jabneh)
   2. Akiva said that all of his learning he owed to _____. (Kalba Savua, Rachel)
   3. Akiva believed that visiting the sick _____. (took too much time from one's studies, was an important duty)
   4. The author of the seven rules, used to explain the Bible, was _____. (Akiva, Hillel)
   5. Because he arranged the oral law in such orderly fashion, Akiva was compared to _____. (Ezra, Zerubbabel)

III. Who was the author of each of the following sayings— Hillel or Akiva? (Review section 3, pages 175 to 177 and pages 135 to 136.)
   1. "Love your neighbor as yourself—that is the most important rule in the Torah."
   2. "Love and pursue peace, love your fellow-men and draw them close to the Torah."
   3. "If I am not for myself, who will be for me?"
   4. "Whatever God does is for the best."
   5. "Beloved is man, for he was created in the image of God."

THE STRUGGLE FOR SURVIVAL 181

6. "A bashful person cannot learn, nor can an irritable person teach."

IV. Answer each question in a complete sentence. (Review section 4, pages 177 to 180.)
1. In what way did Aquila follow the emperor's advice?
2. Why did Gamaliel, Joshua ben Hananya and Akiva go to Rome?
3. How did Akiva console his companions when they passed the Temple ruins?
4. How was Akiva saved from drowning?
5. What Passover ideal did Akiva teach the people?

V. Questions for discussion:
1. How did Rachel help Akiva?
2. Discuss the achievements of other great Jewish women.
3. Why was Akiva called "a second Ezra"?
4. Compare Akiva and Hillel.

THINGS TO DO

1. *Hall of Fame for Jewish Women*—Nominate and elect great Jewish women to a Hall of Fame. In each case discuss why the person deserves to be elected. Devote a section in a scrap-book to each person elected.

Here are some women whom you may choose from:

Sarah, Rebecca, Leah, Rachel, Miriam, Deborah, Ruth and Naomi, Esther, Queen Salome, Queen Helena, Rachel (wife of Akiva).

This is a good project for Mother's Day.

2. *Research*—Report to the class about the life of Rabbi Joshua ben Hananya.

Joshua was one of the pupils who carried Johanan ben Zakkai outside of the walls of Jerusalem. He was the teacher of Akiva. It was largely through him that the Sanhedrin at Jabneh decided to accept the opinion of Hillel in all disputes between Hillel and Shammai.

A good source for his biography is Jack Myers *The Story of the Jewish People*. Anecdotes that the class will enjoy are: "The Nearest Way" (p. 164), "Wisdom In An Ugly Frame" (p. 165), "One of God's Ambassadors" (p. 167).

PUZZLE

Substitute 3-letter words for each of the following phrases. The words will be identical whether read *across* or *down*.

1. A Hebrew word meaning "the son of."
2. Adam's wife.
3. The first word in the English translation of "Rosh Ha-Shanah."

CHAPTER XVI

THE BAR KOCHBA REBELLION

1. A WICKED EMPEROR

WHEN Hadrian became emperor of Rome he was anxious to gain the good-will of all the nations over whom Rome ruled.

"How can I win the friendship of the Jews in the Land of Israel?" he asked.

"Rebuild the Temple," was the advice given to him by his friends. There can be no doubt that the emperor's friends obtained this advice from Jewish leaders such as Joshua ben Hananya and Akiva.

"Inform the Jews that the Temple in Jerusalem will soon be rebuilt," ordered Hadrian.

The righteous convert Aquila was placed in charge of the rebuilding of Jerusalem and of the Temple. 50 years had passed since the destruction of Jerusalem by Titus.

The Jews rejoiced. At last their prayer would be answered.

Soon, however, enemies began to slander the Jews. The Samaritans warned that Jews would rebel if they ever became strong again.

Hadrian quickly changed his mind.

"I shall rebuild the Temple," said Hadrian, "but not in exactly the same spot."

This, of course, was against Jewish law.

In great anger the Jews gathered weapons to rebel against the emperor who broke his promise so easily. Joshua ben Hananya pleaded with the people to be calm.

"I shall tell you a fable," said Joshua to the people.

"A lion once promised a rich reward to any animal that removed a bone which had stuck in its throat. The stork removed the bone with its long beak and demanded the reward.

" 'What,' roared the lion. 'You placed your head in a lion's jaw and removed your head in safety, and still demand a reward! Is not this reward enough that you are still alive?' "

The people realized that Rome was like the lion. They could not expect Rome to keep a promise. The best they could hope for was that Rome would not destroy them.

The leaders of the rebellion obeyed Joshua and returned peacefully to their homes.

"The time will come," they said, "when we will not allow Rome to break her promises."

Akiva agreed with those who wished to rebel. Many of his students studied faithfully for half of the day, and then retired to the forests where they practised with bow and with arrow.

Ten years later Hadrian visited Israel. He knew that the people were restless and that they hated Rome.

"How can I make these people act like Romans?" he asked.

"Build temples in Jerusalem to the Roman gods," said his advisers. "Forbid the Jews to teach the Torah, to gather for worship on the Sabbath, or to celebrate their holidays."

"It shall be done!" replied Hadrian.

This was exactly the same decree with which Antiochus had stirred up rebellion 300 years before. The only difference was that Hadrian did not try to force the Jews to worship idols.

Joshua ben Hananya and Akiva pleaded with the Romans to withdraw the wicked decree. This time Hadrian would not change his mind.

Soon the rebellion began!

2. SIMON BAR KOCHBA

The rebellion was led by a young hero named Simon of the village of Kozeba. He was known at first as Simon Bar Kozeba.

Young though he was Simon had prepared for this moment for many years. He hated the Romans who had put to death members of his family during previous disturbances.

Simon had stored away provisions and ammunition in the caves of the land. He had trained brave young men as soldiers. The pupils of Rabbi Akiva, especially, joined his forces.

Many legends grew up around this brave soldier who had the strength of a Samson. To test the bravery of his recruits Simon would require each soldier to amputate a finger. When the Rabbis protested, Simon required the soldiers to show their strength by uprooting a young tree while riding on horseback.

Another legend states that Simon was able to catch the stones shot from the Roman machines with his knees and to hurl them back at the enemy.

Simon immediately sought the help of Rabbi Akiva. What a great moment it was when these two met—the ancient Rabbi and the brave young general! Both of them were ready to give their lives for the freedom of the Jewish people.

"People call you Bar Kozeba," said Akiva. "But I shall call you Bar Kochba (Son of a Star), for you are like a star leading the children of Jacob to victory."

Simon Bar Kochba soon showed that he deserved his new name. He fell upon the Romans with great fury and drove them from the Land of Israel.

Bar Kochba stopped his pursuit of the Romans at the boundary of Syria. Had he continued, it is possible that all the nations of Asia would have joined in the fight against the hated Romans.

Bar Kochba returned victorious to Judea. Jerusalem, now a city of ruins, was captured by the Jewish soldiers.

Akiva, overjoyed, declared, "Bar Kochba is the Messiah for whom we have waited so long. He is God's anointed."

Simon was proclaimed *Nasi* or Prince of Israel. As a sign of independence he struck Hebrew coins with the name Simon on one side and on the other side the words "For the Freedom of Jerusalem." On the coins were pictures of the Temple gate, the trumpet blown in the Temple, the harp of victory or palm-branches carried in the Sukkot procession.

It seemed as if the days of the glorious Maccabees had returned!

3. THE FALL OF BETAR

For two years Simon Bar Kochba was master of the land.

The Samaritans and Christians also rallied to his support. They too had suffered from the Roman decree against freedom of worship.

Hadrian was dismayed to find that his commanders were helpless before Bar Kochba. At last he sent for his greatest general, Julius Severus, the man who had subdued Britain.

Julius Severus brought a tremendous army into the Land of Israel. His soldiers were supplied with food by a large fleet. Fortress after fortress fell before the giant battering-rams of the Romans.

Simon Bar Kochba chose a city named Betar, not far from Jerusalem, in which to make his stand against the Romans. The city was well-protected since it was situated on a high mountain. Secret underground streams provided an unlimited supply of water.

Within the city there was great activity. Food was brought in from the countryside by way of secret entrances. Schools were open for children and academies for older pupils.

Akiva continued to teach at his academy in Bnei Brak, but his friend Rabbi Eliezer of Modin settled in Betar. Rabbi Eliezer was Simon's uncle and his presence inspired the soldiers with courage.

Could Bar Kochba really hope for victory? Perhaps if he held out long enough he might receive help from the Parthians, a nation whom the Romans never conquered.

Perhaps Bar Kochba might have been victorious if all the people were united in his support.

Not all the Rabbis agreed with Akiva. When Akiva declared Simon Bar Kochba to be the Messiah, one scholar replied mockingly, "Akiva, grass will grow from your jaws before the Messiah comes."

The Samaritans began to desert to the side of the Romans. Those within Betar attached notes to their arrows revealing to the enemy information about secret entrances to Betar.

One by one the entrances began to fall into the hands of the Romans. It became difficult to bring food into Betar. Famine broke out.

The Samaritans even conspired against Rabbi Eliezer and succeeded in bringing about his death.

"Now we know we are lost," said the soldiers when they heard of Eliezer's death.

Bar Kochba fought on in Betar for over a year. The war had already lasted three years.

A messenger came running to Bar Kochba. "The Romans have blocked up our secret springs! They have cut off our water supply!"

The loss of water meant certain death. Had the Samaritan spies informed the Romans of these underground springs? Probably.

Bar Kochba now had to chance all in an open fight to recover his water supply. A fierce battle raged. Badly outnumbered the weary soldiers of Betar fought bravely—but in vain.

Bar Kochba and his gallant men lost their lives on the field of battle. According to tradition Betar fell on the 9th of Av, the very day on which both Temples were destroyed.

4. THE DEATH OF RABBI AKIVA

The fall of Betar was a death-blow to Akiva's hopes for freedom.

"Only the Torah can save us," said Akiva.

To teach the Torah, however, was dangerous. The penalty was death.

Akiva continued to teach without fear.

"Akiva, are you not afraid?" asked his friend Pappus. "I warn you the Romans will put you to death if you teach the Torah!"

"Foolish Pappus!" answered Akiva sadly. "Let me tell you a story.

"The fox walking along the banks of the river saw that the fish were greatly agitated.

" 'What is wrong?' asked the fox.

" 'Men have spread their nets to catch us,' replied the fish.

" 'Then come on shore and I shall protect you,' said the fox.

" 'Foolish fox,' answered the fish. 'If we are in danger in the water which is our natural home, how much greater will the danger be on land!'

"We cannot escape danger by refusing to teach the Torah any more than the fish could escape by leaving the water," added Akiva. "We cannot exist without Torah."

Akiva was soon imprisoned. In prison he met Pappus.

"Alas, you were right, Akiva," said Pappus. "My failure to teach did not save me. I have been arrested for some imaginary offense. You at least were true to the Torah."

Those were sad days, indeed, for Israel. Only a few Rabbis succeeded in escaping. Two of them were famous pupils of Akiva—one a scholar named Meir, and another a scholar named Simon Bar Yohai.

Many Jews pleaded with the Roman government to free Akiva, but Rome showed no mercy.

Akiva was condemned to death. The 80-year old Rabbi was a hero in death as he had been in life.

"Now I know at last what it means to love God with all

one's heart, with all one's soul and with all one's might," said Akiva.

Just before death came he exclaimed: "Shma Yisrael Adonai Elohenu Adonai Echad."

5. LAG B'OMER

Three years after the fall of Betar and shortly after the death of Akiva, came word that wicked Hadrian had died.

The evil decrees were soon revoked. Jews were given their religious freedom once more.

Rabbi Meir, Rabbi Simon Bar Yohai and 5 other Rabbis who had escaped from the Romans gathered in Galilee to establish a new Sanhedrin.

They sent word throughout Israel saying, "Whoever has studied Torah, let him come and teach; and whoever has not studied Torah let him come and learn."

Akiva had died but his spirit lived on.

"If it were not for Rabbi Akiva," the scholars used to say, "Israel would have forgotten the Torah."

The days between Passover and Shavuot, when Akiva's students had suffered great hardships, became days of sadness and mourning for all Israel. One day, however, *Lag B'Omer*, became a day of celebration.* According to tradition this was the day on which a plague, which had broken out among the students of Akiva, ended. It is possible also that on this day Bar Kochba's soldiers and Akiva's pupils won a victory against the Romans. Perhaps the Roman persecution of Akiva's students ended on this day.

---

* On the day after the Passover a sheaf of barley, called an *omer*, was brought to the Temple as a thanksgiving offering. From the time of the bringing of the *omer* to Shavuot, 50 days were counted. This period was known as the time of the counting of the *omer*. The holiday is celebrated on *Lag B'Omer* which means the 33rd day during the period of the counting of the *omer*.

Lag B'Omer is also remembered as the anniversary of the death of Simon Bar Yohai, the great pupil of Rabbi Akiva.

Lag B'Omer is still celebrated as a joyous holiday in Israel and throughout the world. Many weddings take place on this day. School children go on outings on *Lag B'Omer*, and arrange athletic events on this day.

It is a custom on *Lag B'Omer* to practise archery with bows and arrows. This is a reminder of the pupils of Akiva who after their study in the academy would go into the forests to practise with their bows and arrows in preparation for the revolt against Rome.

Huge bonfires are lit in Israel today in memory of Bar Kochba and Akiva and the soldiers of freedom. There are special processions at the tomb of Simon Bar Yohai in the village of Meron.

A *Sefer Torah*, or scroll of the law, is brought to Meron for the festivities. A bonfire is lit and the people join in joyous singing and dancing.

Thus do we honor the memory of those who fought for the two great ideals of Torah and of freedom.

Bar Kochba and Akiva were not successful in their struggle against Rome. But the ideal for which they fought, freedom, lived on in the minds and the hearts of the Jewish people.

Over 1800 years passed before the dream of Bar Kochba and Akiva came true when the state of Israel was proclaimed on May 14, 1948.

EXERCISES

I. Who said to whom? (Review section 1, pages 183 to 184.)

1. "How can I win the friendship of the Jews in the Land of Israel?"
2. "I shall rebuild the Temple, but not in exactly the same spot."

3. "I shall tell you a fable."
4. "You placed your head in a lion's jaw and removed your head in safety, and still demand a reward!"
5. "Build temples in Jerusalem to the Roman gods."

II. Complete each sentence. (Review section 2, pages 184 to 186.)

Akiva, Bar Kochba, Jerusalem, Kozeba, Romans
1. Simon came from the village of _____.
2. _____ believed that Simon was the Messiah.
3. Akiva called Simon by the name of _____ because he was like a star leading the Jews to victory.
4. Simon Bar Kochba defeated the _____.
5. Simon struck coins which read, "For the Freedom of _____."

III. What is my name? (Review sections 3 and 4, pages 186 to 189.)

1. I was the emperor of Rome. I promised to rebuild the Temple but changed my mind. I commanded the Jews to stop teaching the Torah or carrying out the laws of Judaism. I brought my greatest general from Britain to subdue the rebellion of the Jews.
2. I was the uncle of Bar Kochba. I lived in Betar and encouraged the soldiers to fight for freedom. The Samaritans conspired against me and brought about my death.
3. I was the *Nasi* (prince) of Israel. I won many victories against the Romans. I fell on the field of battle in the defense of Betar.
4. I advised Akiva to save his life by not teaching Torah. I too was thrown into prison by the Romans for some imaginary offense.
5. I encouraged the Jews to fight for Torah and for freedom. I continued to teach the Torah even when warned that the Romans would punish me with death. I died with the *Shma Yisrael* on my lips.

IV. Match. (Review section 5, pages 189 to 190.)

Column A	Column B
Meir	1. Tomb of Simon Bar Yohai
50 days between Passover and Shavuot	2. Israel Independence Day
Lag B'Omer	3. Days of sadness in memory of Akiva and his pupils
Meron	4. 33rd day during the counting of the *omer*
May 14, 1948	5. Pupil of Akiva

V. Questions for discussion:

1. How did the Bar Kochba rebellion differ from the rebellion in the days of Johanan ben Zakkai?
2. What were the causes leading to the defeat of Bar Kochba?
3. How can Akiva and Simon Bar Kochba serve as an inspiration to us today?
4. Has your school ever celebrated *Lag B'Omer?* How?

THINGS TO DO

1. *Lag B'Omer Field Day*—Arrange athletic events or a field day for *Lag B'Omer*. Divide the class into teams named after the heroes of *Lag B'Omer*.

2. *Arts and Crafts for Lag B'Omer*

a—Construct a bow and arrow, or a sword and a shield in the form of the Star of David.

b—Draw a map of Israel. Indicate by means of a star or a design places connected with the Bar Kochba story such as Betar, Jerusalem, Bnei Brak, Meron and Kozeba.

c—Draw a poster announcing the *Lag B'Omer* outing. Use as a design one of the pictures stamped on the Bar Kochba coins.

These designs can be found repeated on Israeli stamps.

A MAGIC STAR PUZZLE

If you substitute the correct numbers for the letters on the *Magen David* (6-pointed star), all numbers on each of the six lines will add up to the same sum.

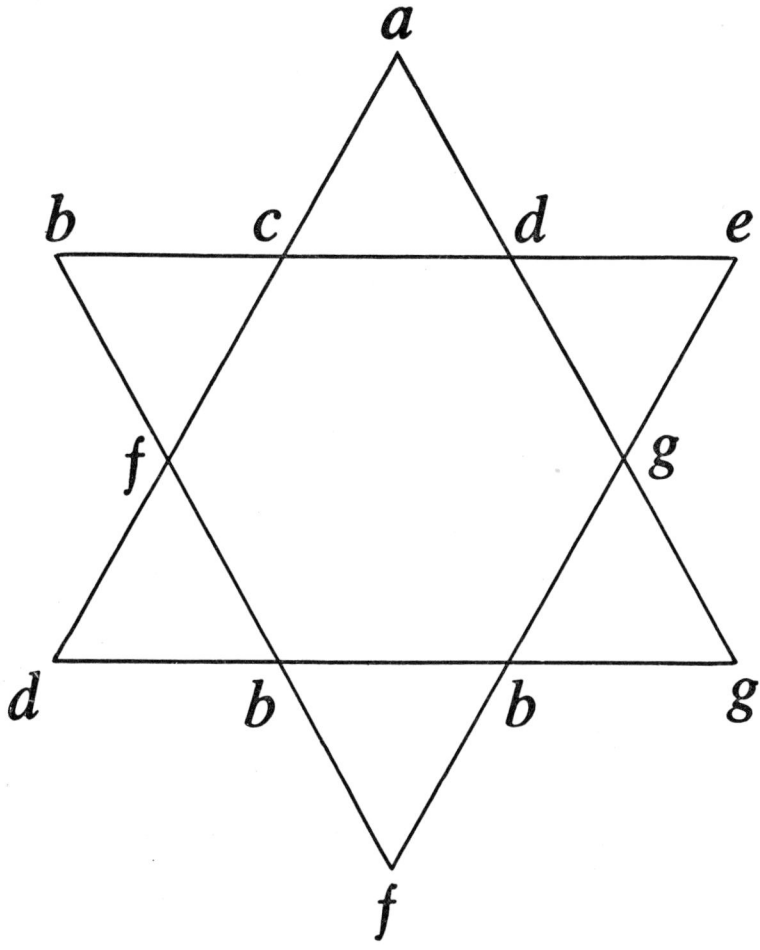

a—The day in the month of *Av* on which Betar and the Temples fell

b—The day of the week on which Adam was created

c—The number of tablets of stone on which the 10 commandments were written

d—The number of sons of Mattathias who fought for Jewish freedom

e—The number of days in the week

f—The number of the commandment which says, "Remember the Sabbath day to keep it holy"

g—The number of years that the Bar Kochba rebellion lasted

CHAPTER XVII

JUDAH THE PRINCE—EDITOR OF THE MISHNAH

1. A PRINCE IN ISRAEL

"ON THE DAY that Akiva died," said the Rabbis, "Judah was born." One great leader passed away but another came to take his place. "As soon as one sun set," added the Rabbis, "another began to rise."

Judah was born to greatness. Was he not descended from the great Hillel? Was not his grandfather, Gamaliel, head of the Sanhedrin in Jabneh for almost 40 years?

Judah's family suffered great hardships during the days of the wicked Hadrian. After Hadrian's death, however, the evil decrees were withdrawn.

Judah's father served as head of the Sanhedrin after the Bar Kochba rebellion. Judah was privileged to study with his father, with Simon Bar Yohai and with other great scholars. His teachers recognized his great ability and learning.

After his father's death, Judah was elected head of the Sanhedrin. People called him Judah the *Nasi* (Prince).

Rome now became friendlier to the Jews than it had been for many years. The emperor recognized Judah as leader of the Jewish people. Judah was permitted to appoint judges and teachers, and to rule with almost no interference.

The Jews paid voluntary taxes to uphold the Sanhedrin and academy as well as Judah's household. Rabbi Judah the Prince became very wealthy. He used his riches to help the people, however, and not for his own personal enjoyment.

Once a famine broke out in all the lands over which Rome ruled. Judah the Prince used his wealth to feed the people in the Land of Israel.

At that time many foreign languages were spoken in the Land of Israel. Judah insisted that all members of his household speak Hebrew. Even his servant was famous because of her command of pure Hebrew.

Judah the Prince enjoyed the friendship of the Roman rulers. Many legends have come down to us about his conversations with one of the Roman emperors.

Once Judah the Prince invited the emperor to dine with him on the Sabbath. Although the food was cold the emperor enjoyed the meal very much.

"This indeed was a meal fit for a king," he said to Judah with a smile.

Judah invited the emperor to dine with him again on a weekday. Hot, tasty dishes were brought before the emperor.

"Wonderful though this food is," said the emperor, "I preferred the first meal."

"It is true that one spice is missing," replied Judah.

"Tell me the name of that spice," urged the king. "My servants can obtain any spice no matter how costly!"

"This is one spice they cannot buy," said Judah smiling. "The spice is the Sabbath. It was because of the Sabbath spirit that prevails in my house that the first meal was so delicious. There is no ingredient in the world as precious as the Sabbath spirit."

Rome's friendship, of course, proved to be very helpful. Judah secured better conditions for the Jewish people.

Judah won the love of all by his unselfish leadership. This gave added importance to the position of *Nasi*.

This position later passed to Judah's son, and after him to his grandson. It remained in Judah's family, passing from father to son, **for over 200 years.**

Thus the Jews once more had a leader to rule over them in time of peace, and to help them in time of trouble.

2. A GREAT RABBI

Rabbi Judah's fame spread far and wide. Pupils from many countries, especially from Babylon, flocked to his academy.

Judah was admired so much that he became known simply as Rabbi.

Judah knew that many of his pupils would become great leaders in Israel. He once said, "I learned much from my teachers, more from my colleagues and most from my pupils."

Judah used to advise his pupils, "Which is the right path for a man to choose—one of which both he and other men will be proud."

Judah the Prince would often give his pupils practical advice. Once at a feast he ordered his servants to serve hard and soft tongues.

The pupils picked the soft meat, but did not eat the hard tongues.

"Are you aware of what you have done?" asked Judah with a smile. "You preferred soft tongues to hard tongues. Thus should it be too in your daily lives. In speaking to your neighbor use a soft tongue, for a hard tongue creates argument and hatred."

He would urge his students to be careful to observe even minor commandments, for one good deed leads to another.

"He who performs a *mitzvah* (good deed) unselfishly need not rejoice over one good deed alone, for that good deed will lead to many other good deeds. And he who commits one sin should not worry about that sin alone, for one sin leads to many other sins."

Rabbi Judah's greatest achievement was the editing of the oral law. For hundreds of years the oral law had grown until it was almost impossible to remember the many, many laws.

Judah completed the work that Akiva had begun of arranging these laws in orderly fashion. Judah's collection of laws was called Mishnah, which means "Teaching." It was written in pure Hebrew.

The Mishnah contains the teachings of the oral law, and thus stands next to the Bible, or written law, in importance.

3. THE MISHNAH

The first section of the Mishnah lists the religious laws connected with farming.

The Bible, for example, commands the farmer to set aside the corner of each field for the poor. How much must the farmer set aside?

"The minimum is one-sixtieth of the field. However there is no fixed maximum," answers the Mishnah. "The more the farmer sets aside—the better."

The Mishnah says that the same is true of charity and of study. There is no set limit—the more the better.

The Mishnah adds that there are some things which bring a reward both in this world and in the world to come—honoring one's parents, charity and bringing about peace.

"But the study of Torah," says the Mishnah, "is equal to all the others put together."

The second section of the Mishnah deals with the festivals.

On Passover, for example, we are commanded to tell about the exodus from Egypt. What exactly must we recite?

The Mishnah lists the passages now found in our Passover *Haggadah* which we recite at the *Seder*. The four cups of wine, the four questions, the explanations concerning the *matzah* and bitter herb, and the songs of praise are mentioned by the Mishnah.

The Mishnah then adds: "In every generation a man must regard himself as if he himself came forth out of Egypt. Therefore are we bound to bless Him who wrought all these wonders for our fathers and for us. He brought us out from slavery to freedom, from sorrow to gladness, from mourning to festivity, from darkness to great light and from bondage to redemption."

The other sections of the Mishnah deal with the laws of marriage, property, the Temple and purity.

The desire for justice and mercy underlies all the laws of the Mishnah. Every effort was made, for example, to prevent capital punishment.

In cases involving the death penalty 23 judges would sit in judgment. No person could be put to death unless there were two witnesses who had seen the crime. Other evidence was not accepted if there were not two eye-witnesses.

Those in favor of acquittal spoke first. A judge who voted "innocent" could not change his vote to "guilty," but one who voted "guilty" could change his vote to "innocent."

Because of these safeguards, it was rare to convict a person. "A Sanhedrin which put one man to death in seven years was called a cruel Sanhedrin," says the Mishnah. "One conviction in 70 years," says Rabbi Eliezer, "would be considered cruel." Rabbi Akiva was completely opposed to capital punishment.

Witnesses were warned of the horror of shedding innocent blood with these words:

"Why did God begin the world by creating one man (Adam)? To teach us that if one causes the death of a single soul it is as if he destroyed the whole world. And if one saves a single life it is as if he saved the whole world."

In the spirit of the Mishnah, the new state of Israel abolished the death penalty in 1954.

4. "ETHICS OF THE FATHERS"

One of the most famous books in the entire Mishnah collection is called "Ethics of the Fathers." Many of the sayings of Hillel, Shammai, Johanan ben Zakkai, Akiva and Judah the Prince are found in this little book.

Some of the sayings remind us of the golden rule.

"Rabbi Eliezer said: Let your friend's honor be as precious to you as your own."

Another Rabbi added, "Let your friend's property be as precious to you as your own."

How can we serve God best? By serving our fellow-men. "He who pleases mankind, pleases God. He who displeases mankind, displeases God."

When we have a task to perform it is good to remember the saying of Rabbi Tarfon, "The day is short, but the work is great."

Is it better to be last among the wise or first among the ignorant? The Rabbis taught, "Be the tail among the lions rather than the head among the foxes."

Rabbi Judah the Prince used to warn his pupils not to judge by appearances. "Do not look at the jar but at what is in it."

What makes a man wise, strong, rich, or famous? This is the answer of Ben Zoma, a friend of Akiva's.

"Who is wise? He who learns from every man.

Who is strong? He who conquers temptation.

Who is rich? He who is content with his portion in life.

Who is honored? He who honors his fellow-men."

There are many witty sayings about pupils. The Rabbis knew that not all pupils are alike.

"There are four types of students:

"He who is quick to learn but quick to forget—his gain is offset by his loss.

"He who is slow to learn but slow to forget—his loss is offset by his gain.

"He who is quick to learn and slow to forget—he is fortunate.

"He who is slow to learn and quick to forget—he is unfortunate."

The purpose of education is to help a person to think for himself. The Rabbis expressed the same thought in a different way.

Some pupils, they said, are like the sponge which soaks up everything—good and bad. Others are like the funnel—in one ear, out the other. Still others are like a strainer which holds on to the dregs but allows the wine to pass through. Those who think for themselves, however, are like the sifter which retains the fine flour but rejects the coarse flour.

Do we all understand the difference between what is yours and what is mine? Even in this matter, according to the Rabbis, we are not alike.

"There are four types of men:

"He who says, 'What is mine is mine, and what is yours is yours'—he is average; but some say that he is like the men of Sodom.

"He who says, 'What is mine is thine, and what is thine is mine'—he is ignorant.

"He who says, 'What is mine is thine, and what is thine is thine'—he is saintly.

"He who says, 'What is thine is mine, and what is mine is mine'—he is wicked."

We owe a great debt to Rabbi Judah who preserved the wonderful laws and sayings of the Rabbis. He served his people as ruler and as scholar. That is why the Rabbis said of him, "Not since Moses was there a man like Judah who combined leadership and Torah."

EXERCISES

I. True or false? (Review section 1, pages 195 to 197.)
   1. Akiva was the last great Rabbi.
   2. Judah the Prince was descended from Hillel.
   3. Rome was as cruel in the days of Judah the Prince as it had been in the days of Bar Kochba.
   4. Judah wanted all the members of his household to speak Hebrew.
   5. The week-day meal was not as tasty as the Sabbath meal because the Sabbath spirit was missing.

II. Choose the correct name or phrase. (Review section 2, pages 197 to 198.)

1. Judah's pupils came _____. (from many countries, only from the Land of Israel)
2. Judah said that he learned most from his _____. (pupils, teachers)
3. Judah advised his pupils to use a _____. (hard tongue, soft tongue)
4. Judah was the editor of the _____. (Bible, Mishnah)
5. The Mishnah contains the _____. (oral law, written law)

III. Answer each question in a complete sentence. (Review section 3, pages 198 to 199.)

1. How much of his field must a farmer set aside for the poor?
2. According to the Rabbis, what are some of the things that bring a reward in this world and in the world to come?
3. What do we recite at the *Seder* table?
4. How many eye-witnesses are required by Jewish law in cases involving the death penalty?
5. According to the Mishnah, why did God begin the world by creating one man?

IV. Fill in the missing words. (Review section 4, pages 199 to 201.)

1. "Let your friend's property be as precious to you as _____."
2. "He who pleases _____, pleases God."
3. "Be the tail among the _____, rather than the head among the foxes."
4. "Do not look at the _____ but at what is in it."
5. "Who is _____? He who is content with his portion in life."
6. "He who is quick to learn and _____ to forget—he is fortunate."
7. A pupil should not be like the _____, because everything comes in one ear and out the other.

8. "He who says, 'What is thine is _____, and what is mine is mine'—he is wicked."

V. Questions for discussion:
1. What were Judah's achievements?
2. What advice given by Judah to his pupils would be most helpful to pupils today?
3. The new state of Israel abolished capital punishment. Do you think this was the right thing to do?
4. Which of the quotations from "Ethics of the Fathers" do you like most? Why?

REVIEW QUESTIONS
for Units Three and Four (pages 109 to 203)

1. Discuss the main achievement of each of the following Rabbis: Hillel, Johanan ben Zakkai, Akiva, Judah the Prince.
2. Write a sentence telling about the importance of each of the following: Salome Alexandra, Simon ben Shetah, Hyrcanus, Herod, Queen Helena, Josephus, Bar Giora, Bar Kochba.
3. What connection does each of the following Roman rulers have with the Jewish people: Pompey, Julius Caesar, Mark Antony, Vespasian, Titus, Hadrian?
4. Mention 2 problems faced by the Jewish people during the Roman period. How did they try to solve these problems?
5. Why do we observe *Tisha B'Av?* Why do we celebrate *Lag B'Omer?*
6. Tell a favorite anecdote about one of the Jewish leaders who lived during the Roman period.
7. Identify or explain each of the following: Pharisees, Sanhedrin, *prosbul*, Shammai, Zealots, Gamaliel, Joshua ben Hananya, Betar, *Nasi*, Simon Bar Yohai, Mishnah.
8. List 5 favorite sayings from the Rabbis.

TEST
for Units Three and Four

I. What is my name? (25 points)
1. I was head of the Sanhedrin in the days of King Herod.

I introduced the *prosbul* to help people who wanted to borrow money. I taught a stranger the rule, "Do not do unto others what you do not want others to do unto you."

2. I helped to save Judaism by establishing an academy at Jabneh where the Torah could be taught. I taught the people that good deeds and prayer would take the place of Temple sacrifices.
3. The Romans freed me after the fall of Jerusalem. I was head of the Sanhedrin at Jabneh for almost 40 years.
4. I was the teacher of Akiva. I made a trip to Rome to plead for my people. I persuaded the people not to rebel when Hadrian broke his promise to rebuild the Temple.
5. I was the editor of the Mishnah. As head of the Sanhedrin I was recognized by Rome and helped secure better conditions for my people.

II. Match. (20 points)

Column A	Column B
Julius Caesar	1. Jewish general who wrote the history of the Jews
Josephus	2. Roman who destroyed Jerusalem in 70 C.E.
Titus	3. Leader of rebellion against Rome who fell at Betar
Akiva	4. Roman ruler who gave Jews many privileges
Bar Kochba	5. Rabbi who was put to death by Rome because he taught the Torah

III. *Tisha B'Av* or *Lag B'Omer?* (15 points)
   1. A plague which broke out among Akiva's students ended on _____.
   2. The two Temples and Betar fell on _____.
   3. Jews visited the Wailing Wall to mourn the loss of the Temple on _____.
   4. Bonfires are lit in Israel on _____.
   5. Students carry bows and arrows and go on outings on _____.

IV. Write out 4 proverbs found in "The Ethics of the Fathers" or sayings by the great Rabbis. (20 points)

V. About which person is each of the following stories told? (20 points)
1. He returned to its original owner a pearl found in a bag tied to a donkey. (Hyrcanus, Simon ben Shetah)
2. She was a queen of Adiabene who converted to Judaism and devoted her life to good deeds. (Queen Helena, Queen Salome Alexandra)
3. Unable to pay the fee required for entrance to the academy he listened through the skylight on the roof. (Hillel, Shammai)
4. He told the fable of the fox and the fish to prove that we must teach Torah even in time of danger. (Akiva, Joshua ben Hananya)
5. He explained to the emperor that the week-day meal was not tasty because the spice of the Sabbath spirit was missing. (Judah the Prince, Simon Bar Yohai)

UNIT FIVE

Jews in Babylon

CHAPTER XVIII

A NEW CENTER OF LEARNING

1. THE PUPILS OF JUDAH THE PRINCE

EVEN in the days of the Temple there were millions of Jews who lived in countries outside of the Land of Israel. The losses during the rebellions against Rome were so great that now the Jews outside of the Land of Israel outnumbered many, many times those who lived in the Holy Land.

Pupils who studied at the academy of Judah the Prince came from far and wide. There were many scholars especially from Babylon who helped to spread a knowledge of Torah in their native land.

One of Judah's greatest pupils was a Babylonian named Abba. Since he was very tall his friends called him Abba Arika, which means Abba the tall one.

In his youth Abba had studied in Babylon. He made such progress, however, that there was no academy in Babylon advanced enough for him.

His uncle, Rabbi Hiya, who was a close friend of Rabbi Judah the Prince, wrote to his nephew, "Come to study at the academy of Rabbi Judah. You can live with me, and I shall take care of your material needs."

As Abba left Babylon to travel to the Land of Israel he must have thought of Hillel who had made this same journey over 200 years before. Perhaps he too would become a famous scholar.

Abba soon became one of Judah's most brilliant pupils. He

was given a seat in the academy right behind his uncle, Rabbi Hiya.

One of the other pupils later reported, "When Rabbi Judah and Abba discussed the Torah it was just as if sparks of fire flew from one to the other."

Another great Babylonian pupil who studied at Judah's academy was named Samuel. Abba Arika and Samuel became close friends. When we read of their friendship we think of that of David and Jonathan.

Samuel was not only a learned Rabbi but a doctor as well. When Judah became ill he called on Samuel to treat him. Samuel remained his doctor as long as he studied in the Land of Israel.

At last Samuel decided to go back to his native land. He bade farewell to his teacher, Rabbi Judah the Prince, and to his dear friend, Abba Arika. He then returned to Nehardea the city in which he had been born. There he was appointed a judge by the head of the Jewish community.

2. ABBA ARIKA

Abba Arika remained for a while in the Land of Israel.

"He deserves to succeed Rabbi Judah as head of the academy when Judah dies," said many of the scholars.

There was a burning desire, however, in the heart of Abba Arika to spread learning in his native country. He left the Land of Israel shortly before the death of Judah, and joined his friend Samuel in Nehardea.

Abba Arika was received with great honor by Samuel and the Jews of Babylon. He was soon offered the position as head of the Nehardea academy, but he declined in favor of Samuel.

"Samuel is a native of Nehardea," thought Abba Arika, "and it is not fair for me to deprive him of this honor in his own city."

Abba Arika left Nehardea and settled in a city named Sura.

There he opened his own academy which became famous throughout the world.

Out of respect for Abba Arika the people began to call him simply Rav (the Master), just as they had called Judah the Prince by the title Rabbi.

The Jews of Babylon, in the days of Abba Arika, were very prosperous. There were about one million Jews living in cities and villages. They had a long history, their ancestors having come to Babylon 800 years before, at the time of the fall of the First Temple.

They had been well-treated by their rulers and enjoyed many privileges. They were much more fortunate, in this respect, than their brothers in Israel who had been persecuted by Greece and Rome.

Many Jews had acquired land and were successful farmers. The fields lay between two large rivers, the Tigris and the Euphrates. Large canals brought water from the rivers to irrigate the land.

Other Jews worked as merchants or as craftsmen. They too were prosperous.

The Persians appointed a descendant of King David to serve as prince of the Jews. He was known as "Head of the Exile."

The Jews had their own courts and officers. They observed their own laws and customs. As long as Jews paid their taxes the Persian kings were satisfied.

Abba Arika, however, was disappointed because the Jews of Babylon knew so little of the Torah.

"We will do what was done in Jerusalem in the days of the Temple," said Rav. "We will build schools for the children, for they are God's anointed. And we will gather the elders to discuss the written law and the oral law."

Twice a year, for a month at a time, hundreds of scholars, eager for learning, gathered in Sura to discuss Torah. During the month before Passover and the month before Rosh Ha-Shanah the visitors camped on the fields belonging to Rav or along the Euphrates River. What an inspiring sight it must have been!

The gathering was called *Kallah* which means "crown" because the pupils sat in a circle giving the appearance of a crown. The Mishnah was Rav's great textbook. At each *Kallah* another book in the Mishnah was discussed.

Rav had succeeded beyond his fondest dreams. Babylon was becoming the center of Torah.

Many of the prayers we still recite in the synagogue were composed by Rav. This was Rav's daily prayer:

> "May it be Thy will, O Lord our God,
> To grant us long life,
> A life of peace,
> A life of goodness,
> A life of blessing,
> A life of sustenance,
> A life of good health,
> A life marked by the fear of sin,
> A life free of shame and reproach,
> A life of prosperity and honor,
> A life of love of Torah and awe of Heaven,
> A life in which Thou wilt fulfill all the requests of our hearts for good!"

This prayer is now recited before each new month. It is a beautiful expression of the Jewish conception of the good life.

3. SAMUEL

Abba Arika and Samuel remained loyal friends throughout their lives.

Besides being an expert in medicine, Samuel excelled in other sciences. He loved to study the stars. "The paths of heaven are as well-known to me," he said, "as the streets of the city of Nehardea."

Samuel used his knowledge of the heavens to arrange the calendar. He calculated the appearance of the new moon, and the dates of the festivals for 60 years in advance. The heads of the academy in the Land of Israel were very grateful to Samuel when he sent them this information.

Rav, or Abba Arika, was greater than Samuel in his knowledge of religious law, but Samuel was greater in his knowledge of civil law. One question that was often asked was, "Do Jews have to obey the civil laws of the country in which they live?"

Samuel ruled, "The law of the country is binding on Jews."

This became an important principle encouraging Jews to live as good citizens in every land.

Samuel was very much interested in fair business practise. "A merchant may charge a profit of $1/6$," said Samuel. "A profit greater than this is unfair, and the buyer may ask for a return of his money."

The following story indicates how clever and patient Samuel was.

A Persian once came to Samuel and said, "Teach me the Torah and the Hebrew language."

Samuel began to teach him the alphabet.

"This is an *aleph*, and this is a *bet*."

Samuel then pointed to the *aleph*.

"*Bet*," said the Persian.

"*Aleph*," Samuel corrected.

"No, it is a *bet*," insisted the Persian.

Samuel pointed to the next letter.

"*Aleph*," said the Persian.

Realizing that the Persian just wanted to mock him, Samuel struck him on the ear.

"Ouch! My ear!" shouted the Persian.

"That's your hand, not your ear," said Samuel.

"What? Everybody knows that's an ear," replied the Persian.

"True," said Samuel, "and everybody who knows Hebrew knows that this is an *aleph* and this is a *bet*. If you want to learn you must trust your teacher."

The Persian then became a model pupil.

The people praised Samuel and quoted in his honor the verse, "The patient in spirit is better than the proud in spirit."

4. GEMARA

The academy established by Rav in Sura remained the largest in Babylon for hundreds of years. Samuel's academy in Nehardea, unfortunately, was sacked by invaders several years after Samuel's death. Many of the scholars fled to Pumbeditha. Here a great school now came into existence which kept alive the traditions of Samuel's academy.

In the Land of Israel the *Nasi* chose Tiberias on the beautiful Sea of Galilee as his home and as the seat of the academy.

Babylon soon forged ahead as the leading center of Jewish life. Roman cruelty had done its deadly work, and only a small and struggling community of Jews remained in the Land of Israel.

The oral law continued to grow. Sura and Pumbeditha in Babylon and Tiberias in the Land of Israel were the centers for the study of the oral law.

New cases were decided by the courts. New problems arose. New discussions took place in the academy.

These decisions and discussions were committed to memory by the pupils who tried to remember every word uttered by the great Rabbis.

The pupils themselves were merchants, farmers and craftsmen who would crowd into the house of study in the morning before they engaged in work, or in the evening after the day's work was done.

After 300 years, about the year 500, the discussions were

written down and collected. This collection is known as Gemara which means "completion," for, in a way, it was a completion of the Mishnah.

The language of the Gemara is Aramaic, a language resembling Hebrew. Aramaic was then spoken in Babylon and in the Land of Israel.

Together the Mishnah and Gemara are called Talmud. The Bible and the Talmud are the Jewish people's most treasured possessions.

EXERCISES

I. Complete each sentence. (Review section 1, pages 209 to 210.)

Abba Arika, Jonathan, Judah, Hiya, Samuel
1. Many Babylonians studied at the academy of _____.
2. Abba Arika stayed at the home of his uncle, _____.
3. It was just as if sparks flew when Judah discussed the Torah with _____.
4. When Judah was ill he was treated by his pupil _____.
5. Abba Arika and Samuel were loyal friends like David and _____.

II. Answer each question in a complete sentence. (Review section 2, pages 210 to 212.)

1. Why did Rav refuse to become head of the academy at Nehardea?
2. Where did Rav open an academy?
3. Why was Abba Arika called Rav?
4. How did the Jews of Babylon earn a living?
5. How did Rav encourage the study of Torah?
6. When do we recite the prayer composed by Rav?

III. Discuss briefly each of the following topics. (Review sections 3 and 4, pages 212 to 215.)

1. Samuel and the calendar
2. Samuel and the civil law
3. Samuel and the Persian pupil

4. Sura and Pumbeditha
5. Gemara

IV. Questions for discussion:
1. How did Rav and Samuel influence the lives of the Jews in Babylon?
2. Compare the Jews of Babylon and the Jews of America.
3. Samuel encouraged Jews to obey the laws of the country in which they lived. What contributions have Jews made as citizens of America?

THINGS TO DO

1. *Research*—The Jewish communities scattered throughout the world outside of Israel are called Diaspora. Bring in a report about the black Jews of Ethiopia (Falashas) who claim descent from King Solomon and the Queen of Sheba; the Beni Israel of India who came to India after the destruction of the Second Temple in 70 C.E.; or the Jews of China.

2. *Siddur*—Construct a model *Siddur*. Include in Hebrew or in English prayers such as *Adon Olam*, the *Shma*, excerpts from the 18 Blessings, a Psalm of David, the Friday night *Kiddush*, etc. Be sure to include the prayer of Abba Arika (see page 212).

WHAT'S MY OTHER NAME?

Each of the following was known by more than one name. What was the other name?

1. Abram
2. Sarai
3. Jacob
4. Simon Bar Kozeba
5. Rabbi
6. Abba Arika

CHAPTER XIX

THE TALMUD

1. IN THE ACADEMY

WE OPEN the Talmud. Here is a discussion that took place in the academy. It's almost as if we ourselves were present....
The discussion is about the Sabbath.
The head of the academy reads and explains the Mishnah.
"There are many oils that may be used to light the Sabbath lamp," he reads. "Some are of the opinion that only olive oil should be used."
"Why only olive oil?" asks one pupil.
"Because it gives a clear light. The Sabbath lamp should beautify the house."
"There is a legend," adds another Rabbi, "that before the children of Israel received the 10 commandments they were notified by Moses of the gift of the Sabbath. 'I have a special gift for Israel in my treasure house,' said God to Moses. 'It is called the Sabbath. Go tell the children of Israel about this gift.'"
The head of the academy then tells a story about Simon Bar Yohai who saw a man carrying two bunches of myrtle on Friday before sunset.
"What are the bunches of myrtle for?" asked Simon Bar Yohai.
"To beautify the house in honor of the Sabbath," replied the man.
"Would not one bunch of myrtle be enough?" asked Simon.
"There is a double command in the Bible," was the reply.

"We are told to *remember* and to *observe* the Sabbath day. We must double the honor which is due the Sabbath!"

"Behold, how Israel loves the commandments of God!" exclaimed Rabbi Simon.

"What kind of oil must be used for the Chanukah lamp?" asks another pupil at this point.

"My teacher used to use poppy-seed oil," answers the head of the academy, "although all types of oil are permitted. Poppy-seed oil burnt slowly and the light lasted longer. But later he insisted on olive oil because it gives a clearer light."

"Why do we light candles on Chanukah?" asks another pupil.

One of the Rabbis repeats the beautiful legend of the cruse of oil which lasted for eight days even though there was only enough oil for one day.

"These eight days," adds the Rabbi, "are days of good cheer when we thank God for the miracle of the victory of the Maccabees, and when we remember the miracle of the cruse of oil."

"The school of Hillel used to light one candle on the first night of Chanukah," comments another scholar. "Each night they would add an extra candle. The school of Shammai, however, would light eight candles on the first night. Each succeeding night they would light one candle less."

"What is the correct practise?" asks one of the students.

"We follow the practise of Hillel who had an excellent reason. He believed we must show that we are trying to increase our knowledge and our good deeds. That is why we increase the number of candles each night."

"In general, the law follows the practise of Hillel," says the head of the academy. "This was the decision of the Sanhedrin at Jabneh in the days of Gamaliel and Joshua ben Hananya."

"A man should always be as modest and as patient as Hillel," remarks another Rabbi. He then relates the wonderful story of how Hillel taught the stranger the golden rule.

And so the discussion goes on and on. . . . But the hour is late and we must close our Talmud.

2. AT COURT

The next day we turn to another section of the Talmud. The house of study, it seems, has been turned into a court. Three Rabbis are sitting as judges.

A merchant enters.

"Learned Rabbis," says the merchant, "this morning as I passed through the market-place I found a ring. Is it my duty to announce publicly what I have found?"

The Rabbis examine the ring.

"The Bible commands us to restore what is lost. There are many ways of identifying this ring and therefore it must be announced."

A court attendant then announces to those assembled that a ring has been found.

A Persian quickly pushes his way through the crowd.

"It is my ring," he claims. He gives many signs of identification, and the ring is returned to him.

"Blessed be the God of the Hebrews," calls out the Persian, "for He has given you good and righteous commandments."

A craftsman then enters.

"I found several Persian coins on the road," he declares.

"You need not announce this publicly," reply the Rabbis. "There is no way of identifying coins. We could not tell whether the person claiming the coins is telling the truth. You may keep the coins."

This is followed by a dispute between a farmer named Reuben and a merchant named Judah.

"Each year for the past three years Judah has bought my crop of dates," says the farmer. "My palm trees are the best in the valley of the Euphrates, and he has always sold them at a good price."

"That is true," remarks the merchant.

"What is your complaint?" asks the chief judge.

"Last autumn these were Judah's exact words," replies the farmer. "He said, 'Next year I shall buy your crop of dates again.' But now he refuses to keep his word and will not pay for the dates."

"I have a good reason," argues Judah. "I have been ill for the past few months and can no longer go from house to house selling the dates. It is not my fault."

The three Rabbis consider the case. At last the chief Rabbi renders the decision:

"It is a principle of Jewish law that you cannot sell what has not yet come into existence. There was no real sale since the dates did not yet exist when Judah made the offer to buy next year's crop. Each man, of course, is warned by the Torah to keep his word. In this case, however, Judah cannot be held responsible since he is prevented by illness from re-selling his fruit."

Those in the courtroom agree that it is a fair decision, especially since the farmer can still sell his dates and has really lost nothing.

The next case involves an argument between two neighbors named Joseph and Benjamin.

"Benjamin took lumber belonging to me and built a shed for his donkey and goat," complains Joseph.

"I found the lumber near the public road," replies Benjamin. "I did not realize it belonged to Joseph. I shall gladly pay him what the lumber was worth. He wants me, however, to destroy the shed and return the original lumber."

"It is not my concern what he did with the lumber. I only want what is mine," argues Joseph. "Return my wood."

The judges quickly render a decision.

"The Mishnah clearly states that where a beam of wood is built into a house, the value of the beam must be returned. The house need not be destroyed."

STUDYING THE TALMUD

This is the last case that morning, and the court is adjourned.

3. IN THE SYNAGOGUE

It is Sabbath afternoon. Students, merchants, farmers and workers have gathered in the academy for a lecture by the Rabbi and for the afternoon service.

The Rabbi comments on the verse, "Death and life are in the power of the tongue."

He relates the story of Rabbi Gamaliel and his servant, Tavi.

"Go to the market-place," said Gamaliel to his servant, "and buy me some meat."

"What kind of meat?" asked Tavi.

"The best," replied Gamaliel.

Tavi went to the market and bought tongue.

The next day Gamaliel again said to his servant, "Buy me some more meat."

"What kind?" asked Tavi.

"Today I want the worst kind," said Gamaliel.

Tavi went to the market and again bought tongue.

"What have you done?" asked Gamaliel in amazement. "When I asked for the best you bought tongue, and when I asked for the worst you bought tongue."

"True," replied Tavi. "That is because there is nothing better than a good tongue, and nothing worse than a bad tongue."

The Rabbi begins to explain the importance of speaking in a kindly manner to one's friends and neighbors. Seeing that the attention of some of the listeners is wandering, he decides to tell another story.

A sick king was once advised that only the milk of a lioness would cure him. One of the servants found a lioness in the forest, tamed it and then obtained its milk.

On the way home the servant dreamed that the members of his body began to argue.

"We deserve the credit," said the legs. "If not for the legs the servant could never have gone to the forest."

The hands claimed credit for taming and milking the lioness. The heart and mind claimed credit for the entire plan.

At last the tongue spoke up. "If not for me," said the tongue, "the plan would never have succeeded."

The members of the body all turned in anger to the tongue and exclaimed, "You deserve no credit at all!"

"Wait and see," replied the tongue.

The servant came before the king and said, "Here is the milk of the *kalbeta* (dog)."

"What?" shouted the king. "I send you for the milk of a lioness and you bring me dog's milk. Hang him!"

As they were bringing the servant to the gallows the members of the body began to weep.

"Will you admit that I am your ruler, if I save you?" asked the tongue.

"Gladly," they replied.

"I demand the right to see the king," said the tongue to the executioners. "I have an important message for him."

When the servant was brought before the king the tongue said, "O your Majesty, is this how you reward a faithful servant? I brought you the milk of a lioness which will cure your illness. In some languages a lioness is called *kalbeta*."

The milk was tested and found to be the milk of a lioness. The king was cured and the servant was given a rich reward.

Death and life, indeed, are in the power of the tongue!

As we turn the pages of the Talmud we hear once again the scholarly academy discussions, the wise court decisions and the inspiring synagogue lectures of the ancient Rabbis.

EXERCISES

I. Fill in the correct name or phrase. (Review section 1, pages 217 to 219.)

1. In the days of the Talmud, _____ were used to honor the Sabbath. (candles, lamps)
2. The man brought two bunches of myrtles to his home to honor the _____. (Sabbath, wedding feast)
3. The Chanukah lights remind us of the dedication of the Temple by _____. (the Maccabees, Zerubbabel)
4. Lighting one candle on the first night of Chanukah and adding an additional candle for each succeeding night was the practise of _____. (Hillel, Shammai)
5. Jewish law follows the practise of Hillel was the decision of the Sanhedrin under the leadership of _____. (Gamaliel, Judah)

II. Why? (Review section 2, pages 219 to 222.)
1. Why did the court decide that the finder of the ring had to announce what was found?
2. Why did the Persian exclaim, "Blessed be the God of the Hebrews?"
3. Why didn't the finder of the Persian coins have to announce what he found?
4. Why did the court decide that there was no sale when the merchant promised to buy next year's crop?
5. Why did the Rabbis decide that the shed need not be torn down?

III. Who said to whom? (Review section 3, pages 222 to 223.)
1. "Go to the market-place, and buy me some meat."
2. "There is nothing better than a good tongue, and nothing worse than a bad tongue."
3. "You deserve no credit at all."
4. Here is the milk of the *kalbeta* (dog)."
5. "I demand the right to see the king. I have an important message for him."

IV. Questions for discussion:
1. The Talmud is known for its wit and wisdom. Give examples from the lives of the Rabbis (chapters 11, 14, 15,

16, 17, 18), the Mishnah (chapter 17), or the Gemara (chapter 19).

2. Discuss whether each of the following Talmudic laws is fair and just:

a—The *prosbul* (p. 131)
b—Redemption of house within one year (p. 132)
c—Corner of the field (p. 198)
d—Two eye-witnesses (p. 199)
e—Rules for capital punishment (p. 199)
f—Profit of ⅙ (p. 213)
g—Returning lost objects (p. 219)
h—Selling crops not yet in existence (p. 220)
i—Returning property no longer in original form (p. 220)

THINGS TO DO

1. *Interview*—Invite a lawyer to class to discuss how American law would decide each of the matters listed in IV, 2, or in the section following this called "Research."

2. *Research*—What is Talmudic law in the following cases? Find the answers by consulting a Rabbi or teacher who has studied the Talmud. The answers can also be found in a book about the Talmud such as *Everyman's Talmud* by A. Cohen (chapter X, pages 342-352).

a—If a person dug a hole in a public road and somebody fell into it and hurt himself, must the one who was negligent pay damages?

b—If a farmer did not lock his barn, and his horse escaped into his neighbor's field causing damage to the crops, is the farmer responsible?

c—One man sees a lost ring first, but the second man picks it up first. Who is entitled to the ring if the original owner does not appear to claim it?

d—If coins are found scattered in the road they need not be announced publicly. Must the finder try to locate the loser if the coins are in a purse?

e—How long must a finder try to locate the owner of a lost object?

f—If a borrower loses what he has borrowed must he pay for the loss?

g—A farmer hires equipment to plough land in a valley, but uses it for stony land on a hill. Must he pay damages if he breaks the plough?

RHYTHM—A GAME

The players are seated in a circle. Each one is given the name of a person famous in Jewish history. The players tap their legs, clap their hands and snap the fingers of the left and right hands in rhythm.

The leader calls out his name and the name of one of the other players. The one whose name is called must respond in rhythm, by repeating his name and adding the name of another player. Those who do not respond properly in rhythm drop out of the circle.

CHAPTER XX

UNDER ARAB RULE

1. JEWS IN ARABIA

IN THE DAYS of the Talmud, Arabia was a stronghold for the Jewish people.

"There is a legend," the Arabian Jews would say, "that Joshua sent soldiers here to fight against wicked Amalek, and that the land was so beautiful in their eyes that some settled here."

Many of Solomon's sailors passed through Arabia. When the Temple fell in the days of Jeremiah, more Jews settled in Arabia. Later during the wars against Rome, Jewish refugees found their way to Arabia.

Jews remembered that Arabs were the children of Ishmael, son of Abraham. The Arabic language resembled the Hebrew language.

Jews began to prosper in Arabia. They planted palm trees, or wandered with the sheep looking for pasture. Merchants would travel as far as India, loading their goods on camels that crossed the desert.

Arabs and Jews made treaties of peace and lived as brothers. Many Arabs began to believe in one God and became Jews.

Once, for example, the king of Yemen, a warrior named Abi Karib, fought against the city of Medina. He cut down the palm trees and stopped the wells, filling them with earth.

Fearful of starvation and thirst, the city of Medina begged for peace. Now many of the inhabitants of Medina were Jews.

Among the messengers that came to Abi Karib to sue for peace were two Jewish scholars.

"Why do you cause bloodshed?" asked the Jewish messengers. "Surely God will bless you if you show mercy and spare the lives of the people of Medina."

"Who is God?" asked Abi Karib.

"God is the creator of the world. There is but one God, and all men are the children of God. It is His wish that we do justice and that we love our neighbors."

Abi Karib pleaded with the Jewish scholars to teach him more of the Torah. He accepted the Jewish religion and returned to Yemen with the two Jewish scholars.

The subjects of Abi Karib followed the example of their ruler and accepted the religion of Israel. History tells us that this happened about 500 C.E.

Alas, the Jewish kingdom of Yemen lasted only 30 years. The last Jewish king was Joseph, the son of Abi Karib.

Ethiopia and the lands of the West made war against Joseph and defeated him. Rather than fall into the hands of his enemies, Joseph mounted on horseback a cliff overlooking the Red Sea. He threw himself from his horse into the waters of the Red Sea, thus ending his life.

Although no longer rulers of Yemen, the Yemenite Jews remained true to the Jewish religion. It is possible that some of the Yemenite Jews moved into Ethiopia, and that the Falashas, or black Jews, are partly descended from them.

2. MOHAMMED AND THE JEWS

When Mohammed was born there were many independent tribes of Jews living in Arabia. They were proud of their freedom and of their religion.

Mohammed, as a boy, would meet Jewish merchants in the bazaars of Mecca. He would listen as they spoke of their belief in one God. He enjoyed hearing the delightful tales of Abraham, Isaac and Jacob.

Mohammed became a camel-driver. As he drove his camel he would think about the belief in one God and about the

Bible. He called the Jews "The People of the Book," because they studied the Torah, and lived according to its laws.

An uncle of Mohammed's wife had become a Jew. He taught Mohammed, who could not read or write, many of the laws of the Torah.

Mohammed soon began to believe that he was a prophet of God, and that he was sent to teach the Arabs the belief in one God.

In this way Judaism became the mother of another new religion. The Christian religion and the religion of Mohammed were both taken from the Jewish religion.

Mohammed's neighbors in Mecca were not friendly to his new religion. Mohammed, in fear of his life, fled to Medina. Here he found Arabs who already knew about the belief in one God which they had learned from the Jews.

Some of Mohammed's followers were warlike soldiers. They believed that the new religion must be spread by the sword.

They swept across Arabia shouting, "There is no God but Allah and Mohammed is his prophet." Within 10 years all of Arabia had been conquered by Mohammed.

At first Mohammed was very friendly to "The People of the Book." He thought that Jews would gladly accept the new religion which taught the belief in one God.

When Mohammed saw that Jews would never leave their own religion, he showed no mercy. Many were slain; others were forced into exile.

The Arabs continued their march of conquest after the death of Mohammed. They conquered one land after another. But soon they learned to treat the Jews more kindly.

The Jews of Palestine, as the Land of Israel was now called, welcomed the new rulers. Jerusalem became an Arab city, and a Mohammedan mosque was built where the Temple once stood.

In Egypt, in North Africa and in Spain, Arabs and Jews began to build a new civilization. The Arabs treated "The

People of the Book" with kindness, and Jewish learning began to flourish in Arab countries.

3. BOSTANAI

The leader of the Jewish community in Babylon, at this time, was a man named Bostanai. He was called *Resh Galuta*, which means "Head of the Exile." He came from a family of princes who were descended from King David.

There is a famous legend told about Bostanai.

After the close of the Talmud the Jews of Babylon were persecuted by the Persian rulers.

"I will destroy all the princes of Israel," said the wicked Persian king. "No more will a descendant of King David rule as leader of his people."

After the king had carried out his evil plan he dreamed a fearful dream. He dreamed that he was in a strange Persian garden which had many beautiful trees and flowers. He seized an axe and began to cut down the trees, one by one.

At last only one small tree remained. Just as the king was about to destroy this tree, an old man appeared in the garden. His appearance was like that of an angel of God.

"Why do you destroy this tree?" demanded the old man angrily.

He smote the king on his forehead. The king fell to his knees begging for mercy.

"I swear that I will guard this tree so that none will harm it," said the king.

When the king awoke he sent for a learned Rabbi to interpret his dream.

"The garden stands for the princes of Israel," explained the Rabbi. "You have destroyed all the descendants of King David. Happily, one child has not yet been destroyed. You have been warned to guard and to protect him."

The king showered riches on this child, the last descendant

of King David. The child was named Bostanai, since a garden in Persian is called "bostan." The child was taught the Torah by great scholars, and he clung to the religion of Israel with all his heart.

Bostanai was appointed *Resh Galuta* by the king, and he led his people with wisdom and with kindness.

Bostanai was 35 years old when the Arabs, sweeping away all obstacles in their path, defeated the Persian king.

Bostanai and the Jews welcomed the Arabs. The Arabs honored Bostanai recognizing him as one of the princes of the land.

Bostanai married the daughter of the former Persian king, a beautiful princess named Dara. She accepted the religion of Israel and helped Bostanai to rule the Jewish community.

Bostanai was given an escort of horsemen who accompanied him when he rode through the streets of the city. He was dressed in kingly clothes. When he visited the Arab court, the Caliph would rise to greet him. Bostanai would sit on a throne opposite the Caliph, and the other princes would rise to show him honor.

Bostanai's rise to greatness ushered in a new and happy period for the Jews of Babylon. The heads of the academies in Sura and Pumbeditha served as spiritual leaders, and the *Resh Galuta* served as the political leader.

From all parts of the world, Jews continued to turn to Babylon for guidance and instruction in Torah.

EXERCISES

I. Arrange in the order in which these events happened. (Review section 1, pages 227 to 228.)

1. Abi Karib fought against the city of Medina.
2. Solomon's sailors passed through Arabia.
3. Abi Karib, the king of Yemen, became a Jew.
4. Joseph threw himself into the waters of the Red Sea.

5. After the wars against Rome, Jewish refugees fled to Arabia.
6. Jewish scholars from the city of Medina explained the teachings of the Torah to the king of Yemen.

II. Complete each sentence. (Review section 2, pages 228 to 230.)
  1. Mohammed called the Jews "The People of the Book" because _____.
  2. Mohammed fled from Mecca because _____.
  3. Judaism is known as the mother of religions because _____.
  4. Mohammed became unfriendly to the Jews because _____.
  5. Jews of Palestine welcomed the new Arab rulers because _____.

III. Select the phrases which correctly describe Bostanai. (Review section 3, pages 230 to 231.)
  1. Descended from King David
  2. A native of Jerusalem
  3. Named after a great prophet
  4. A lover of Torah
  5. *Resh Galuta* (Head of the Exile)
  6. A friend of the Arab Caliph
  7. A great Rabbi
  8. A wise leader

IV. Questions for discussion:
  1. Judaism is known as the mother of religions. What teachings did the Christian and the Mohammedan religions borrow from Judaism?
  2. Mohammed harmed the Jews, but later, Jews were helped by the new religion. Show how this is true.
  3. "We are the people of the book" is a slogan often used during Jewish Book Month. How can we encourage young people to read more Jewish books?

THINGS TO DO

1. *Diorama*—Construct a diorama dealing with a subject mentioned in this chapter. Suggested subjects:

   a—Jews in Arabia taking care of sheep, planting palm trees or digging wells
   b—Jewish merchants and their camels
   c—At the bazaar (market-place)
   d—Jewish scholars in the tent of Abi Karib discussing the Torah
   e—In a Persian garden
   f—The *Resh Galuta* at the court of the Caliph

2. *Jewish Book Month*

   a—Prepare an assembly program including a play, songs and recitations, in honor of Jewish Book Month.
   b—Prepare a list of books for Jewish Book Month which students will enjoy reading. Include books about great Jews, stories of Jews in many lands, Jews in America, Jewish holidays etc.

Describe each book briefly in a sentence or two. Star the books that you enjoyed most. Consult the librarian. Also, write to the Jewish Book Council of America for suggestions.

NUMBER-LETTER PUZZLE

If letters of the alphabet are substituted for the numbers, the word will spell out a well-known phrase used to describe the Jewish people.

20	8	5				
16	5	15	16	12	5	
15	6					
20	8	5				
2	15	15	11			

CHAPTER XXI

SAADIA GAON—BABYLON'S GREATEST SCHOLAR

1. THE KARAITES

THE PEOPLE honored the head of the academy by calling him Gaon ("Excellency"). The Geonim, or heads of Sura and Pumbeditha, and the Prince of the Exile, ruled Babylonian Jewry for hundreds of years.

A serious dispute broke out about 100 years after the death of Bostanai. The candidate for the position of *Resh Galuta* was a descendant of Bostanai named Anan ben David. Unfortunately, Anan had often criticized the Talmud and the oral law.

"How can we elect Anan?" asked the Geonim. "He will not enforce the laws of the Talmud. We will pick his younger brother, Hananya, instead."

Anan protested against this decision. Several members of the community supported Anan.

The Caliph approved the choice of Hananya. Fearing revolt the Caliph placed Anan in prison. Later he freed Anan who promised to leave Babylon.

Anan and his followers settled in the Land of Israel.

"We no longer accept the oral law," declared Anan. "Our practises will be based on the Bible only."

The followers of Anan were called Karaites because they followed the Scriptures (*Mikra*).

The Karaites refused to celebrate Chanukah. Purim was changed into a two-day fast in memory of Queen Esther who fasted when she appeared before the king to plead for her people.

"We will not call upon doctors to treat our sick," said the Karaites, "since God heals us."

The Karaites refused to accept the calendar. Basing their calculations on the work of Judah the Prince and Samuel, the Rabbis had fixed the calendar permanently without depending any longer on witnesses to observe the new moon. Since the Karaites refused to accept this calendar they often observed Yom Kippur, Passover and the other holidays on different days of the year. All meat was forbidden except the meat of the deer and the dove. The Karaites rejected the laws concerning the separation of meat and milk.

The Sabbath which was a day of joy and happiness became a day of gloom, "We are commanded not to kindle any fires on the Sabbath," argued the Karaites.

In all Jewish homes it had been the custom to kindle the lights before the Sabbath, and to use the light after the Sabbath had begun. The Karaites, however, remained in total darkness throughout the Sabbath eve.

The Karaites helped Judaism in one respect. They encouraged the study of the Bible and of Hebrew. Vowel signs were placed beneath the Hebrew words to help the reader pronounce the text. Grammar became an important subject.

The Karaites attracted many followers in Babylon, Palestine, Egypt and Asia Minor. It was easier to read the Bible than to study the complicated laws of the Talmud.

There was great danger that the Jewish people would be split into two groups!

2. SAADIA

The greatest champion of the Rabbis against the Karaites was Saadia ben Joseph.

Saadia was born in Egypt. There he mastered the Torah as well as science.

While still a young man Saadia wrote a book against the beliefs of Anan and of the Karaites.

"Judaism is a religion of reason," argued Saadia. "The Karaites do not really understand the Bible. The oral law helps us to interpret the Bible. We need the Talmud as our guide."

The Karaites were very angry at Saadia because of his book against Anan. Shortly thereafter Saadia left Egypt. Some historians believe that he was forced to leave because of the threats of his Karaite enemies.

Saadia went to Palestine and continued his studies in the city of Tiberias. Later he traveled to Babylon where he became a teacher in the Academy of Sura.

Meanwhile a new dispute arose over the calendar. A Rabbi in Tiberias, not a Karaite, challenged the Geonim.

"The next Passover," he declared, "must be celebrated on a Sunday not on a Tuesday."

Saadia immediately wrote an answer. He proved that the Geonim were right, and that the Rabbi in Tiberias was wrong.

At first the people were confused. Who was right? But when they read Saadia's arguments they knew that the Geonim had arranged the calendar correctly.

The *Resh Galuta*, who was named David ben Zakkai, and the Geonim thanked Saadia for his great help in the dispute.

Several years later the Gaon of Sura died.

"Whom shall I appoint as Gaon?" David ben Zakkai asked one of his advisers. "I believe that Saadia deserves the honor," he added.

"I warn you not to appoint Saadia," replied the adviser. "He is a man of independent spirit who will not be afraid to challenge you if he disagrees with you. Besides, Saadia was born in Egypt, and the Gaon of Sura has always been a native of Babylon."

"Saadia has proved that he is a brilliant scholar and a wise leader," replied David ben Zakkai. "He is known to all because of his writings in answer to the Karaites. He upheld the honor of the Babylonian Geonim by proving that they had arranged the calendar correctly. We need a man like Saadia as our leader."

Thus, Saadia was appointed Gaon of Sura.

3. THE QUARREL WITH THE *Resh Galuta*

Unfortunately, David ben Zakkai soon changed his mind. He discovered that Saadia was a man of high principles who believed in strict justice.

After two years a fierce argument sprang up between Saadia and David ben Zakkai. The *Resh Galuta* was asked to make an important decision concerning a large inheritance. According to the law the papers required the signatures of the Geonim.

When the papers were brought to Saadia he saw that David ben Zakkai had made a serious error.

Unwilling to create a dispute, Saadia said to the messengers, "Bring the papers to the Gaon of Pumbeditha since he is older than I."

The Gaon of Pumbeditha quickly signed. The papers were brought once more to Saadia.

"You have the signature of the *Resh Galuta* and of the Gaon of Pumbeditha," said Saadia. "Why do you need my signature?"

Realizing that Saadia had a reason for not signing, the messengers urged him to explain what was wrong. Saadia was forced to reveal that an error had been made.

The *Resh Galuta*, in great anger, sent his son, Judah, to Saadia.

"I have been asked to inform you that the *Resh Galuta* orders you to sign," said the son.

"Tell your father," replied Saadia calmly, "that the Bible commands us to show no favoritism in justice."

The son repeated Saadia's words to his father.

"Warn Saadia not to be a fool," shouted David ben Zakkai, "or he will live to regret what he has done."

Saadia would not yield. At last the matter almost came to blows.

The *Resh Galuta* finally appointed another Rabbi as Gaon in place of Saadia. Knowing that he was right, Saadia refused to resign. He retaliated by appointing a new *Resh Galuta*.

After some time David ben Zakkai succeeded in winning over the Caliph to his side. Saadia was forced into retirement for four years.

The people admired Saadia's courage and sense of justice. They were angry with David ben Zakkai because he refused to make peace with Saadia.

One of the leading members of the community of Bagdad boldly stood up before the *Resh Galuta* and said, "How long will you allow this foolish quarrel to continue? Should you not do what is right and just? Saadia has proved that he is a true man of God and should be allowed once more to serve as Gaon."

David ben Zakkai meekly nodded.

"I am willing to make peace," he said.

There was great rejoicing when David ben Zakkai and Saadia made peace with each other. That day happened to be Purim, and David ben Zakkai celebrated the holiday at the home of the Gaon.

Saadia, great man that he was, sincerely forgave David ben Zakkai. When David died he was succeeded by his son, Judah. But the son passed away after a few months leaving a child of twelve.

Saadia took the grandson of David ben Zakkai into his own home. He provided for his education and treated the orphan kindly.

The people admired this great scholar who had shown both courage and kindness.

4. THE WRITINGS OF SAADIA

Saadia Gaon worked day and night to educate the people.

"We cannot combat the teachings of the Karaites if our people are not acquainted with the Bible," said Saadia. "I shall translate the Bible into Arabic so that all will know its true meaning."

This translation became very popular. Those who studied it saw that the Karaites did not appreciate the true spirit of the Bible. The Karaites soon began to lose their influence; today there are only a few Karaites left.

Saadia also compiled a dictionary and wrote a grammar book to help the students learn Hebrew.

Questions about Jewish law were sent to Sura from many lands. With the help of the other scholars Saadia would answer these questions. Usually messengers carrying the responses would pass through Egypt, Saadia's native country. Here copies of the letters would be made and stored away in a dry place where the letters would be preserved.

Finding that some synagogues did not observe the correct order of prayers, Saadia edited a *Siddur*. He added several poems written by great Hebrew poets. Saadia himself was a poet, and he included a few of his own poems.

Saadia was the first great Jewish philosopher of the Middle Ages. A philosopher is one who loves truth and wisdom.

"There are many Jews who do not understand the teachings of Judaism," complained Saadia.

To help them Saadia wrote *The Book of Beliefs and Opinions*.

"My soul was stirred on account of our people, the children of Israel," he wrote. "For I saw in this age of mine many believers whose belief was not pure. I saw men who were sunk in seas of doubt and there was no diver to bring them up from the depths."

In *The Book of Beliefs and Opinions* Saadia explained the belief in one God and the reasons for obeying the commandments of the Bible. He showed how people were responsible for their acts, and how God commanded them to do what is good and right.

Saadia attacked superstitious beliefs and explained that Judaism is based on reason.

Saadia taught the people to believe that the Messiah would come some day. Above all, he urged the Jews never to lose faith in the redemption of Israel. God would gather in the exiles from the four corners of the earth to the Land of Israel, and Zion would be rebuilt.

Saadia died in the year 942 C.E. Jews the world over celebrated his 1000th anniversary in 1942.

Saadia will always be remembered for his many achievements:

1. He was Babylon's greatest Gaon.
2. He helped to preserve the Talmud and the oral law by preventing the spread of Karaite teachings.
3. He helped to spread a knowledge of the Bible through his Arabic translation.
4. He helped to establish the Jewish calendar now in use.
5. He was one of the early editors of the *Siddur*.
6. He was the first great Jewish philosopher of the Middle Ages.

EXERCISES

I. The Rabbis or the Karaites? (Review section 1, pages 234 to 235.)

1. The _____ believed that Jewish law should be based on the Bible only.
2. The _____ believed in the Talmud and oral law as well as the Bible.
3. The _____ celebrated Chanukah as a joyful holiday.

4. The _____ refused to consult doctors.
5. The _____ ate no meat except the meat of the deer and dove.
6. The _____ taught that Sabbath candles should be lit before the Sabbath.

II. True or false? (Review sections 2 and 3, pages 235 to 237.)
   1. Saadia was born in Babylon.
   2. Saadia attacked the teachings of the Karaites.
   3. Saadia proved that the Geonim had arranged the calendar correctly.
   4. Saadia was appointed by Bostanai to serve as Gaon of Sura.
   5. An argument sprang up between Saadia and the *Resh Galuta* because Saadia refused to agree to an unfair decision.
   6. Saadia and David ben Zakkai finally made peace with each other.

III. Choose the correct name or phrase. (Review section 4, pages 239 to 240.)
   1. Saadia translated the Bible into _____. (Arabic, Aramaic)
   2. Because of Saadia, people continued to follow the teachings of the _____. (Karaites, Rabbis)
   3. Saadia was one of the editors of the _____. (Mishnah, *Siddur*)
   4. *The Book of Beliefs and Opinions* was written by _____. (Anan ben David, Saadia)
   5. In 1942, Jews celebrated the _____ anniversary of Saadia. (500th, 1000th)

IV. Questions for discussion:
   1. What changes did the Karaites try to introduce?
   2. Saadia's dispute with David ben Zakkai reminds us of other occasions in Jewish history when the spiritual leader rebuked the political leader. Compare Saadia's dispute with one of the following events:

a—Samuel rebukes King Saul for having failed to punish the wicked king of the Amalekites.
b—Nathan rebukes King David for taking Bathsheba from Uriah.
c—Elijah rebukes King Ahab for having taken the vineyard of Naboth.
d—Jeremiah rebukes King Zedekiah for not keeping his promise to free the Hebrew slaves.

3. Saadia was one of the editors of the *Siddur*. The Bible, the Talmud and the *Siddur* are the three most precious books we possess. Why?

THINGS TO DO

1. *Class Newspaper*—Prepare a newspaper about events ocurring during *Adar* 4697 (937 C.E.), just before David ben Zakkai and Saadia settled their quarrel. These are some of the topics that might be assigned to the members of the staff:

a. An interview with Saadia ben Joseph
b. A review of Saadia's book, *The Book of Beliefs and Opinions*
c. An editorial about peace between the Gaon and the *Resh Galuta*
d. A human interest story about the grandson of the *Resh Galuta* (the child was then 9 years old)
e. A late bulletin about peace rumors
f. A letter from Saadia to relatives in Egypt
g. A report about preparations for the Purim holiday
h. A diary of a student in the Sura academy describing a discussion in the academy or the *Kallah* which had just taken place
i. An original story about the son of a Jewish family in Bagdad who fell in love with a Karaite girl
j. An interview with a Karaite
k. Drawings: Bagdad scenes, the Purim celebration, Jews of Bagdad, in the Sura academy etc.

2. *Research*—Bring in a report about Bagdad, the city of *The Arabian Nights*.

CATEGORIES—A GAME

The leader announces a category. Each player must mention a name that belongs in this category. Suggestions for categories: a famous Rabbi; a Jewish king; a great Jewish woman; a famous Jewish leader; a Biblical character; a place famous in Jewish history; a Jewish book; a Jewish holiday; 12 tribes of Israel; a prophet; a Hebrew word; a letter of the Hebrew alphabet.

UNIT SIX

New Centers of Jewish Life

CHAPTER XXII

THE KINGDOM OF THE KHAZARS

1. IN THE LAND OF THE KHAZARS

THE STORY of the Jewish kingdom in the land of the Khazars is a strange and romantic one. It sounded so fantastic that many historians thought it was only a legend. But now we know for certain that this kingdom really existed. We know too that the Khazars were a powerful nation and that their rulers were firm believers in the Jewish religion.

The Khazars lived in that part of Russia now called the Ukraine. Their lands reached from the Black Sea to the Volga River near the Caspian Sea.

The first Jews reached the land of the Khazars about the time of Bostanai. Many fled from persecution in Europe and in Asia.

They brought with them their scrolls of the Torah.

"Let us hide these holy books in a cave," they said, "so that nobody will destroy them."

Often they would enter the cave to pray.

The Khazars at first worshiped idols until they heard about the belief in one God.

At last there arose a king named Bulan who put away the idols. One night he dreamed that the angel of the Lord appeared unto him.

"What you have done is pleasing in the eyes of God," said the angel. "Now pray to God and follow His laws."

2. BULAN ACCEPTS JUDAISM

King Bulan was still confused.

"I do not know how to worship God," he said. "Shall I worship Him according to the belief of the Christians, the Mohammedans or the Jews?"

King Bulan sent for representatives of the three religions. Each one argued that his was the true religion.

The king then turned to the Christian and asked, "I know that you believe in the truth of the Christian religion. Of the two remaining religions, which is the better?"

"The Jewish religion," was the reply, "for their Bible is truly the word of God."

Bulan sent for the Mohammedan and asked him a similar question.

"I know that you believe in the words of Mohammed. Of the two remaining religions, which is the better?"

"I would prefer Judaism," said the Mohammedan, "since the Jews have a pure belief in one God."

According to one account the king asked that the scrolls be brought from the cave. He was pleased when he heard that these scrolls contained the Jewish laws.

"I see that the Jewish religion is the true one," said Bulan. "Judaism is the mother religion from which other religions learned about the belief in one God. I will worship God according to the laws of Moses."

Bulan and the princes of the kingdom became Jews. The people, however, were given full freedom to worship as they pleased.

Synagogues were built and Rabbis were invited from Babylon and Palestine to teach the Torah.

3. KING JOSEPH

Jews continued to rule in the land of the Khazars for over 200 years. The kings had pure Hebrew names such as Benja-

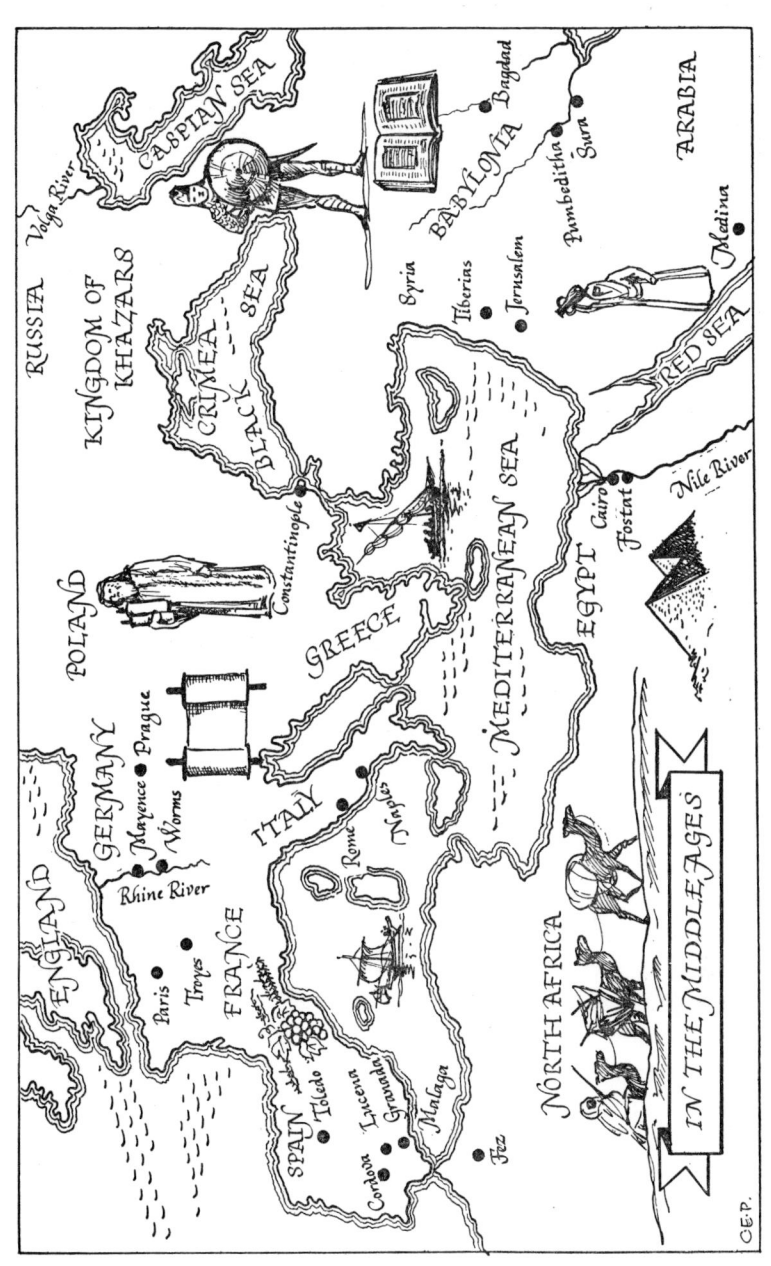

min, Aaron and Manasseh. One king was named Chanukah.

From time to time the Khazars were attacked by the Russians, or the Turks, or the emperor of Constantinople. But the Khazars fought bravely and their powerful armies turned back the invaders.

Unfortunately, the Jews of the outside world had almost no contacts with the Khazars. A few years after the death of Saadia, however, there was an exchange of letters between the Jews of Spain and Joseph, the king of the Khazars.

At that time the adviser and physician to the king of Cordova in Spain was a great Jewish leader named Hasdai Ibn Shaprut. It was his duty to receive the ambassadors who came from all parts of the world to visit the king of Cordova. Hasdai heard from merchants who lived in Asia about the Jewish kingdom of the Khazars.

Soon thereafter Hasdai received the messengers of the emperor of Constantinople.

"Is it true," asked Hasdai, "that there is a Jewish kingdom northeast of Constantinople?"

"It is true," was the reply. "It is called the land of the Khazars, and it is a fifteen day journey by sea from our land to theirs. Their king is a great general named Joseph, but there is peace between our king and King Joseph."

Hasdai's joy knew no bounds. "No longer will the nations taunt us by saying that only the Jews are a people without a country," said Hasdai.

He then wrote a long letter to King Joseph asking for more information about the Khazars.

"If I knew that this report is true," he wrote, "I would give up my high and honored position; I would take leave of my family, and I would travel over mountains and across the seas and continents until I came to your land. And when I saw your greatness my eyes would light up and I would offer a prayer giving thanks to God that He had not forgotten His people."

Hasdai sent the letter by means of Jewish ambassadors to the emperor in Constantinople, hoping that the ambassadors would be shown the way to the land of the Khazars.

After six months the emperor asked the ambassadors to return to Cordova.

He wrote to Hasdai, "It was impossible to send your messengers to the land of the Khazars since the journey is such a dangerous one."

Hasdai was disappointed but he continued his efforts. At last his letter reached the land of the Khazars by way of Russia.

King Joseph wrote a long reply to Hasdai. He told how King Bulan dreamed about the angel of God, and how he became convinced that the Jewish religion is the true one. He described the land of the Khazars, and gave the names of the Jewish kings who had ruled over the Khazars.

He invited Hasdai to settle in his country saying, "You will be unto me like a father, and I shall be your son."

King Joseph also expressed the hope that the exile would soon end.

"May the God of Israel," he wrote, "hasten the day of our redemption and gather our exiles to the Land of Israel."

4. THE END OF THE KHAZARS

What was Hasdai's response to this letter? Did he ever try to visit King Joseph? History cannot answer these questions for no further letters have come down to us.

Hasdai remained the adviser to the king of Cordova for many years. He encouraged Jewish poets and scholars to continue their work and thus helped usher in the Golden Age in Spain.

Many enemies, meanwhile, gathered against King Joseph. A few years after the letter to Hasdai was written, the Russians invaded the land of the Khazars.

King Joseph fought bravely for four years, but at last was forced to yield. The Khazars surrendered most of their possessions, and withdrew to Crimea above the Black Sea. Here the Khazars ruled for about 50 years.

The Khazars remained independent until the year 1016. In that year they were defeated by the armies of Russia and Constantinople.

The Khazar princes fled to Spain. They and their children settled in the city of Toledo where they were greatly honored by the Spanish Jews. Some of the children of the Khazar princes became great scholars.

A small community of Khazar Jews remained in Russia. They later intermarried with other Jews who came to settle in Russia.

The Khazar kingdom had lasted for about 300 years. News of this kingdom stirred the imagination of the Jewish people.

Legends were told by father to son about a Jewish kingdom beyond the mountains of darkness where lived the lost ten tribes. This kingdom, it was said, was separated from the rest of the world by the Sambatyon River. It was believed that the Sambatyon River constantly throws up large stones except on the Sabbath when it rests. Here the descendants of the lost ten tribes, giants in strength, waited for the day when all the children of Israel would be reunited.

Above all, the story of the Khazars revived the hope that the day would come when Israel would once more enjoy freedom in its own land.

EXERCISES

I. Complete each sentence. (Review sections 1 and 2, pages 247 to 248.)

Babylon, Bostanai, Bulan, Russia, Volga
1. The Khazars lived in the land of _____.
2. The Khazar kingdom reached from the Black Sea to the _____ River.
3. The first Jews reached the land of the Khazars about the time of _____.

NEW CENTERS OF JEWISH LIFE

4. _____ listened to representatives of the three religions, and then decided to accept Judaism.
5. Rabbis were invited from _____ to teach the Torah to the Khazars.

II. Answer each question in a complete sentence. (Review section 3, pages 248 to 251.)

1. Who were some of the Jewish kings of the Khazars?
2. How did Hasdai Ibn Shaprut learn about the Khazars?
3. What did Hasdai write in his letter to King Joseph?
4. How did the letter reach King Joseph?
5. What did King Joseph write in his letter to Hasdai?

III. Match. (Review section 4, pages 251 to 252.)

Column A	Column B
Hasdai Ibn Shaprut	1. A river which rests on the Sabbath
Joseph	2. A city in which the Khazar princes found refuge
Russia	3. Adviser to the king of Cordova
Toledo	4. King of the Khazars
Sambatyon	5. The country which destroyed the Khazar kingdom

IV. Questions for discussion:

1. What effect did the story of the Khazars have on the Jewish people?
2. Judaism discourages converts. Do you think that Judaism should become a missionary religion?

THINGS TO DO

1. *Story*—Write an original story about a traveler who learns that he has arrived in the land of the lost ten tribes.
2. *Letter*—Write a letter to a former teacher telling about your progress in the study of Jewish history. Mention the topics that you enjoyed most.

CROSSWORD PUZZLE

Across

1—A Jewish kingdom in Russia
5—The first and fifth letters of the capital of Israel
6—The garden in which Adam was placed
8—The Karaites rejected the oral _____ (spelled backwards)
9—The birth place of Abraham
10—Bar Kochba's first name

Down

2—Jewish adviser to the king of Cordova
3—A mountain in Jerusalem near which the Temple was built
4—The Sambatyon _____
5—Another name for Hebrews
7—Name of a tree
9—United Nations (abbreviated)

CHAPTER XXIII

THE GOLDEN AGE IN SPAIN

1. THE DECLINE OF BABYLON

AFTER Saadia's death Babylon began to lose its central position in Jewish life.

For one thing, the Arab rulers and people became harsh in their treatment of the Jews. The man who succeeded David ben Zakkai and his son as *Resh Galuta* was accused of cursing Mohammed and was put to death. There were anti-Jewish riots.

Wars and taxes placed a heavy burden on Jewish merchants and farmers.

Above all, the land was losing its fertility. Canals broke down and were not repaired. When the Mongols destroyed the irrigation system, several centuries later, Babylon (now Iraq) became a desert.

Unable to support its scholars the academy of Sura, in despair, sent four Rabbis to the West to plead for help. The leader of the group was Rabbi Moses who sailed with his wife and a young son named Enoch.

The Rabbis collected funds and then set sail from Italy to return to Babylon. It was their hope to reach Sura in time for the *Kallah*, the Torah gathering in which all the scholars of Babylon took part.

The Arabic kingdom of Cordova was then at war with several Christian countries. The king of Cordova sent the admiral of the fleet to sea with orders to capture all strange ships.

The ship in which the four Rabbis sailed was captured by

the Arabic admiral not far from Greece. In the struggle the wife of Rabbi Moses lost her life.

The admiral brought each of the Rabbis to another port and demanded ransom of the Jewish communities. One Rabbi was ransomed by the Jews of Egypt, another by the Jews of Tunis in North Africa and a third by the Jews of France.

Rabbi Moses and his young son were brought to Cordova. Here his learning was soon recognized and he set up an academy for the study of Talmud. After his death his son, Enoch ben Moses, served as head of the academy.

A remarkable thing happened. Each of the Rabbis, like Rabbi Moses, set up a school for the study of Talmud. Thousands of students born in Europe or Africa flocked to these new schools.

It was just as if the torch of learning, held high for 700 years by the Jews of Babylon, was now carried aloft by the Jews of the West.

Unfortunately, less and less money reached Babylon. The academy of Sura closed its doors, leaving only the academy of Pumbeditha.

Meanwhile, for the Jews of the West, especially Spain, a new era of greatness had begun.

2. THE JEWS OF SPAIN

The first Jews probably reached Spain in the days of King Solomon whose ships sailed the seven seas. Spain was called Sefarad in Hebrew. That is why the descendants of Spanish Jews are known as Sefardim.

Many Jewish prisoners were sent to Spain by the Romans. Several cities, like Granada, were built up by the Jewish setlers. Granada, in fact, was originally called "Jews' Town."

The Jews in Spain increased in number. Their lot was made miserable, however, by religious persecution.

Spain fell before the conquering Arabs in 711. Jews were

treated kindly by their new rulers. Learning was encouraged. Some Jews were appointed to public office. Others became doctors, astronomers, poets, teachers and learned Rabbis.

The first great Jewish leader in Spain was Hasdai Ibn Shaprut. At first Hasdai served as court physician. He discovered a cure which made him famous among the Arabs.

The king of Cardova soon began to rely on Hasdai's advice in matters of state. Hasdai would receive ambassadors from all countries of the world. He also advised the king on financial matters.

Hasdai knew many languages. When the emperor of Constantinople sent an important medical book as a gift to the king of Cordova, Hasdai was asked to translate the book from Latin into Arabic.

Hasdai never forgot his people.

He would ask each ambassador, "How are the children of Israel treated in your country?"

When he discovered that the emperor of Constantinople treated Jews harshly, Hasdai asked for better treatment of the Jewish people. We have already seen how Hasdai spared no effort to gain more information about the Khazars.

Hasdai was a great admirer of Saadia Gaon. He invited a pupil of Saadia, a fine Hebrew poet named Dunash, to come to Cordova. He sent generous sums of money to Sura and was given an honorary title, "Head of the *Kallah*."

After Saadia's death, Hasdai asked Saadia's son to send him a biography of his father.

Hasdai invited another poet to serve as his secretary. The letter to King Joseph of the Khazars was written partly in Hebrew poetry by this poet.

Hasdai was an ardent supporter of Rabbi Moses, the founder of the academy in Cordova. Hasdai introduced Rabbi Moses to the king who showered honors upon him.

When the academy of Sura closed its doors, Hasdai bought

many of the copies of the Talmud. Each copy was written by hand. These copies were given to the students of Rabbi Moses in the academy of Cordova.

Hasdai's praises were sung by the poets. It was he, indeed, who ushered in the Golden Age in Spain.

3. SAMUEL *Ha-Nagid* (THE PRINCE)

Samuel ben Joseph was born in Cordova a few years after the death of Hasdai. He studied at the famous academy of Rabbi Enoch ben Moses.

When Samuel was 20 years old civil war broke out among the Arabs. Samuel fled to Malaga, a city in the Spanish kingdom of Granada. Here he opened a small spice-shop.

Not far from his spice-shop stood the beautiful castle of the vizier, or prime minister. One of the servants of the vizier, who bought spices in Samuel's shop, noticed how beautiful his handwriting was.

"Will you write a letter in Arabic for me?" asked the servant.

"Gladly," replied Samuel.

The letters written by Samuel for the servant came to the attention of the vizier. Samuel soon became the vizier's secretary and adviser. The vizier followed Samuel's advice at all times, and the kingdom prospered. King Habbus rewarded his vizier with riches and honor.

When the vizier was about to die, King Habbus wept.

"Who will guide our kingdom in time of trouble?" asked the king in tears.

"Fear not," replied the vizier, "It was not I who gave you good counsel but Samuel ben Joseph. Let him be your adviser and all will be well."

King Habbus appointed Samuel to be vizier. No Jew in Spain had ever received such honor before. Even Hasdai, great though he was, was never given an official title.

Under Samuel's rule Granada flourished. Samuel even led the armies of Granada into battle and was victorious.

Samuel also served as leader of the Jewish community. He was called Samuel *Ha-Nagid* (The Prince) and was loved by all because of his wisdom and kindness.

4. IN THE DAYS OF SAMUEL *Ha-Nagid*

There were many Arabs who envied Samuel. Near the palace of King Habbus lived an Arab merchant who would curse Samuel.

One day the king heard the Arab's vile insults and curses. The king turned in anger to Samuel.

"That man deserves to die. Punish him by cutting out his evil tongue!" ordered the king.

The merchant was brought to Samuel. The Jewish vizier spoke kindly to him and learned that he had suffered greatly in life.

Instead of punishing him, Samuel gave the merchant a gift and allowed him to depart in peace.

A few days later King Habbus and Samuel rode in the king's carriage through the streets of Granada.

The merchant appeared in the doorway of his store and shouted, "May Allah bless King Habbus and Samuel, his vizier!"

Recognizing the merchant, King Habbus turned to Samuel and asked, "Did I not order that his evil tongue be cut out? Why did you not carry out my command?"

Samuel explained what had happened and then added, "Your Majesty, I have carried out your command. I have removed his evil tongue and have given him a kind tongue instead."

Samuel's great ambition was to make Spain a center of Jewish learning. He himself was an outstanding scholar, and he served as head of the academy. He wrote several books to explain the Talmud to his students.

Samuel *Ha-Nagid* was also a fine Hebrew poet. Even on the battlefield, he would retire to his tent at night to write poetry. In pure Hebrew verses he would pour forth his feelings of gratitude for victory or for escape from danger.

From all parts of Spain, Hebrew poets gathered at the court of Samuel *Ha-Nagid*. Often he would support them until they found a means of livelihood.

Greatest of these poets was Solomon Ibn Gabirol. After years of wandering and hardship Solomon found a haven of peace at the court of Samuel *Ha-Nagid*. Here he wrote many of his golden Hebrew verses which found their way to the heart of his people.

Samuel *Ha-Nagid's* Hebrew library was the finest in Spain. He employed scribes to copy the Bible and Talmud for the students of the academy.

He was also famous for his charity. He sent money to the academy of Pumbeditha in Babylon, and helped support synagogues in the Holy Land.

When Samuel *Ha-Nagid* died in 1063 his loss was mourned by Jews throughout the world. They knew that a prince had fallen in Israel.

EXERCISES

I. Choose the correct name or phrase. (Review section 1, pages 255 to 256.)

1. Babylon began to lose its importance in Jewish life after the death of _____. (Bostanai, Saadia)
2. Babylon became like a desert because of _____. (destruction of the canals, drought)
3. The four Rabbis were captured by a ship from _____. (Egypt, Spain)
4. Because of lack of support the academy of _____ closed its doors. (Pumbeditha, Sura)
5. Rabbi Moses and his son Enoch were ransomed by the Jews of _____. (Cordova, France)

II. True or false? (Review section 2, pages 256 to 258.)
   1. Descendants of Spanish Jews are called Sefardim.
   2. Jews were treated well in Spain before the Arabs arrived.
   3. Hasdai Ibn Shaprut was a physician and statesman.
   4. Hasdai encouraged Hebrew poetry and learning.
   5. Hasdai was Gaon in Sura.
   6. Hasdai ushered in the Golden Age in Spain.

III. Who said to whom? (Review sections 3 and 4, pages 258 to 260.)
   1. "Will you write a letter in Arabic for me?"
   2. "Who will guide our kingdom in time of trouble?"
   3. "It was not I who gave you good counsel but Samuel ben Joseph"
   4. "That man deserves to die. Punish him by cutting out his evil tongue!"
   5. "I have removed his evil tongue and have given him a kind tongue instead."

IV. Questions for discussion:
   1. Why did Babylon decline in importance as a center of Jewish life?
   2. How did Hasdai Ibn Shaprut and Samuel *Ha-Nagid* promote Jewish learning?
   3. Why is this called a "Golden Age"?

THINGS TO DO

1. *Time-line*—A time-line will help the students understand the periods of time during which the great events of Jewish history took place. Mark off six equal distances on the walls of the classroom—one for each 500 years. In each section put up dates, names and pictures. Some of the important events for the first period, 2000 B.C.E.—1500 B.C.E., are: the birth of Abraham in Ur, the migration to Canaan, the renewal of the covenant by Isaac and Jacob, Joseph's rule as prime minister of Egypt, the migration to Egypt, the enslavement of the children of Israel.

The second period, 1500 B.C.E.—1000 B.C.E., includes the

exodus from Egypt, the granting of the 10 commandments, the conquest of Canaan under Joshua, the period of the Judges, the appointment of the first king by Samuel, the rule of King Saul.

In the third period, 1000 B.C.E.—500 B.C.E., we learn of the following events: the reign of King David, the building of the Temple by Solomon, the revolt of the 10 tribes of Israel, the prophecy of Elijah, the fall of the 10 tribes in the days of Isaiah, the destruction of the First Temple in 586 B.C.E., Jeremiah's prophecy of hope, the return from exile and the building of the Second Temple.

In the fourth period, 500 B.C.E.—1 C.E., some of the notable events are: the strengthening of Jerusalem by Nehemiah, the editing of the Bible by Ezra, the defeat of Haman by Esther and Mordecai (Purim), the conquest of Jerusalem by Alexander, the translation of the Bible into Greek, the winning of religious freedom by Judah the Maccabee in 165 B.C.E. (Chanukah), the winning of political independence by Jonathan and Simon, the conquest of Judea by Pompey, the teaching of the golden rule by Hillel.

The following events should be noted for the fifth period, 1C.E.—500 C.E.: the fall of the Second Temple, the establishment of the academy in Jabneh by Johanan ben Zakkai, the revolt of Akiva and Bar Kochba (135), the editing of the Mishnah by Judah the Prince, the formation of the Babylonian academies by Rav and Samuel, the completion of the Talmud.

The sixth period, 500-1000, includes: the establishment of the Jewish kingdom of Yemen, the Arab conquest, the appointment of Bostanai as *Resh Galuta*, the leadership of the Geonim of Sura and Pumbeditha, the rise of the Karaites, the teachings of Saadia Gaon, the reign of the Khazar kings, the rule of Hasdai Ibn Shaprut, the birth of Samuel *Ha-Nagid*.

Consult the table, "Important Dates in Jewish History" on pages 298 and 299.

2. *Keren Ami* ("My People's Fund")—Organize a class or school *Keren Ami*. Arrange for the collection of funds. Decide to which charities funds are to be sent. Discuss the work of each charitable organization.

NAMESAKES

In Jewish history we often read of two or three famous people with the same name. In this chapter, for example, we read of a Rabbi Moses who established the academy in Cordova; he had the same name, of course, as the great leader who led the children of Israel out of Egypt.

Can you identify the following famous leaders and their namesakes? 1. Jonathan 2. Joseph 3. Joshua 4. Judah 5. Rachel 6. Samuel 7. Simon

CHAPTER XXIV

RASHI—PRINCE OF COMMENTATORS

1. THE JEWS OF EUROPE

THE FIRST JEWS came to France and Germany in the days of the Romans. There were Jewish soldiers in the armies of Rome. Jewish merchants engaged in trade. Later they were joined by Jewish craftsmen. Jewish refugees settled here after the rebellions against Rome.

The barbarians who then lived in these countries were later driven out by the Goths and other tribes. That is why it is sometimes said, "The Jews came to France and Germany before the French and Germans."

The centuries following the fall of Rome in 476 are often called "The Dark Ages." Jews, however, kept the torch of learning burning brightly. Jewish children were taught to read and write at a time when the people around them were illiterate.

Jews studied the Bible and Talmud. Some learned Jews served as physicians.

The wise Charlemagne treated the Jews kindly. In this respect he was like Cyrus, Alexander and Julius Caesar—all of whom were friends of the Jews. Many Jewish merchants were given charters promising them protection and other privileges.

Charlemagne sent a Jew named Isaac as one of the ambassadors to the Caliph of Bagdad. Unfortunately, the other ambassadors died during the journey. Isaac, however, returned safely bringing with him an elephant as a gift from the Caliph to Charlemagne. Trade between East and West revived.

In the year 800 Charlemagne was crowned Emperor of the Holy Roman Empire. His empire included France and a large portion of what is now Germany, Italy, Holland and Belgium.

Throughout his empire Jews prospered. There were many synagogues in Italy, France and in the communities along the Rhine River. Charlemagne prevented any religious persecution. He refused to enforce the anti-Jewish laws that had been passed by rulers before him.

Charlemagne encouraged Jewish scholars to come to his empire. We read of one Rabbi who left Italy to teach in Mayence along the Rhine. Another Rabbi came from Bagdad to France. It is said that Charlemagne himself requested the Caliph to allow the Rabbi to come to France.

By the time that Samuel *Ha-Nagid* ruled in Granada there were many flourishing schools of Torah in France and Germany.

2. RASHI

France's greatest scholar was Solomon ben Isaac. He is best known as Rashi. This name was formed from the initial letters of his Hebrew name, *R*abbi *Sh*elomo ben *I*saac.

Solomon was born in Troyes, France in 1040. (In Spain the Jews were then enjoying the Golden Age. Samuel *Ha-Nagid* was at the height of his power.)

Many legends are told about the birth of the beloved Rashi. Isaac, his father, was a jewel merchant. Once two men lured Isaac into a boat and tried to force him to surrender a precious jewel. Rather than allow the jewel to fall into their hands, Isaac cast it into the water.

At that moment a voice was heard saying, "Be consoled about your loss. A son will be born to you whose learning will shine like a jewel, and who will enlighten the eyes of all Israel."

The story, of course, is only a legend. It is true, however, that Rashi's learning did shine like a jewel which seemed to gain in brilliance as the years went by.

RASHI'S SYNAGOGUE

Troyes was not a large city. But many visitors would come to Troyes for its winter and summer fairs. From these visitors Solomon ben Isaac learned about the larger communities where there were academies of Torah.

Solomon's father was his first teacher. Later, as a young man, Solomon went to study at the academy in Worms. He continued his studies in Mayence until he was 25 years old.

The young man mastered the study of Bible and Talmud. There was little opportunity for Rashi to study science, for the Arab countries had made much more progress in science than the Christian countries of Europe. In Jewish studies, however, there was no equal to Rashi.

3. TEACHER OF ISRAEL

Rashi returned to Troyes where he served as Rabbi. He accepted no salary for his services.

Troyes was known for its excellent grapes, and Rashi earned a living from his vineyards. Except during the vintage season Rashi devoted most of his time to teaching and study.

Many students gathered in Troyes to learn from this great teacher. Never had the Bible and Talmud been taught in such a clear and interesting manner.

Rashi wrote down his comments on the Bible and Talmud in book form. These commentaries were widely copied, and Rashi's fame spread far and wide.

Rashi's commentaries became the guide to the Bible and Talmud wherever these subjects were studied.

Students would speak of the great teacher in words of the highest praise.

"The Talmud was like a closed book to me," one student would say, "until Rashi's explanations cleared away the difficulties."

"Rashi can explain in one word what it takes others pages to explain," remarked a second student.

"He always seems to find the right word," added a third

scholar. "With Rashi a drop of ink is worth a piece of gold."

"When I read Rashi," observed another student, "it is as if I am being helped by a kind and understanding teacher who stands at my side. The sweetness of his gentle words speaks to the heart."

The legends which grew up around Rashi's commentary are an indication of the love which the people felt for Rashi's work.

It is said that Rashi traveled the world over seeking material for his commentaries. In the East, says the legend, Rashi met a priest.

The two engaged in a friendly discussion. Suddenly the priest fell ill. Rashi cared for him like a brother. He prepared a special remedy about which he had learned from a great Jewish doctor.

Soon the priest recovered.

"I owe my life to you," said the priest. "Even though we are not of the same religion, you cared for me unselfishly."

"Charity unites all men," replied Rashi. "If ever you find a Jew in trouble, I am sure you will come to his aid."

Rashi continued his travels consulting the great Rabbis wherever he went about difficult passages in the Bible or Talmud.

When Rashi came to Prague he found the city in a turmoil. The Jews were threatened with exile. There was danger of a riot.

Rashi went to the Duke to plead for the safety of the Jews.

"You must act quickly or lives will be lost," pleaded Rashi.

The Duke called in the Bishop to ask for advice.

As soon as Rashi saw the Bishop he recognized the priest whose life he had once saved.

The Bishop too recognized Rashi.

"This man once saved my life," said the Bishop. "He taught me that charity unites all men. The Jews must be treated kindly. They should be allowed to live here in peace."

The Duke accepted the Bishop's advice. His soldiers protected the Jews and they continued to live in Prague in peace. Rashi was hailed as their savior.

There is always a kernel of truth in every legend. Because Rashi was noble in character, legends grew up which ascribed noble deeds to him.

4. THE BIBLE COMMENTARY

Let us turn the pages of Rashi's commentary on Genesis, the first book of the Bible. We find not only clear explanations of difficulties, but many fascinating quotations from the legends of the Talmud.

Here is a quaint legend about the creation of the sun and moon.

At first the sun and the moon were equal in size. The moon, however, was eager to become larger than the sun.

Appearing before God the moon said, "Almighty God, you have made the sun and the moon equal in size. Would it not be wiser to make one larger than the other? Can two kings share one crown?"

"Very well," replied God, "let the sun become the greater light and the moon the lesser light."

The moon was greatly disappointed.

Seeing the moon's disappointment God said, "Since the moon is smaller than the sun, I shall create the stars to escort the moon at night."

We turn the page and read that God created man of the dust of the earth.

"The dust was taken from every country of the world," says Rashi. "Thus man feels at home in every land." Rashi understood that Adam was father of all men. All countries share in the creation of mankind.

We turn to the story of the flood.

"God could have saved Noah in many ways," quotes Rashi. "But He asked Noah to build an ark to attract the attention of the people around him. When they heard about the flood that would come down upon the earth they might repent. God could then forgive the people if they no longer sinned. Alas, instead of repenting the people scoffed at Noah."

Rashi notes that at first the Bible says that God brought down "rain"; later the Bible says that there was a "flood." Why are two different words used?

"At the beginning," says Rashi, "God brought down light rain. This was the last chance for repentance. If the people repented, the rain would merely have served to water the earth. But when God saw that the people refused to repent the rain became a flood."

We read Rashi's charming comments on Abraham, Isaac and Jacob. At last we come to the story of Joseph.

What was the sin of the butler and baker who were placed in prison by Pharaoh?

"A fly was found in the wine and a pebble in the bread," answers Rashi. "Later it was discovered that the butler was not at fault, but that the baker had been negligent."

Meanwhile Rashi explains that the basket which the baker saw in his dream was made of open wicker-work. "In the section of France in which I live," adds Rashi, "we see many such baskets. Those who sell cookies and sweets usually place their wares in such baskets."

Rashi then translates the word into Old French. (A list of the French words used by Rashi has been collected in order to learn exactly how Charlemagne spoke. Rashi is the best source for Old French!)

In commenting on Pharaoh's dream Rashi describes how the Nile River overflows its banks filling the small canals with water used for irrigation.

Pharaoh rejected the interpretation of his dream given by the Egyptian magicians. What was their interpretation? The Bible does not tell us. Rashi, however, finds an explanation in the writings of the Rabbis and presents it to the reader.

"The seven fat cows," said the magicians, "stand for seven fat daughters. The seven lean cows stand for death. Pharaoh will become the father of seven daughters all of whom will die."

Is it any wonder that Pharaoh preferred Joseph's interpretation?

We are told by the Bible that when Jacob and his family went down to Goshen in Egypt they were not sure of the exact road. Judah was sent ahead to instruct them as to the correct way.

Rashi explains the verse. Then he adds: "The Rabbis have another explanation. Judah was sent ahead to set up a school which would instruct the children of Israel as to the correct way."

Thus we see that Rashi lost no opportunity to stress the importance of the Jewish school!

We are told that those who came down to Egypt numbered seventy *soul*. Why doesn't the Bible use the plural, "souls"?

Rashi explains that "soul" may be singular or plural. But then he adds, "Idol-worshipers who worship many gods are indeed like many different souls. The children of Israel, however, were all united in the worship of One God, and thus the Bible speaks of them as one soul."

Rashi's wit, wisdom and learning have won for him the title, "Prince of Commentators."

5. RASHI'S LAST DAYS

Rashi had three daughters but no sons. His daughters married learned scholars. Rashi's grandchildren were famous Rabbis, second only to Rashi in greatness. One of Rashi's grandchildren became known as Rabbenu Tam which means "Our Rabbi, the Perfect One."

Another of Rashi's grandchildren, Samuel ben Meir, helped Rashi with his commentary.

"I would explain the verse differently," Samuel once said to Rashi.

"Perhaps you are right," replied Rashi modestly. "Each day new explanations are suggested that I would like to include in my commentary. If I had the leisure I would rewrite my commentary."

Rashi was as modest as Hillel. Often he would write in his commentary or in his letters, "I do not know the answer." Nor was he ashamed to admit that he had made a mistake.

Once when Rashi became ill his grandson finished the commentary which Rashi had begun. Try as he might Samuel could not learn the secret of putting a thought into one or two words.

Rashi lifted his grandson's manuscript as if weighing the paper.

"If you commented on the entire Talmud in such a lengthy manner," said Rashi with a smile, "I am afraid your commentary would be as heavy as a chariot."

Jews in Europe had lived in peace for hundreds of years. Rashi's last days, however, were saddened by the Crusades which began in 1096.

Sometimes we read that the Crusaders were noble men whose one purpose was to win the Holy Land from the Arabs. Alas, history shows us that many of the Crusaders were murderers and robbers who destroyed without mercy.

Many Jews were victims of the fiendish Crusaders.

"Death to all Jews!" shouted the Crusaders.

They fell upon the peaceful Jewish communities lying along the Rhine River. The waters ran red with the blood of the Jewish slain.

Some were given the choice between conversion and death. The Jews disdained the offer. Bravely they went to their death with the *Shma Yisrael* on their lips.

Fortunately, Rashi's city was spared. But Worms and

Mayence, the cities in which he had studied, were almost completely wiped out.

According to a legend Duke Godfrey, the famous Crusader, sought Rashi's advice before he set out on his journey.

"Will I succeeed in my mission?" the Duke asked the wise Rabbi.

"You will capture Jerusalem," replied Rashi. "But after reigning for a few days you will be put to flight by the Arabs. When you return to this city only three horses will be left to you."

"Woe unto you if your prediction is wrong!" said Godfrey in anger. "If I return with four horses instead of three, the Jews of France will be put to death!"

After many years Godfrey returned from the Holy Land accompanied by only three riders. But still there was one more horse than Rashi had predicted. Vengeance burned in the eyes of the Duke.

Just as Duke Godfrey was about to enter the city of Troyes, a loose stone fell from the gate upon one of the cavaliers, killing horse and rider.

Only three horses were left. Rashi's prediction had come true.

Thus ends the legend.

In reality Godfrey never returned to France. He died in Jerusalem in 1100.

Rashi passed away in Troyes five years later, in 1105. His commentaries have won for him a lasting place in the hearts of the Jewish people.

EXERCISES

I. Answer each question in a complete sentence. (Review section 1, pages 264 to 265.)

1. When did the first Jews arrive in France and Germany?

2. What was the attitude of Jews to education during the Dark Ages?
3. Mention the names of some great rulers who were friendly to the Jews.
4. Tell about Isaac's journey to Bagdad.
5. How did Charlemagne help the Jews?

II. Match. (Review sections 2 and 3, pages 265 to 269.)

Column A	Column B
Rashi	Father of Rashi
Isaac	Rabbi Shelomo ben Isaac
Troyes	Cities where Rashi studied Torah
Worms and Mayence	Learned from Rashi that charity unites all men
Bishop of Prague	Birthplace of Rashi

III. What is Rashi's answer to each of the following questions concerning the book of Genesis? (Review section 4, pages 269 to 271.)

1. Why is the moon smaller than the sun?
2. Where was the dust with which Adam was created taken from?
3. Why does the Bible use the word "rain" at first, but later use the word "flood"?
4. Why were the butler and baker placed in prison?
5. How did the magicians interpret Pharaoh's dream?
6. Why was Judah sent to Goshen ahead of Jacob and the rest of the family?
7. Why does the Bible say that those who went down to Egypt numbered 70 *soul*?

IV. Rashi or Godfrey? (Review section 5, pages 271 to 273.)

1. _____ modestly admitted there were many questions he could not answer.
2. _____ set out for the Holy Land to capture Jerusalem.
3. The Crusaders almost completely wiped out Worms and Mayence the cities in which _____ had studied.

4. _____ died in Jerusalem.
5. _____ died in Troyes, France.

V. Questions for discussion:
1. Compare Rashi and Samuel *Ha-Nagid*.
2. Why did Rashi's commentaries become so popular?
3. What do the legends teach us about Rashi's character?

THINGS TO DO

1. *Essay Contest*—Let the school sponsor a contest on "What Torah Means to Me." The winner might receive a book as a prize. The winning essay should be read at an assembly.
2. *Chumash and Rashi*—Each week a different portion of the *Chumash*, or 5 Books of Moses, is read in the synagogue.
Prepare a brief explanation, based on Rashi's commentary, of some of the verses in the weekly portion of the Bible. Consult the Rabbi or one of the teachers in preparing the talk. The talk might be delivered at the Sabbath service of the Junior Congregation.

WHAT WAS MY BIRTHPLACE?

We have studied about many lands which were centers of Jewish life. In which country was each of the following leaders born?
1. Nehemiah
2. Judah the Maccabee
3. Hillel
4. Akiva
5. Judah the Prince
6. Rav
7. Saadia
8. King Joseph
9. Samuel *Ha-Nagid*
10. Rashi

CHAPTER XXV

JUDAH HALEVI–SWEET SINGER OF ZION

1. A GREAT POET

RASHI was the prince of commentators. Judah Halevi was the prince of poets.

Judah Halevi was born in 1085 when Rashi was in the prime of his life. He was born in Toledo, Spain. Toledo was captured from the Arabs by the Christian king of Castile in the very year that Judah Halevi was born. Jews were treated kindly.

Many Jews served as advisers to the king of Castile. Toledo soon became the largest Jewish city of Spain.

Judah was an only son. He was sent by his father to Lucena, a city near Granada, where he received his Jewish education. He studied not only Bible and Talmud, but science and medicine.

Judah became a lover of Hebrew poetry. He was inspired by the poems of Samuel *Ha-Nagid*, Solomon Ibn Gabirol and the other great Hebrew poets of Spain.

Soon he too began to write poetry. He wrote songs of youth, songs of friendship, songs of springtime and songs of love.

Judah Halevi returned to Toledo where he practised medicine. Still he found time to devote many hours to the writing of poetry.

But now his poems became more serious in tone.

He sang of the joy of the Sabbath. He describes how he

toils throughout the days of the week, while he yearns for the peace of the Sabbath. He rejoices as the Sabbath approaches:

"The morrow shall my freedom bring,
At dawn a slave, at eve a king."

He sang of his love for his people. Israel will be redeemed. Israel is as eternal as the stars of heaven.

"Let them not cry despairing, nay, nor say
Hope faileth and our strength is near to die.
Let them believe that they shall be alway,
Nor cease until there be no night nor day."*

He sang of his soul's yearning for God. He finds God everywhere:

"O Lord, where shall I find Thee?
All-hidden and exalted is Thy place;
And where shall I not find Thee?
Full of Thy glory is the infinite space."*

2. *The Book of the Khazari*

Judah Halevi, like Saadia Gaon, wrote a book to explain the teachings of Judaism. The book pretends to be a conversation between the king of the Khazars and a Rabbi, and is therefore called *The Book of the Khazari*.

According to the way Judah Halevi tells the story, the king was troubled because of his dreams.

Each night an angel appeared to the king and said, "Your intentions are satisfactory, but not your deeds."

The king sent for representatives of the various religions, but was not pleased with their explanations. At last he invited a Rabbi to appear before him.

"What is your belief?" asked the Khazari.

"We believe in the God of Abraham, Isaac and Jacob," re-

---

* Translated by Nina Davis.

plied the Rabbi. "It is He who sent Moses to lead the children of Israel out of slavery in Egypt, and who gave us the Torah."

The Khazari was surprised to hear the words of the Rabbi.

"Why do you say that you believe in the God of Abraham, Isaac and Jacob?" asked the king. "Is it not enough to say you believe in one God who created the world?"

"It is true," answered the Rabbi, "that our religion taught the peoples of the world the belief in one God. But that is not enough. Because of our history we have learned what laws to follow and what customs to practise. We accept the traditions of Abraham, Isaac, Jacob, Moses and the prophets. These traditions are found in the Torah which we must follow."

"Is Judaism a religion of beliefs or of deeds?" asked the Khazari.

"Both," replied the Rabbi. "We believe in God, but our tradition teaches us what good deeds to practise."

"You were the last person I invited to appear before me," said the Khazari, "because I see that the Jewish nation is weak and powerless. Why do the other nations have power and wealth? Is that not a sign that theirs is the true religion?"

"God does not judge righteousness by wealth or power," replied the Rabbi. "Israel among the nations is like the heart among the organs of the body. The heart is most sensitive and feels pain when any part of the body suffers. The heart too is purest and rejects whatever is impure. Israel suffers, but from Israel the world learns the pure teachings of religion."

"I see now," said the king, "that I must accept the religion of Judaism. In this way I shall know what deeds to perform in life. This is what the angel meant when he said my deeds as well as my intentions must be satisfactory."

The king then confided in one of his trusted generals. Together the king and the general journeyed to the cave where the Jews had placed the scrolls of the law. Here they were received into Judaism by those who gathered to pray each Sabbath.

Returning to his court the king persuaded his officers and subjects to follow his example. They set up a synagogue in the shape of the tabernacle built by Moses in the desert.

The king then invited the Rabbi to be his adviser. The rest of *The Book of the Khazari* tells about their conversations.

The Rabbi explained to the king the need for prayer, the purpose of the Sabbath, of the Day of Atonement and of other holidays. He discussed the beauty of the Hebrew language and the longing of the Jew for the Land of Israel.

The Rabbi and the Khazari conversed about the pure belief in one God and about man's responsibility to choose between good and evil. The Rabbi also showed how the oral law is needed for the proper understanding of the written law.

At last the Rabbi said, "Now that I have accomplished my mission, with your permission, O your Majesty, I hope to journey to Jerusalem."

"Please do not leave the Land of the Khazars," replied the king. "God is everywhere. Surely you can worship Him here as well as in Jerusalem."

"All my life I have prayed for the day when I could kiss the soil of Jerusalem," replied the Rabbi. "Now the time has come."

"You endanger your life," said the king. "You must cross seas and desert. You will meet unfriendly nations."

"Love knows not the meaning of danger," said the Rabbi with a smile. "When the Jews have shown that their love for Jerusalem is so great that nothing can stand in the way of their return, then indeed will Zion be rebuilt."

"Go in peace," said the King. "I pray that you will reach the Holy Land safely. May God be with you!"

Thus ends this great book by Judah Halevi.

3. THE JOURNEY TO JERUSALEM

The Rabbi's words really expressed Judah Halevi's longing for Jerusalem.

"My heart is in the East," wrote the poet, "although I am in the far-off West."

His love for the city of Jerusalem is beautifully expressed in another famous poem.

To Jerusalem

O joy of the world, on lofty height,
Proud city of the Lord's delight,
So great my love—
How can I rest?
I yearn for thee
From distant West.

My soul is filled with deepest sadness
When I recall thine ancient gladness,
The departed glory
Of days of yore,
Thy holy Temple
Which is no more.

On eagle's wings, O would that I
Homeward to Zion might swiftly fly!
I'd pour my tears
Upon the earth,
And sorrow then
Would turn to mirth.

Judah Halevi resolved to leave the comforts of Spain and to make the journey to Jerusalem. His wife was no longer alive; but in tears he bade farewell to his daughter and to his grandson who was also named Judah.

At sea a terrible storm almost destroyed the boat. The poet describes how the raging heavens and the stormy waters were like two seas. Between them his heart was like a third sea, lifting up waves of praise to God that at last he was on his way to Zion.

For a moment the poet is sad as he thinks of his grandson whom he has left behind in Spain.

"How can Judah forget Judah?" he asks.

But his love for Zion is so strong that no sacrifice is too great.

The poet arrived by boat in Egypt. Here he was shown great honor.

"Stay with us," pleaded the members of the Jewish community, just as the king of the Khazars had pleaded with the Rabbi.

"I cannot tarry," was the poet's reply. "If only my boat had the wings of dawn to bring me ever more quickly to the shores of the Holy Land!"

At last Judah Halevi reached the land of his dreams. With ecstasy he kissed the soil and the stones of the Holy City, and prayed for the rebuilding of Jerusalem.

What happened to Judah Halevi after he reached Palestine? Did he continue to live there for many years? Was he ever reunited with his daughter and with his grandson?

Alas, we do not know. All records of what happened to Judah Halevi after he arrived in the Land of Israel have disappeared. History does not know the answer to these questions.

There is a legend that when Judah caught sight of Jerusalem that he composed one of his greatest poems. In the poem he lamented that the Holy City was now in ruins. A passing Arab horseman, hearing his words, was jealous of the poet's love for Jerusalem. Riding up to Judah he pierced him with his lance. The poet died with the word Zion on his lips.

But this is only a legend. Judah Halevi's death and burial-place remain shrouded in mystery.

Judah Halevi's poetry is a lasting monument to the memory of the greatest poet of the Golden Age. Rightly has he been called "The Sweet Singer of Zion."

EXERCISES

I. Choose the correct name or word. (Review section 1, pages 276 to 277.)

1. Judah Halevi was born in _____. (France, Spain)
2. Toledo was captured from the Arabs by the king of _____. (Castile, Granada)
3. Judah was inspired by the poems of _____. (Hasdai, Solomon Ibn Gabirol)
4. Judah Halevi made a living as a _____. (merchant, physician)
5. Besides his religious poems, Judah Halevi wrote many famous poems about _____. (friendship, war)

II. True or false? (Review section 2, pages 277 to 279.)

1. The angel who appeared to the king in a dream said he was satisfied with the king's deeds.
2. The Rabbi explained that not only must we believe in God, but that we must also learn from tradition what good deeds to perform.
3. According to the Rabbi, Israel among the nations is like the heart among the organs of the body.
4. The Rabbi denies the importance of the oral law.
5. At the end of *The Book of the Khazari* the Rabbi informs the king that he hopes to make a journey to Jerusalem.

III. Complete each sentence. (Review section 3, pages 279 to 281.)

Egypt, Jerusalem, Judah, Spain, West

1. The poet wrote, "My heart is in the East, although I am in the far-off _____."
2. The poet expresses the hope that he might fly on eagle's wings to _____.
3. The poet left the comforts of _____ and traveled to the Holy Land.
4. At sea the poet sadly remembers his grandson _____.
5. The Jews of _____ pleaded with Judah Halevi to

remain with them but the poet continued on his journey to Zion.

IV. Questions for discussion:
  1. What subjects did Judah Halevi choose for his poetry?
  2. What differences are there between the story of the Khazars found in Chapter 22 and the story told by Judah Halevi in *The Book of the Khazari?*
  3. Why is Judah Halevi called "The Sweet Singer of Zion"?

THINGS TO DO

1. *Memory Gem*—Memorize the poem "To Jerusalem" (page 280.)

2. *Story*—Write a story giving a different ending for the life of Judah Halevi. Show how he was reunited with his daughter and his grandson.

3. *Original Poems*—Write a poem using one of the subjects about which Judah Halevi wrote. Suggested titles: a—Friendship b—Youth c—Spring d—Sabbath Eve e—My People f—The Sea g—To Jerusalem

RIDDLES BY JUDAH HALEVI

Judah Halevi composed many riddles in verse form. Here are two:

> Happy lovers learn our law
> Be joined in one as we.
> Aught that passes through we saw,
> And again are one, you see.
>   (A pair of scissors)

> What is it that's blind with an eye in its head,
> And the race of mankind its use cannot spare;
> Spends all its life in clothing the dead,
> And always itself is naked and bare?
>   (A needle)*

---

* Translated by Joseph Jacobs.

CHAPTER XXVI
RABBI MOSES BEN MAIMON (RAMBAM)

1. THE WANDERER

MOSES BEN MAIMON was born in Cordova in 1135. He was a lad of about six when Judah Halevi began his journey to the Holy Land. Moses received his love of Torah from his father who served as a judge in the Jewish community of Cordova. Even as a boy Moses' genius was recognized.

But the Golden Age of Spanish Jewry was quickly coming to an end. A few weeks after Moses ben Maimon had become Bar Mitzvah, tragic news spread like wildfire through the streets of Cordova.

"The Almohads are approaching! Flee for your lives!"

The Almohads were a fanatical sect of Mohammedans who spread their beliefs at the point of the sword. They swept through North Africa and now successfully invaded southern Spain.

Those who escaped death were given a choice:

"Convert or go into exile!"

Once more the Jews took up the staff of the wanderer. Families were forced to leave the cities of Spain where their ancestors had lived for hundreds of years.

Maimon and his family wandered from city to city. Despite these hardships Moses ben Maimon continued his studies. He mastered the writings of the Hebrew sages, the wisdom of the Greeks and the science of the Arabs.

In what cities and under what masters did he study? We do not know. But we do know that the young scholar ex-

משה בר מימון זצ״ל

RAMBAM

celled in every branch of learning known in his day—Bible and Talmud, botany and medicine, philosophy and astronomy.

After 12 years of wandering the Maimon family settled in Fez, North Africa. Apparently, Moses ben Maimon was attracted to Fez by the fame of several great scholars under whom he wished to study. The Almohads ruled in Fez, but perhaps they were becoming more tolerant.

For several years Moses remained in Fez. But again there arose the fanatical cry, "Death to the Jews!"

One of the teachers of Moses ben Maimon was cruelly put to death. Moses and his family, however, were warned in time by an Arab poet.

"Your lives are in danger," they were told. "If you remain in Fez any longer it means certain death!"

Moses and the members of his family boarded a boat for Palestine in the middle of the night. After several days at sea a violent storm arose. The boat was tossed about wildly by the waves until it seemed that the boat would be torn asunder.

But suddenly the storm subsided, and the sea grew calm. The boat landed, after a month at sea, in Palestine. The passengers raised their voices and gave thanks to God that their lives had been spared. Moses ben Maimon observed the anniversary of their arrival ever after as a day of gladness and joy.

25 years before Judah Halevi had come to the Holy Land. Did Moses ben Maimon find any trace of the great poet? Alas, we do not know.

Moses and his family remained in the Holy Land for about six months. Moses prayed at the Wailing Wall in Jerusalem near the ruins of the Temple, and visited the grave of Abraham in Hebron.

The land itself, however, was almost a desert. The Jews had suffered greatly at the hands of the Crusaders, and only a handful remained.

Like Jacob of old, Moses ben Maimon and his family decided to go down into Egypt.

2. THE COMMENTARY ON THE MISHNAH

Moses ben Maimon settled in Cairo. His fame began to spread.

He became known as the Rambam, an abbreviation formed from the initial letters of his full name *R*abbi *M*oses *b*en *M*aimon. (He is also called Maimonides, the Greek for "son of Maimon.")

During all these years of wandering, Moses ben Maimon had been busy writing an Arabic commentary on the Mishnah.

At the end of his commentary he explained the many difficulties he had to face in carrying out his task. Then he adds, "I was troubled by suffering and exile since I was driven from one end of the world to the other. God knows that I have explained some chapters while on my wanderings and others on board ship."

The Rambam was a descendant of Judah the Prince, and indeed no one has done as much as Moses ben Maimon to explain the Mishnah which Judah had edited.

In his commentary the Rambam listed 13 articles of faith which were widely accepted as the basis of Judaism.

In these articles of faith Moses ben Maimon stated:

1. I believe that God is the creator of all things.
2. I believe that God is one.
3. I believe that God has no physical shape or body.
4. I believe that God is eternal.
5. I believe that we must worship only God.
6. I believe that the words of the prophets are true.
7. I believe that Moses was the greatest prophet of all time.
8. I believe that our Torah was revealed unto Moses.
9. I believe that our Torah will never be replaced by a new Torah.
10. I believe that God knows our innermost thoughts.
11. I believe that God rewards the righteous and punishes the wicked.

12. I believe in the coming of the Messiah.
13. I believe in the resurrection of the dead.

The Jewish religion has never officially accepted the 13 articles of faith. In fact, there was much controversy over the exact meaning of some of Rambam's statements. Nonetheless, Moses ben Maimon's creed has become widely known. One of the most popular poems in the *Siddur*, the *Yigdal*, is based on the 13 articles of faith.

Hundreds of years later when Jews were led to their death by Hitler's soldiers, a heart-rending song burst from the lips of the victims:

"I believe ...
I believe ..."

The melody grew louder and louder as all joined in the song of hope:

"I believe ...
I believe ...
I believe ...
I believe in the coming of the Messiah!"

Those who marched to their death sang the words of Moses ben Maimon to show that they had not lost hope. They knew that their sacrifice was not in vain.

They believed in the redemption of Israel. They had faith, just as the Rambam did, that the Jewish people could not be destroyed!

3. THE *Code* OF MOSES BEN MAIMON

As Rabbi of the Cairo community, the Rambam received questions from Jews in many lands. People looked up to him in the same way that they had once regarded the Gaon of Sura or Pumbeditha.

"Our judges find it difficult to arrive at a correct decision because the Talmud is so vast," said Moses ben Maimon. "I shall help them by listing briefly all the laws scattered throughout the Talmud. In times of persecution like these not all judges have the peace of mind to search through the 'sea of the Talmud' for the answers to our problems."

For 12 long years the Rambam worked to complete his *Code*. He wrote the *Code* in pure Hebrew using the style of the Mishnah. The *Code* soon became the handbook for Rabbis and judges wherever Jews lived.

One of the most famous sections of the *Code* deals with the laws of charity. The highest form of charity, according to Moses ben Maimon, is the prevention of poverty. Here are his own words:

There are 8 degrees of charity:

1. Giving reluctantly to the poor.
2. Giving cheerfully but less than one can afford.
3. Giving only after the poor man has requested charity.
4. Giving before the poor man has requested charity, but embarrassing him by giving him charity directly.
5. Giving so that the donor does not know who receives the charity, even though the poor man knows the name of the donor.
6. Giving so that the poor man is not embarrassed by knowing who is the donor, even though the donor may know the name of the one who is receiving charity; thus, our great sages used to go secretly and leave money near the doors of the poor.
7. Giving so that donor and recipient are unknown to each other, for this is doing a good deed unselfishly; thus, there was a secret chamber in the Temple where donations were made and gifts were received privately. Giving to an organized charity would be similar in nature; but one should not give to an organized charity unless he is sure that those in charge are trustworthy and efficient.
8. The highest type of charity is the prevention of poverty by providing a poor man with a means of livelihood. That is

why the Bible says, "If your brother grows poor, uphold him." This really means, "Uphold him before he grows poor."

4. THE PHYSICIAN

The Rambam did not accept a salary as Rabbi of Cairo. At first he and his younger brother, David, supported themselves by dealing in jewels.

Unfortunately, David was drowned in the Indian Ocean when the boat in which he was sailing was wrecked. Moses ben Maimon became ill as a result of his brother's death, and did not recover for an entire year.

After David's death, Moses ben Maimon began to devote himself to the practise of medicine. He became one of the greatest doctors of the Middle Ages. His books on medicine were widely studied in every country.

Recognizing his greatness as a physician, the vizier appointed Moses ben Maimon to serve as court doctor. Each day Moses would travel from Fostat, just outside of Cairo, to the court to attend the officials of the court.

At this time King Richard the Lion-Hearted of England was in the Holy Land fighting against the Arabs. When he heard of Moses ben Maimon's skill as a physician he invited him to come to England as the royal physician. Moses ben Maimon, however, refused to leave Egypt.

As court physician the Rambam attended Saladin, the great Sultan who had defeated the Christians during the Third Crusade. Later he was physician to Saladin's son.

In an interesting letter Moses ben Maimon describes his daily activities. This is what he wrote to a scholar in France who wished to visit him:

"I dwell in Fostat and the Sultan resides at Cairo (about $1\frac{1}{2}$ miles away). My duties to the Sultan are heavy. I must visit him early every morning; if he feels weak or any of his children or the inmates of his harem are ill I do not leave Cairo but spend the greater part of the day in the palace. Also if one or two of the officials fall ill I have to attend to them, and thus spend the whole day there.

"In brief, I repair to Cairo every day in the early morning, and even if nothing unusual happens I do not return to Fostat until after the noon hour.

"By that time I am fatigued and hungry. I find the courts of my house full of people, both Jews and Gentiles, of every station in life—judges and officers, friends and opponents, all awaiting my return.

"I dismount from my animal, wash my hands, and go forth to them to entreat them to wait for me while I partake hastily of some food, my only meal in twenty-four hours.

"After that I attend to the patients and prescribe medicine for them. Patients go in and out until nightfall, and sometimes, I assure you, until two hours after nightfall or even later. I talk to them and advise them while lying on my back, so fatigued am I. By night-time I am so weak I am unable to speak.

"As a result, no Israelite can have a private discussion with me except on the Sabbath. Then most of the members of the community come to me after the services and I advise them what activities to carry out during the week. Afterwards they study a little until noon and depart. Some of them return and study again until the evening prayers.

"This is my daily routine. I have only related to you part of what you will see if, please God, you come to visit me."

5. GUIDE AND PHILOSOPHER

One of the Arab poets wrote in praise of the Rambam, "He is the greatest of all doctors because he cures not only the body but also the soul."

Indeed, Jews of many lands turned to Moses ben Maimon for spiritual guidance.

At the very time that Saladin, the great lover of justice,

treated the Jews with kindness, the rulers of Yemen persecuted the Jews.

"How can we encourage the Jews of Yemen to remain true to their faith?" wrote one Rabbi to the Rambam. "Some of our own people have become renegades, and have tried to convince the Jews that even the Bible predicted the coming of Mohammed and that he is the true prophet."

The Rambam wrote an eloquent reply urging the Jews to remain true to their religion. "The Mohammedan religion," he wrote, "in comparison with the Jewish religion is like a lifeless statue in comparison with a real person of flesh and blood. In time of trouble one must show courage and not betray the religion which we have received from our ancestors."

Many copies were made of the Rambam's reply and were sent to every Jewish community in Yemen. There was great danger for the Rambam because he had criticized the Mohammedan religion, but he felt that no danger was too great since we must defend our religion at all costs.

The Rambam used his influence at court to better the conditions of Jews in Yemen and in other countries. The Jews of Yemen were so grateful that they mentioned the name of Moses ben Maimon each day in their prayers. They remained firm in their faith and at last their persecution ended.

Other Jews wrote to the Rambam saying, "We hear many arguments which seem to contradict the teachings of the Bible. Is there a conflict between reason and religion?"

To help all those who were struggling with this question Moses ben Maimon wrote *The Guide to the Perplexed*.

The Rambam showed how the search for the truth is man's noblest goal in life. "There can be no contradiction between Judaism and reason," he wrote, "for Judaism is based on reason."

The Rambam believed that we must know how to interpret the Bible correctly. We must not take every word in the Bible literally since the Bible often uses poetic language.

"The Bible spoke in the language of man," wrote Moses ben Maimon, quoting the Rabbis of the Talmud.

The Rambam then explains our belief in one God. He shows how the purpose of the Torah is to teach us loving-kindness, justice and righteousness.

"A king once commanded his subjects to come to his palace," wrote the Rambam. "Some ignored his command; others could not find the palace. Still others could not find the gate of the palace. A few, however, entered and were rewarded by the king.

"So it is," added the Rambam, "with the understanding of the Torah. Ignorant people cannot find the truth. Reason and wisdom, however, help us to find the gate which leads to the palace of true knowledge of the Torah."

The Guide to the Perplexed was the Rambam's crowning achievement. Moses ben Maimon was the greatest Jewish philosopher of the Middle Ages.

The Rambam died at the age of 70 and was buried in the Holy Land near the city of Tiberias.

Jews the world over mourned his death and said, "From Moses the law-giver to Moses ben Maimon there was none like Moses ben Maimon."

The Rambam ends *The Guide to the Perplexed* with the words of the prophet, "The people that walked in darkness have seen a great light."

There were dark days ahead for Israel. Teachers like Rashi and Moses ben Maimon, however, had taught the Jewish people to uphold their faith with courage, and to drive away the darkness by lifting on high the torch of learning.

EXERCISES

I. Arrange in the order in which these events happened. (Review section 1, pages 284 to 286.)

   1. Moses ben Maimon prayed at the Wailing Wall in Jerusa-

lem near the ruins of the Temple, and visited the grave of Abraham in Hebron.
2. Moses ben Maimon and his family went down into Egypt.
3. Judah Halevi left Spain and traveled to the Holy Land.
4. The Jews were driven from Cordova by the Almohads.
5. Moses ben Maimon and his family set sail in the middle of the night for the Holy Land.
6. Moses ben Maimon and his family settled in Fez after 12 years of wandering in Spain.

II. Commentary on the Mishnah or *Code?* (Review sections 2 and 3, pages 287 to 290.)
1. The 13 articles of faith are found in the _____.
2. The _____ was meant to help judges in making their decisions.
3. The poem *Yigdal* is based on a section of the _____.
4. The laws of charity are listed in the _____.
5. "Prevention of poverty is the highest form of charity," is an idea expressed by the Rambam in the _____.

III. Eliminate the name or phrase that does *not* belong. (Review section 4, pages 290 to 291.)
1. (David, Moses, Saadia) were sons of Maimon.
2. (Judah Halevi, Moses ben Maimon, Rashi) were doctors.
3. Moses ben Maimon's skill as a physician was recognized by (Charlemagne, Richard the Lion-Hearted, Saladin).
4. Among the countries in which Moses ben Maimon lived were (Egypt, England, Spain).
5. Moses ben Maimon became famous as a (doctor, poet, Rabbi).

IV. Answer each question in a complete sentence. (Review section 5, pages 291 to 293.)
1. Why was Moses ben Maimon called the greatest of doctors?
2. How did the Rambam encourage the Jews of Yemen?
3. Why was it dangerous for the Rambam to write to the Jews of Yemen?

4. Why did the Rambam write *The Guide to the Perplexed?*
5. Where was the Rambam buried?

V. Questions for discussion:
1. In what way does the United Jewish Appeal carry out the rules for wise giving mentioned by the Rambam?
2. "The prevention of poverty is the highest form of charity." How can we prevent poverty today?
3. What contributions have Jews made in the field of medicine?
4. Why was it said, "From Moses the law-giver to Moses ben Maimon there was none like Moses ben Maimon"?

REVIEW QUESTIONS
for Units Five and Six (pages 207 to 295)

1. Show how each of the following countries was an important center of Jewish life: Babylon, Arabia, Spain, The Land of the Khazars, France, Egypt.
2. Discuss the main achievements of each of the following leaders: Rav, Samuel, Saadia, Rashi, Judah Halevi, the Rambam.
3. The Talmud records discussions in the academy, court decisions and synagogue lectures. Give an example of each.
4. Describe the political conditions under which each of the following worked: Abi Karib, Bostanai, Hasdai, King Joseph, Samuel *Ha-Nagid*.
5. Tell a popular legend or anecdote about each of the following: Samuel, Bostanai, Samuel *Ha-Nagid*, Rashi.
6. Describe briefly the contents of each of the following books: Saadia's *The Book of Beliefs and Opinions*, Rashi's commentary on Genesis, Judah Halevi's *The Book of the Khazari*, the Rambam's *The Guide to the Perplexed*.
7. Identify: Abba Arika, Anan ben David, David ben Zakkai, King Bulan, Charlemagne, Saladin.
8. Tell why each of the following cities is important in Jewish history. (Also indicate the country in which each city is located.) Nehardea, Sura, Pumbeditha, Tiberias, Medina, Bagdad, Cordova, Granada, Troyes, Cairo.

9. How did the Karaites differ from the rest of the Jewish community?

10. What progress did Jews make, beginning with Saadia, in the fields of Bible, Talmud, poetry and medicine?

TEST

for Units Five and Six

I. Name the country in which each of the following events took place. (20 points)

1. Rav and Samuel established academies of learning at Sura and Nehardea. The Talmud was completed in this country about 500 C.E.
2. Many independent Jewish tribes flourished here. Mohammed learned the belief in one God from the Jews in this country.
3. The Jews enjoyed a Golden Age in this country. Poetry, science and the study of Torah flourished. Leaders like Samuel *Ha-Nagid* occupied important positions.
4. The rulers of this country in southern Russia converted to Judaism.
5. The Rambam served as leader of the community in this country. As physician to the Sultan he used his influence to help his people.

II. Match. (28 points)

Column A	*Column B*
Abi Karib	1. Was called "Sweet Singer of Zion"
Bostanai	2. Corresponded with the Khazars
Saadia Gaon	3. First *Resh Galuta* under Arab rule
Hasdai Ibn Shaprut	4. Author of a commentary on the Mishnah
Rashi	5. King of Yemen who converted to Judaism
Judah Halevi	6. Wrote a book against the ideas of the Karaites
Moses ben Maimon	7. Lived in France during the First Crusade

III. Mention 3 ways in which the Karaites differed from the rest of the Jewish community. (12 points)

IV. What is my name? (25 points)
1. I was a pupil of Judah the Prince and also served as his doctor. I was a close friend of Abba Arika. I founded a great academy of learning. Many of our discussions are quoted in the Talmud. A well-known story about me tells how I taught the Hebrew alphabet to a Persian.
2. I was the founder of the Karaite movement. They made my younger brother *Resh Galuta* instead of me. I was descended from Bostanai.
3. I was king of a powerful country. After consulting representatives of many religions I decided to follow the laws of Judaism. My descendants ruled for 300 years in a country situated in southern Russia.
4. I was vizier to the king of Granada. I encouraged Hebrew poets and scholars. I also wrote Hebrew poetry. Through kindness I changed an enemy's evil tongue into a gentle tongue.
5. I was author of a *Code* and of *The Guide to the Perplexed*. Richard the Lion-Hearted invited me to serve as his physician but I decided to remain at the court of Saladin.

V. True or false? (15 points)
1. A discussion between Hillel and Shammai about the kindling of the Chanukah lights is found in the Talmud.
2. Saadia's *The Book of Beliefs and Opinions* is a translation of the Bible into Arabic.
3. There is a legend about why the moon is smaller than the sun in Rashi's commentary on the first book of the Bible.
4. An angel told the king of the Khazars that his intentions were good but that his deeds were not satisfactory, according to Judah Halevi's *The Book of the Khazari*.
5. *The Guide to the Perplexed* is a book about medicine.

Important Dates in Jewish History

1900 B.C.E.* (approximate) Abraham migrated to Canaan.
1300 B.C.E. (approximate) The children of Israel left Egypt.
1260 B.C.E. (approximate) Joshua conquered Canaan.
1000 B.C.E. (approximate) David became king.
961-922 B.C.E. (approximate) Solomon reigned as king.
722 B.C.E. Assyria exiled the 10 tribes of Israel. In Jerusalem, Isaiah the Prophet foresaw an era of universal peace.
586 B.C.E. Babylon destroyed the First Temple. Jeremiah prophesied the rebuilding of Jerusalem.
536 B.C.E. Cyrus the Great permitted the Jews to return to Zion.
516 B.C.E. Zerubbabel completed the building of the Second Temple.
445 B.C.E. Nehemiah became governor of Jerusalem. Ezra the Scribe helped edit the Bible.
332 B.C.E. Alexander the Great conquered Jerusalem.
165 B.C.E. Judah the Maccabee rededicated the Temple (Chanukah).
142 B.C.E. Simon won complete independence for Judea.
62 B.C.E. The Romans under Pompey conquered Jerusalem.
10 C.E. (or A.D.) Hillel died.
70 C.E. The Romans destroyed the Second Temple. Johanan ben Zakkai established an academy at Jabneh.
135 C.E. The Bar Kochba rebellion ended. Rabbi Akiva was put to death shortly thereafter.
200 C.E. (approximate) Judah the Prince completed the editing of the Mishnah.
247 C.E. Rav, founder of the Sura Academy in Babylon, died.
500 C.E. (approximate) The Babylonion Talmud was completed.
624 C.E. Mohammed attacked the Jews of Arabia.
660 C.E. Bostanai, the *Resh Galuta*, died.

---

* B.C.E. means "Before the Common Era." C.E. means "Common Era;" it is the same as A.D.

700 C.E. (approximate) Bulan, king of the Khazars, was converted to Judaism.
711 C.E. The Arabs conquered Spain.
770 C.E. Anan ben David founded the Karaite movement.
800 C.E. Charlemagne became Emperor of the Holy Roman Empire. He encouraged Jewish merchants, scholars and physicians.
928 C.E. Saadia became Gaon of Sura. He died in 942.
960 C.E. Hasdai Ibn Shaprut corresponded with Joseph, the king of the Khazars.
993 C.E. Samuel *Ha-Nagid* was born. He died in 1055.
1040 C.E. Rashi was born. He died in 1105.
1085 C.E. Judah Halevi was born. He traveled to the Holy Land in 1140.
1135 C.E. Moses ben Maimon (Rambam) was born. He died in 1204.

Guide to Pronunciation

KEY

ärm	thēre	nŏt
hăt	thêy	môre
câre	înk	rūle
āte	īce	ŭp
ēat	ĭll	fûr
ĕnd	ōld	ṡ as in "was"

Index

Aâr'on, 13
Äb-bä' Ä-rî'ka, 209
Ä-bî' Kä-rîb', 227
Ā'bra-hăm, 13
Ā'bram, 216
Äc-re, 102
Ăd'am, 153
Ä-där', 60
Ăd-i-ăb'e-ne, 139
Äd-lô-yä'da, 67
Ä-dôn' Ô-läm', 216
Ā'hăb, 242
A-hăṡ-u-ē'rus, 58-66
Ä'kä-ba, 168
Ä-kî'va, 172-190
ä'leph, bêt, 213
Ăl-ex-ăn'der, 71-75
Ăl-ex-ăn'dri-a, 75
Ăl'lah, 229
Ăl'mō-hăds, 284
Ăm'a-lĕk, 227
A-măl'e-kīte, 227
Ăm'mo-nītes, 46
Ä-nän', 234

Ăn-tī'o-chus ("ch" as in "Jericho"), 81
Ăp-ol-lō'ni-us, 85
Ā'qui-la, 177
A-rā'bi-a, 227
Ăr-a-mā'ic, 215
Ăr-is-tŏb'u-lus, 113
Ăr'non, Map
Ăr-ta-xer'-xēṡ, 45
Ăs-syr'i-a, 14
Äv, 151
Ăv-tăl'yon, 128

Băb'y-lŏn, 19-33
Băc'chus, 116
Băg'dăd, 238
Băl'foŭr, 41
Bär Kôch'ba (guttural "ch"), 184-187
Bär Mĭtz-väh', 284
Bā'ruch, 19
Băth'she-ba, 242
Bē'er-shē'ba, Map

Bĕl, 24
Bĕl'giŭm, 265
Bĕl-shăz'zar, 22-24
Be-nî' Iṡ'ra-el, 216
Bĕn'ja-min, 249
Bĕn Zô'ma, 200
Bê-tär', 186
Bĕth'le-hĕm, Map
Bĕth-zūr', 96
Big'than, 59
Bnêi Bräk, 174
bôs-tăn', 231
Bôs-ta-naī', 230
Bu'lan, 247

Caē'ṡar, 115
Caī'rō, 287
Cā'liph, 231
Cā'naan, 13
Cär'mĕl, Map
Căs'pi-an, 247
Căs-tîle', 276
Chä-nu-kah' (guttural "ch"), 81-92

300

INDEX 301

Chär′le-māgne, 264
Chū-mäsh′ (guttural "ch"), 275
Clē-o-păt′ra, 121
Con-stan-ti-nō′ple, 251
Côr-dō′va, 255
Crī-mē′a, 252
Crū-sāde′, 272
Cȳ′rus, 24-26, 31-36

Dā′mon, 80
Dăn′i-el, 19-28
Dä′rä, 231
Da-rī′us, 26-28, 37-39
Dā′vĭd, 14, 19
Dĕb′o-rah, 14
Dī-ăs′po-ra, 216
drêi′del, 92
Dū-näsh′, 257

Ē′dom, 34
Ē′do-mīte, 113
Ĕl-e-ä′zar, 96
Ĕl-i-ē′zer, 200
E-lī′jah, 14
Ē-lūl′, 171
Ĕm-mä′us, 87
Ē′nŏch, 255
Ep-i-mä′nes, 81
Ep-i-phä′nes, 81
Ē′sau, 13
Ĕs′ther, 59-67
Ē-thî-ō′pi-a, 228
Eu-phrā′teṡ, 31
E-zē′ki-el, 20-22
Ĕz′ra, 43-56

Fa-lă′shaṡ, 228
Fĕz, 286
Flôr′us, 143
Fŏs′tăt, 290

Ga-bî′rol, 276
Găl′i-lee, 95, 146

Ga-mā′li-el, 142, 169
Gä-ôn′, 234
Gā′za, 72
Ge-mä-rä′, 215
Gĕn′e-sĭs, 269
Ge-ô-nîm′, 234
Ge-rī′zĭm, 57
Gĭl′e-ăd, 95
Gŏd′frēy, 273
Go-lī′ăth, 14
Gôr′gi-as, 88
Gō′shen, 271
Gŏths, 264
Gra-nä′da, 258
grŏg′-gerṡ, 65

Häb′bus, 258
Ha-dăs′sah, 59
Hā′dri-an, 183
Häg-gä-dah′, 178
Haī′fa, 29
Hä-lê′vî, 276
Hā′man, 59-68
hä-man-tä′shen, 65
Hä-Nä-gîd′, 258
Ha-nā′nī, 51
Hăn′a′nī′ah, 51
Hä-nän′ya, 234
Hăn′nah, 83
Har-bō′nah, 63
Hăs′daī Ibn Shăp-rut, 250, 257
Hä-tik-vah′, 22
Hē′bron, Map
Hĕl′e-na, 139
Hĕr′od, 119-125
Hĕsh-vän′, 170
Hil-lĕl′, 128-138
Hī′ya, 209
Hyr′ca-nus (first syllable pronounced "her"), 113

Ĭr-ăq′, 255
Ī′ṡaac, 13

Ī-ṡāī′ah, 14
Ĭsh′ma-el, 227
Iṡ′ra-el, 14, 22, 57, 190
Ĭṡ-rā′e-li, 41
Ĭt′a-ly , 265
Î-yär′, 170
Ī-zā′tes, 140

Jăb′neh, 164
Jā′cob, 13
Jăf′fa, Map
Jăn′naī, 111
Jĕr-e-mī′ah, 19
Jĕr′i-chō, 14
Je-rū′sa-lem, 33-54
Jĕsh′u-a, 33-38
Jĕz′re-ĕl, Map
Jō-hăn′an, 161-169
Jŏn′a-than, 95-102
Jôr′dan, 100
Jō′ṡeph, 250
Jō-sē′phus, 146-150
Jŏsh′u-a, 184
Jō-ta-pä′ta, 147
Jū′dah, 83-99; 195-201
Jū′dā-iṡm, 139, 278
Jū-dē′a, 111
Jū′pi-ter, 82

Käl′ba Sä-vū′a, 172
käl′be-ta, 223
Käl-läh′, 212
Kā′rā-ītes, 234
Kätz′ya, 73
Kē′rĕn Ä-mî′, 262
Khā′zär, 247-252
Khā-zä′ri, 277
Kid-dūsh′, 216
Kĭn-nē′rĕt, 147
Kis-lĕv′, 82
Knĕs′ sĕt Hä-g′dô-lah′, 54
Kô-hä-nîm′, 34, 54

INDEX

Kô-hĕn', 33
Kô-hĕn' Gä-dôl', 33
Ko-zē'ba, 184

Läg B'Ô'mer, 189
lät'kes, 92
Lē'ah, 181
Lĕb'a-non, 34
Lē'vīte, 34
Lū-cē'na, 276
Lўs'i-as, 86

Măc'ca-bēe, 85
Măc-e-dō'nî-a, 72
Mä-gĕn' Dä-vîd', 193
Maī'mon, 284
Maī-mŏn'i-dēŝ, 284-295
Măl'a-ga, 258
Ma-năs'seh, 250
Măr-i-ăm'ne, 120
Märk An'to-ny, 121
Măt-ta-thī'as, 83-85
mä-tzah', 198
Mä-yence', 267
Mĕc'ca, 228
Mēdes, 26-27
Me-dî'na, 227
Mĕd-i-ter-rā'nē-an, 168
me-gĭl'lah, 65
Mê-ir', 188
Mĕn-e-lā'us, 81
Mē'ne Mē'ne Tē'kel U-phär'sin, 23, 25
me-nô-rah', 37-38, 89
Me-rôn', 190
Mĕs-sī'ah, 125
me-zū-zah', 141
Mĭk-rä', 234
Mĭr'i-am, 181
mĭsh-lô'ach mä-nôt', 67
Mĭsh-näh', 198
mĭtz-väh', 197

mĭtz-vôt', 174
Mō'äb, Map
Mō'din, 83
Mō-hăm'med, 228
Mŏn'gol, 255
Môr'de-caī, 59-68
Mō'šeŝ, 13

Nā'bŏth, 242
Nā-ōmî, 181
Nā'pleŝ, 249
Nä-sî', 130, 195
Nā'than, 242
Năz'a-reth, Map of Israel
Nĕb-u-chăd-nĕz'zar ("ch" as in "Jericho"), 20
Nĕ'gĕv, Map
Ne-här-dē'a, 210
Nē-he-mī'ah, 44-54
Nē'rō, 146
Nĕs Gä-dôl' Hä-yah' Shäm, 92
Ni-cā'nor, 87
Nīle, 270
Nĭn'e-veh, 139
Nî-sän', 170
Nūn, Gim'el, Hêh, Shîn, 94

Ô'mer, 189

Păl'-es-tīne, 229
Păn-dô'ra, 80
Păp'pus, 188
Pär'thi-a, 140
Per'sia (s as in "measure"), 31, 58
Phā'raōh, 13
Phăr'i-seeŝ, 111
Phĭl-a-dĕl'phus, 76
Pŏm-pêi'î, 171
Pŏm'pēy, 114
Pŏn'tius Pī'late, 141

Pŏp-pē'a, 149
Prägue, 268
prōs'bul, 131
Pŭm-be-dî'tha, 231
Pū-rîm', 58-68
Pўth'i-as, 80

Räb-bê'nu Täm, 271
Rā'chel, 172
Räm-bäm', 284-295
Räsh'î, 264-275
Räv, 211
Re-bĕc'ca, 13
Rêsh Gä-lū'ta, 231, 237
Reū'ben, 219
Rhīne, 272
Rōme, 111-201
Rūth, 14

Säad'i-a, 234-240
saith (pronounced "sĕth"), 20
Săl'a-din, 291
Sa-lō'me Ăl-ex-ăn'dra, 111
Sa-mā'ri-a, 101
Sa-măr'i-tan, 34-37, 45-48
Säm-bät'yôn, 252
Săm'son, 14
Săm'u-el, 210
Săn-băl'lat, 46-48
Săn-hĕd'rin (silent "h"), 111
Sā'rah, 181
Sā'rai, 216
Saul (rhymes with "ball"), 14
Scō'pus, 72
Sê'der, 178
Se-fä-räd', 256
Se-fär-dîm', 256
Sê'fer Tô-rah', 190
Sĕv'e-rus, 186

INDEX

shä-lôm', 162
shä-mäsh', 94
Shäm-maī', 132, 161
Shä-vū-ôt', 13, 34
Shē'ba, 14
She-lô-mô', 265
She-mä'ya, 128
Shmä Yis-rä-ĕl', 139
shô-fär', 47
Shvät, 170
Shū'shan, 44, 58
Sid-dūr', 216
Sī'mon, 71-72; 99-103
Sī'mon Bär Gi-ō'ra, 150
Sī'mon Bär Yô-haī', 188
Sī'mon ben Shē'tah, 111
Sî-vän', 170
Sŏd'om, 201
Sŏl'o-mon, 14
Spär'ta, 101
Suk-kôt', 14, 33, 53

Sū'ra, 210
Syr'i-a, 81-103

Tăl'mud, 217-223
Täm-mūz', 170
Tär'fon, 200
Tar-pēi'an, 152
Tä'vî, 222
Tĕl-A-vîv', 20-22
Tē'resh, 59
Tê-vêt', 170
Tī-bē'ri-as, 147
Tī'gris, 211
Tish-ä'B'Äv, 151
Tĭsh-rî', 170
Tī'tus, 150
To-lē'dō, 252
Tō'rah, 52, 54, 75
Tranŝ' jôr'dan, 101
Troyes (pronounced "Trwä"), 265
Trȳ'phon, 101
Tu Bî-shvät', 170
Tu'nis, 256
Tȳre, 33, 71

U-krāine', 247
Ûr, 13
U-rī'ah, 242

Văsh'tī, 58
Vĕs-pā'sian, 147
vi-zî'er, 258
Vol'ga, 247

Worms, 267

Yär-mūk', Map
Yĕm'en, 227
Yôm Kip-pur', 33, 47, 53

Zā-dôk', 165
Zäk-kaī', 161
Zĕal'ŏts, 143
Zĕch-a-rī'ah, 37-38
Zĕd-e-kī'ah, 29
Zē'resh, 63
Ze-rŭb'ba-bĕl, 33-4ḇ
Zī'on, 19-68
zūz, 133